WHO KILLED SAM SHEPPARD? THE EXPLOSIVE INSIDE STORY!

There were two victims in one of the century's most sensational murders: Marilyn *and* Sam Sheppard. One was brutally slain, and the other totally ruined in a shocking example of the misuse of the power of the press.

Now, after years of research uncovering hidden facts, a top investigative reporter has finally told the complete story of the tragedy. Here is Jack Harrison Pollack's fully documented insider's account of the murder—and the following travesty of justice that resulted from a campaign of character assassination unparalleled in journalistic annals.

Dr. Sam

An American Tragedy

Dr. Sam

An American Tragedy

BY JACK HARRISON POLLACK

AVON
PUBLISHERS OF BARD, CAMELOT, DISCUS, EQUINOX AND FLARE BOOKS

AVON BOOKS
A division of
The Hearst Corporation
959 Eighth Avenue
New York, New York 10019

Published by arrangement with the author.
Library of Congress Catalog Card Number: 70-183801

ISBN: 0-380-00488-7

First Avon Printing, December, 1975

AVON TRADEMARK REG. U.S. PAT. OFF. AND FOREIGN COUNTRIES, REGISTERED TRADEMARK—MARCA REGISTRADA, HECHO EN CHICAGO, U.S.A.

Printed in the U.S.A.

For
Margit

"My punishment is greater than I can bear."

—*Genesis* 4:13

CONTENTS

PREFACE

"OH, he's the doctor who killed his wife."

Across America and Europe Dr. Sam Sheppard is still generally identified in this way. However, countless persons doubtfully add, "But did he *really* kill her? I never was sure."

Whether Sheppard murdered his first wife Marilyn on July 4, 1954, has been argued in numerous courts, and from California living rooms to Riviera beaches. Despite an Ohio court's acquittal of Sheppard of the crime in his late 1966 retrial, doubt still persists over the controversial osteopath's guilt or innocence. Few are neutral or lukewarm about Dr. Sam or his case. Fights still erupt in Cleveland and Columbus bars between Sheppard defenders and critics. Ohioans who visit other parts of the United States and the world are still frequently asked: "Do you live anywhere near Dr. Sheppard's house?"

The man's strange life and his equally unusual death, at the age of 46 in April, 1970, haven't stopped this speculation. Sam Sheppard died as he lived—cloaked in mystery. The case remains an albatross around Ohio's neck. He is the one murder defendant about whom crime reporters are most often asked. I rediscover this whenever someone hears that I knew Sam personally and wrote extensively about his case. I must have been asked at least a thousand times, "Did Sam do it?"

Hence this book. Yet many friends have asked me, "Why do you want to write a book about Sheppard? He's an unsavory, unimportant character."

Was he really as unsavory as he was reputed to be?

Certainly he was impractical, irresponsible, self-destructive, and willfully wasteful. His medical idealism was diffused. The last third of his life was an endless legal, medical, social, and marital struggle against authorities, in and out of prison. Yet we know little of the man inside. Again, that is why I wrote this book, especially since, disappointingly, Dr. Sam's brilliant, flamboyant lawyer, F. Lee Bailey, disclosed in his autobiography merely a fragment of his knowledge of his tortured client. Bailey's briefs in the case revealed more than did his book.

The bizarre Sheppard saga has inspired several partisan books; a long-running television series; one worthless movie; and a three-hour NBC-Universal colorcast on which this author was the technical consultant. Yet the hidden Sheppard story has never fully emerged. There has been scant psychological probing of this case, in which many of the flesh and blood principals have been portrayed as black and white ivory chessmen.

Regrettably, Dr. Sam's own hurriedly ghost-written 1966 autobiography added little to the truth about his life. Its title's fervent hope—*Endure and Conquer*—was never fulfilled. Sam Sheppard neither endured nor conquered except inadvertently, in helping to define the fair trial law for news media in many parts of the United States. This is perhaps his greatest legacy. The delicate proper balance, as the Warren Supreme Court expressed it, between a defendant's right to a fair trial and the right of a free press in a democracy is still an issue, as it was in the Ruby, Sirhan, Seale, Manson, Black Panther, Bremer, and other cases.

In any case, a proper discussion of the question of a fair trial does not explain Dr. Sam Sheppard himself. Ten years in prison, especially in the prime years, do something to any man. What turned this promising young doctor's life into a classic American tragedy? Was he an American Dreyfus or merely a dupe? A wife swapper or a wife killer? A monster or masochist? And why, after his acquittal, did he become such a tormented lost soul? Was he a prisoner of his own human frailties; or was he chained by the mores of life in midwestern America during the 1950s and 1960s? And if he didn't kill Marilyn, who did?

This book attempts to answer some of these questions, if only in part. For nearly a decade I have carried some missing Sheppard jigsaw pieces in my mind and in unpublished files. I trust that as I use them here, they will help to illuminate one of twentieth-century America's most baffling murder cases, whose plot might have intrigued Dostoevski and whose characters might have fascinated Dickens.

Jack Harrison Pollack

Westhampton Beach
New York

1

THE CRIME

IT WAS AN EVENT that later spawned millions of words and thousands of headlines and affected hundreds of lives, including half a dozen suicides, for at least a generation. The crime launched a case that was heard around the world.

The scene was a white-frame four-bedroom, two-story modernized Dutch Colonial house at 28924 Lake Road in Bay Village, Ohio (population 11,000), a fashionable suburb on the shore of Lake Erie, thirteen miles west of Cleveland.

The mistress of this home was Marilyn Reese Sheppard, a comely, spirited 31-year-old housewife who was a year older than her husband. She had sparkling hazel eyes, long dark-blonde hair, and a pleasing 5′ 7″, 125-pound figure. She lived in this comfortable suburban home with her high school sweetheart husband Samuel Holmes Sheppard, a doctor of osteopathic medicine, and their only child Samuel Reese (Chip), age seven. On a quiet Saturday evening of July 3, 1954, she was four months pregnant and was looking forward to the birth of her second child.

Dr. Sam, as he soon became known to the world, was a 6′0″ athletic man of 30, weighing 180 pounds. His boyish good looks and dimpled chin invariably turned female heads. He was associated in the practice of medicine with his surgeon father, Dr. Richard Allen Sheppard, and two older brothers, Dr. Richard Niles Sheppard and Dr. Stephen Sheppard, both osteopathic physicians. He was a neurosurgeon on the staff of the prosperous osteopathic Bay View Hospital, founded by his father, in Bay Village. He also maintained a private office.

In addition, Dr. Sam served as the unsalaried police physician for Bay Village and neighboring Westlake. At any hour of the day or night he responded to emergencies, especially in traffic accident cases. Some of the victims he treated free of charge. But many others became paying patients in the Sheppard family's Bay View Hospital or were later treated in the offices of the Sheppard Clinic, in nearby Fairview Park, of which Dr. Sam was a one-fourth partner with his father and two brothers.

The popular, hard-working young doctor sporting the silver spoon was earning approximately $33,000 a year, and his income was expected to soar. He owned his home, a Jaguar, and a Lincoln Continental convertible. When he leisurely drove through Bay Village's tree-shaded streets, young and old, men, women, and children would frequently shout: "Hi, Dr. Sam!" The attractive physician would smile appreciatively and sound his horn.

In the Bay View Hospital he was rapidly distinguishing himself as a daring, skillful surgeon, especially in delicate brain operations. Nurses eagerly trailed after him to assist him with his medical needs. Female patients from debutantes to dowagers were often disappointed if they were checked by physicians other than Dr. Sam, the most handsome of the three Sheppard sons.

Life Was Lovely

The young surgeon seemed headed for a promising career and a happy life thanks to his excellent health, prosperous practice, prominent medical family, and pleasant home life. What else could a man want?

Life had always been, as the saying goes, Sam Sheppard's oyster. At Cleveland Heights High School he had been president of his class for three years. In his senior year he was voted the school's outstanding athlete for having excelled in football, basketball, and track. He was considered tops in pitching woo in parked cars, though evidence is lacking to substantiate his reputation. Classmates remember friendly, outgoing Sam Sheppard as a charmer with perhaps an inner arrogance but an unmistakable outer modesty. He was deemed the man "Most Likely to Succeed."

At first Sam flirted with the notion of becoming a professional athlete. Several small colleges had offered him athletic scholarships, wanting him ultimately to become a coach at their institutions. But the lure of osteopathic medicine—sparked by the example of his father and brothers—proved deeper.

Marilyn Reese, who was a year ahead of Sam in school, went off to Skidmore College in Saratoga, New York, for a year while he was a senior in high school. Brother Steve had dated Marilyn first and introduced her to his younger brother. Steve recalls, "She was slender and had a tremendous sense of humor. But the most characteristic thing about her was a delightful little-girl quality in the way she looked at you."

World War II had broken out, and Sam wanted to enlist in the army, but his overpowering father persuaded him that he would be more useful to his country as a physician than as a soldier. From that time his fate as Dr. Sam was sealed.

The youngest Sheppard entered small Hanover College, in Hanover, Indiana, in an accelerated preosteopathic course. He completed it in two years by taking supplementary courses at Western Reserve University in Cleveland in the summer of 1943. While enrolled in Hanover, he gave Marilyn Reese his fraternity pin to signify that they were engaged. Sam was faithful to her and she to him.

Sam matriculated at the Los Angeles Osteopathic School of Physicians and Surgeons, where his grades were above average. From California the young medical student corresponded regularly with Marilyn, who was then back in Cleveland, but he could see her only during holidays and vacations. Frustrated by their physical separation, in September, 1945, Sam asked Marilyn to come to California. They were quickly married in the First Hollywood Methodist Church without any members of their families present.

The young couple rented an apartment. Marilyn took a

secretarial job but still found time to type her husband's medical papers. Her husband was a dreadful speller, and she corrected all of his mistakes. While she washed and he dried the dishes, she quizzed him for his exams.

They decided to have a baby right away. In her first attempt Marilyn had a miscarriage. Her O blood type was found to be the dangerous Rh negative. In early 1947 their healthy son Samuel, whom they quickly nicknamed Chip, was born. It was a painful birth; Marilyn was in labor for 16 hours.

After the proud young father graduated from medical school, completed his internship, and received his D.O. (Doctor of Osteopathy) degree, he became a resident in neurosurgery under Dr. Randall Chapman at the busy Los Angeles County Hospital. There he treated gun and knife wounds, accident and fire victims, and brain injuries. Though he and Marilyn loved living in southern California, in response to family pressure, they returned to Ohio in the summer of 1951. Sheppard joined his father's growing hospital and family practices.

The Sheppards lived in a rented apartment in Rocky River until Sam's father loaned them the money to purchase their Lake Road home. A 60-year-old house, it had been modernized. Surrounded by many lovely trees, it was perched on a high cliff nearly a hundred feet above the winding shore of Lake Erie. The house included a private beach below the bluff, and there were steps leading to their bathhouse. It was less than a five-minute drive to the Bay View Hospital from the Sheppard house.

Marilyn was an excellent homemaker. She did all of her own shopping and housework except what was handled by a one-day-a-week maid. She made nearly all of the family's meals, and they rarely ate out, except at relatives' or friends' homes.

The Sheppards were members of the local Methodist Church, and Marilyn taught in the Bible class. One day she was baptized in their living room. Their young son Chip, who witnessed the ceremony, later brought smiles to the Sheppard family when he bragged to playmates, "Mommy's been advertised."

Like her husband, Marilyn was also a sports devotée. She generally bowled and played golf without her husband, but she frequently water skiied with him. They used the 14-foot, 25-horsepower aluminium boat they co-owned with their friends and neighbors J. Spencer and Esther Houk. Water skiing was then relatively new to the Cleveland area, but Dr. Sam ravenously read books and magazine articles about it in order to perfect their performances. They taught their neighbors Don and Nancy Ahern and many other friends how to water ski.

The athletic Sheppards encouraged sports even in neighborhood youngsters. On the back of their two-car garage Sam had erected a basketball hoop and backboard, which the local teen-age boys regularly shared with him. He taught them the fine art of shooting. The boys, including 16-year-old Larry Houk, their neighbor's son, worshipped Dr. Sam. The Sheppards, who delighted in being with youth, improvised a clubroom for the boys above the garage in which they provided a chinning bar, barbells, and a ping-pong table. The boys were also invited to use the punching bag in the basement of the Sheppard home. Whenever Sam introduced them to a sports hero, such as his friend Otto Graham, then the star quarterback of the Cleveland Browns, the boys were ecstatic. Dr. Sam was intolerant of any occasional drinking, even beer, by the boys and scolded them for this.

As they approached their ninth wedding anniversary, Sam and Marilyn Sheppard were happier than they had been at any time since the early days of their marriage. Sam had been involved in at least one extramarital affair, and Marilyn knew about it. But in recent months they had made a fresh start in attempting to revitalize their marriage. They discussed dispensing with their twin beds and sharing a double bed, as they did when first married.

The Sheppards rarely spent money on outside entertainment except at an occasional local movie. They never went to nightclubs; Sam considered them a waste of money. He would rather come home from the hospital, have a few drinks, and curl up on the couch with an auto racing or foreign car magazine. This was all that he generally had time to read in addition to his medical publications and the newspapers.

Still, Sam and Marilyn managed to have a full social life. They had informal parties, "pot luck suppers," and beach picnics, and they frequently entertained people whom they hardly knew. Both were always gracious hosts.

On this relaxed July 3 Independence eve, Sam and Marilyn Sheppard were entertaining their neighbors Donald and Nancy Ahern and Michael and Leslie, their two young sons. After Marilyn had cleaned the house, she had made a blueberry pie, her husband's favorite dessert. Shortly before dinner Dr. Sam was sipping a martini when he was telephoned to rush to the hospital to set a fractured leg. He sped to the hospital.

Marilyn changed from her white shorts, took a shower, and put on light slacks and a colored blouse. After the dinner on the screened lakefront porch—the three children ate dinner in the kitchen—the Aherns walked their two young sons home.

When they returned, the Sheppards and Aherns sat in the living room, congenially chatting over drinks. Don Ahern listened to the Cleveland Indians-Chicago White Sox baseball game on the radio until all gathered around the television set to see a movie titled *Strange Holiday*.

During the film Sam sat in a large armchair near the television set. Marilyn snuggled on her husband's lap, her slender arms affectionately caressing him. They had agreed to name their forthcoming child, if a boy, Stephen, in honor of Sam's older brother and his wife Betty, who had recently lost a baby in infancy. Marilyn no longer feared pregnancy despite her difficult delivery of Chip and the death of her own mother in childbirth when Marilyn was six years old. Sam, a pipe smoker, chided his pregnant wife for smoking too many cigarettes. Nancy Ahern, who feigned jealousy at this lovey-dovey scene, snuggled up against her husband, saying, "You two aren't the only lovebirds."

The Aherns left at approximately 12:30 A.M. Marilyn drowsily ushered them to the Lake Road door, which was often left unlocked. Sam was—or appeared to be—asleep on a couch in the living room in his white T-shirt, brown corduroy jacket, and beige slacks.

His snoring astonished no one present because Sam Sheppard was known to doze off anywhere, anytime. He fell asleep during parties at other people's homes as well as his own. He had fallen asleep while watching television even though Marilyn had vainly nudged him, "Wake up, Sam, the movie's getting good." That evening the surgeon was exceptionally tired because he had toiled for several hours trying to save the life of a boy about Chip's age who had been hit by a telephone company truck. When the youngster's heart had stopped, Dr. Sam had opened the child's chest and massaged the heart until his hands were numb and the boy's heart began to beat. Unfortunately the youngster died an hour later.

The following day, though, Sam Sheppard had to be awake. He and Marilyn had invited eighteen couples to a Fourth of July picnic on their private lakefront. They were mostly Bay View Hospital interns and Ohio surgeon friends. Swimming, water skiing, boating, and a wienie roast were on the agenda. The Sheppards were hoping for good weather.

Shortly before daybreak that morning, around 5:45 A.M., the scheduled picnic host made a telephone call. It was to his friend John Spencer Houk, part-time Mayor of Bay Village, who lived three houses away. The voice said, "For God's sake, Spen, come quick! I think they've killed Marilyn!"

Spencer Houk, 45, the owner of a local butcher shop, arose and dressed. So did his wife Esther. The Houks didn't walk or run to the aid of their friends. Instead, they quickly jumped into their station wagon and drove the hundred yards to the Sheppard home, arriving about ten minutes after the call.

Upon entering, the Houks found the first floor a mess, indicating that it had been ransacked or burglarized. The den's desk drawer had been yanked out, and the contents of a medical bag were scattered on the floor. Sam was slumped in a chair in the first floor den naked from the waist up. His trousers were wet, his face appeared bruised, and he seemed groggy. He was holding his neck and writhing in pain.

Esther Houk went upstairs to the bedroom alone. Her husband remained downstairs. Mrs. Houk saw the victim lying in her blood-soaked bed, her pajama top yanked up over her breasts, her outspread legs dangling under the crossbar of her fourposter twin bed. Marilyn's lower body was covered with a sheet. Not only the bed but the entire room was spattered with blood: the walls and doors as well as the bedspread of her husband's twin bed. Marilyn's skull was fractured in many places but not crushed. She seemingly had been beaten savagely on the head with some blunt instrument—thirty-five times, it was later testified.

Marilyn Sheppard was dead, and the only adult known to have been in the house with her at the time of her murder began the long fight for his life.

Sam's Story

The dazed Sheppard told the Houks his recollection of what had happened.

During the 16 years that followed he told this story countless times, and he never substantially changed it.

This is Sam Sheppard's story.

While he was sleeping soundly on the couch, he was awakened by a noise coming from the second floor. He heard Marilyn screaming and calling his name for help, followed by loud moans and noises. He thought Marilyn was having some painful convulsions; she'd had them during her first pregnancy when she was carrying Chip. He did not know how much time had elapsed from when he dozed off until he heard the sound from above. All the lights were out except a 40-watt bulb in the upstairs dressing room.

Still drowsy, he jumped off the couch and rushed up the stairs. As he entered the bedroom, he saw a "white form" standing next to the bed where his wife slept. He was unable to distinguish whether this shadowy figure was a man or a woman, and he did not know how many intruders were in the room. He started to grapple with the form but was suddenly struck from behind on the back of his neck and skull and knocked unconscious. He did not know how long he remained unconscious.

When he recovered, he found himself, injured and groggy, on the floor beside Marilyn's bed, coming to in a sitting position facing the bedroom door. His police badge, which had been in his wallet, was on the floor. He saw his wife on her twin bed in a pool of blood, beaten and battered on the head and face. She had no discernible pulse when he felt it, and she showed no sign of life when he examined her. He ran into their son's adjacent bedroom and determined that Chip was sound asleep and unharmed.

He then heard a noise on the first floor and ran down the stairs. He saw and chased what appeared to be a male figure through the screen door and down the 36 steps to the beach. Despite the moonless darkness, he saw what appeared to be a large, powerfully built man with a "good sized head and bushy hair." He lunged at this figure but was caught in a stranglehold of some sort, choked, hit, and knocked unconscious for a second time, again for an undetermined period.

The next thing he remembers was regaining consciousness while lying at the water's edge, his head on the shore, legs in the water and body swaying back and forth in the waves. Dazed, he staggered back to the house, where he went upstairs again to look at the body of his murdered wife. In his foggy state he thought that it was all some horrible nightmare. Then he called the first person that he thought of—Spencer Houk.

Houk telephoned for an ambulance, the Bay Village Police Department, and Sam's eldest brother Richard, who called brother Stephen.

Telephones began buzzing all over Bay Village and Cleveland about the gruesome murder. Soon the rest of the world was to hear about it.

2

THE TRIAL

IT *was* a "Strange Holiday" on that Fourth of July, 1954.

The Sheppard murder house was a veritable picnic grounds. Dozens of persons trooped through it, ranging from Bay Village and Cleveland police to neighbors' curious children. Bay Village Patrolman Fred Drenkhan was the first to appear, at 6:03 A.M., five minutes after sunrise.

At 6:10 A.M. Dr. Richard Sheppard, a husky, 6′0″, 38-year-old man, arrived with his wife Dorothy, a former teacher. The eldest Sheppard brother considered trying to revive Marilyn by cutting open a chest cavity and massaging her heart. But after examining her with his stethoscope, he decided that she had been dead anywhere from 18 minutes to 2 hours. He walked into the den and quietly said, "She's gone, Sam." According to Mayor Houk's later trial testimony as a prosecution witness, Richard then asked his brother, "Did you do this?" or "Did you have anything to do with this?"

"Hell, no!" snapped Sam, according to Houk.

Richard heatedly denied that he ever asked this question; yet the mere suspicion of the remark was damaging to the defendant because of the possibility that any devoted brother could possibly harbor such a thought. Richard is a conservative, reserved, soft-spoken physician, in sharp contrast to his articulate, outgoing brother Stephen.

When Stephen Sheppard, prematurely white haired at age 34, arrived about ten minutes later with his wife Betty and examined his brother's head and neck injuries, he quickly concluded that Sam needed immediate hospital treatment. Because the Sheppard family's Bay View Hospital on West Lake Road in Bay Village was the closest one—only three miles away—Steve swiftly decided that his brother would receive more personal attention there. After his brother was helped into his station wagon, Steve drove Sam there.

Richard woke Chip and quickly drove the sleepy boy to his own home.

On his hospital bed, Sam Sheppard moaned, "Chip needs his mother more than me. Why didn't they kill me instead of Marilyn?"

Hospital attendants later recalled the patient's physical and emotional pain. Anna Franz, a registered nurse, testified that Sheppard showed subnormal temperature and that his feet were "all shriveled up." Eileen Huge, an X-ray technician swore that Sheppard mumbled to himself, "I heard Marilyn scream, and I tried to get to her, but I couldn't." Marcella Hahn, another nurse, reported, "I tried to give him a drink of water. But he couldn't stand the pain of opening his mouth. His lips were all cut." Other hospital attendants noted that upper right teeth were loose and that he was in a state of shock.

Sheppard was driven to the hospital by his brother Steve after permission was granted by aged John Eaton, chief of the Bay Village eight-man police force. Chief Eaton raised no objection to moving the patient to the Bay View Hospital. However, the *Cleveland Press,* the most vocal Sheppard family critic, later charged that the prime suspect had been "spirited" and "whisked" away from the murder scene and "protected" by his family who "covered up" for him and hampered police efforts to question him.

Actually, after Dr. Sam had arrived at the hospital and was greeted by his austere but comforting father, he was interrogated, at 9:00 A.M., for about half an hour by Cuyahoga County Coroner Dr. Samuel R. Gerber. At 11:00 A.M. he was questioned for about 20 minutes by two of Cleveland's best homicide detectives, Patrick Gareau and Robert Schottke. Gareau and Schottke returned at

3:00 P.M. to question Sam further. Though the bedridden patient was under heavy sedation with a hundred milligrams of Demoral, Detective Schottke shouted at him, "I don't know what my partner thinks, but I think you killed your wife."

"Don't be ridiculous!" retorted the patient, twisting his neck, which was lodged in a felt collar.

When the patient's father entered the room and was informed by his son of Schottke's statement, he briskly snapped at the departing detectives, "Get the hell out of this hospital!"

All night long the patient was restless, tossing from side to side despite his heavy medication.

Dr. Steve spent the entire night at his brother's bedside. As boys, both had shared the same room and had always exchanged confidences. "If Sam had killed Marilyn, he would have told me that night," Steve later insisted. At the trial Steve testified, "He was restless all night despite the heavy medication. He would roll from side to side. He would cry out in his sleep. He was in pain." One of Steve's many unpleasant tasks related to the case was informing Marilyn's father, Thomas Reese, an engineer and inventor, and Reese's second wife Jane of the murder.

To Steve and Richard the only explanation was that their sister-in-law, of whom both were very fond, had been murdered by some crazed, homicidal plunderer who was perhaps searching for narcotics in a doctor's house.

However, authorities speedily concluded—some on that Fourth of July morning—that Dr. Sam had killed his wife. They considered his intruder story preposterous. Within a week men and women all over the United States were saying the same thing: "Sheppard did it himself!"—a judgment based largely upon information disseminated by Ohio newspapers, television reports, and radio broadcasts.

Because of the absence of any other suspect, Ohio authorities, according to their later testimony, swiftly decided that Sheppard had quarreled with his wife, killed her in a rage, washed her blood off his clothing in the lake, faked a clumsy burglary by ransacking drawers in the downstairs den to support his intruder story, inflicted trivial injuries upon his neck by falling down the stairs to the beach, and delayed calling the authorities in order to gain time to conceal the evidence against him, including the murder weapon. When his two brothers and their wives arrived, they quickly wiped off the fingerprints and blood and hid other incriminating evidence.

This is the hypothesis that Cleveland authorities later leaked to the press; it was the official version of the crime presented by the state at the trial—despite the absence of *any* concrete proof.

Three days later, on July 7, Sam Sheppard left the hospital for the day in a wheelchair accompanied by Bay Village Police Sergeant Jay Hubach to attend the funeral of his murdered wife. He was photographed wearing dark glasses and an orthopedic collar, which Steve had prescribed to relieve the patient's head weight on his neck muscles.

The collar quickly became a distasteful Sheppard public symbol. Newspaper cartoons featured caricatures of the collar. Stories were printed about how some Cleveland children improvised Sheppard-like collars and played a game that they called "Murder."

On the drive in Steve's car to the Knollwood Cemetery in East Cleveland, Sergeant Hubach, who was driving, questioned the suspect further about the murder.

"For God's sake," Steve exploded, "Can't you wait until a man's wife is buried before you question him?"

Sam remonstrated that he didn't object to answering questions then or at any other time if the answers would help to solve his wife's murder.

Morbid onlookers at the cemetery craned their necks, even peering into the families' funeral procession cars. Newsmen scurried around for colorful copy. Photographers' flashbulbs popped, and their pictures were blown up in the Cleveland newspapers that evening and the following morning—including large photographs of Sam Sheppard standing beside his wife's coffin.

When Sam was driven back to the hospital in a numb state, Deputy Sheriff Carl Rossbach was waiting to question him.

On the day after Marilyn's funeral one Cleveland newspaper published a story in which Assistant Cuyahoga County Attorney John Mahon—later the chief prosecutor of Dr. Sam—was quoted as sharply criticizing the Sheppard family for refusing to permit his immediate questioning. From then on, local headline stories repeatedly stressed Sheppard's and his family's lack of cooperation with police and other officials. Authorities claimed there were "discrepancies" in Sheppard's story but declined to name them.

Distressed by the growing public belief that Sam had killed Marilyn, the Sheppards consulted their family lawyer, Arthur Petersilge. Because his specialty was corporate law, Petersilge suggested that the Sheppards engage William J. Corrigan, a prominent veteran criminal lawyer, which they promptly did.

The Sheppard family also posted a $10,000 reward in a trust fund for the arrest and conviction of Marilyn's murderer. Lawyer Corrigan issued a press statement in which Sheppard was quoted as saying that he hoped the reward would bring his wife's murderer to speedy justice. Nevertheless, the offer of the reward was seen as a clumsy public relations effort, and it boomeranged on the Sheppard family.

On the evening of July 8 Sheppard was discharged from the hospital. Since his own home had been impounded by the police, without a court order, and he was forbidden to enter it except when accompanied by a policeman, he decided to stay at the spacious home recently purchased by his parents.

That same evening Deputy Sheriffs Carl Rossbach and David Yettra visited the senior Sheppard home, requesting that they be allowed to take fingerprints and palmprints of the entire family. The family quickly obliged. The sheriffs even demanded that seven-year-old Chip be questioned by them. Steve reluctantly drove to his home and returned with his nephew, who was staying with him. The boy was interrogated for an hour. The investigators learned nothing more than what they already knew. The boy had gone to sleep about 9:00 P.M. and did not know anything about his mother's murder until his uncle Richard had awakened him at about 6:20 A.M. the following morning.

The next day Sam Sheppard voluntarily accompanied authorities to his home to reenact his movements on the murder morning. Steve and Richard then voluntarily agreed to go to Prosecutor Mahon's office in Cleveland for further questioning. Result: more newspaper headlines and photographs including a page-one, six-column story headlined in the *Cleveland Press: Doctor Varies Story.*

On the following day suspect Sam Sheppard was again interrogated for nearly ten hours by Detectives Schottke and Gareau, Sheriffs Rossbach and Yettra, and Gertrude Bauer, an assistant in Prosecutor Mahon's office.

During his first free moment Sam Sheppard telephoned his father-in-law, Thomas Reese, with whom he had always enjoyed warm relations. Reese, a quiet, capable man, had invented a wood grain metal process that was used in manufacturing automobile dashboards. His son-in-law suggested that they have a private talk on Reese's boat at the Forest City Yacht Club, which only a week earlier Sam and Marilyn had helped to repair.

"Fine. I'll be glad to see you, Sam," Reese told his son-in-law.

An hour later Reese telephoned, saying apologetically, "Sam, I think we ought to delay our meeting until the situation straightens out.

"What situation?"

"Now, Sam, I don't for a minute think—"

"For Christ's sake, Tom, do you honestly think that *I* had anything to do with Marilyn's murder?" Sam exploded.

"Sam, I have complete confidence in you. But my womenfolk seem to think that maybe we ought to wait before . . ."

"Tom, are you worried about what your womenfolk think or about what happened to Marilyn and what *is* happening to your grandson and son-in-law?"

"I'm sorry, Sam, but that's the way the ball bounces." He hung up.

Later that day Sheppard again voluntarily accompanied Coroner Gerber and police authorities to his murder home to retell his story. Among those tramping through the house then was nine-year-old Michael Ahern, who fingered everything in search of a turtle Sam had rescued for him.

During the next 22 days 5 different public agencies stumbled over each other in probing the case: the Bay Village and Cleveland Police Departments (members of the latter scoffed at those in the former as Keystone Cops) and the Cuyahoga County offices of the Coroner, Sheriff, and Prosecutor. Coroner Gerber and Dr. Lester Adelson, his aide, were photographed on July 17 holding up Marilyn Sheppard's blood-streaked pillow and pajamas for news photographers.

However, none of these arms of the law came up with *any* hard murder evidence against their prime suspect. The evidence remained *entirely* circumstantial. The murder weapon was *never* found or even determined. Exactly how the crime was committed was *never* clearly established. There were *no* fingerprints, *no* strange footprints, *no* concrete clues. Yet suspicion focused entirely on Dr. Sam.

Perplexed, the police publicly demanded that Sheppard and his family immediately take lie detector tests. Lawyer Corrigan strongly advised them not to for two reasons, which then seemed valid: (1) they would be administered in a hostile atmosphere by police who were already convinced of Sam Sheppard's guilt; (2) Sheppard's thinking may still have been somewhat groggy because of the head and spinal injuries he claimed he received while struggling with his wife's murderer.

"The only way to convict yourself, Sam," his new lawyer assured him, "is by opening your mouth."

The suspect's rejection of this polygraph test was a major prearraignment issue of the Cleveland police and press. Had the main suspect been able to "pass" the lie detector test, the case against him would have theoretically collapsed. Corrigan, however, did not trust the Cleveland police.

As late as July 29—25 days after the murder—Cleveland Police Chief Frank Story told reporters, "Our feeling is that Sam Sheppard killed his wife even though we can't prove it. If we had a single shred of solid evidence against him, I'd send the janitor out to make the arrest."

Indeed, the evidence would determine whether Dr. Sam went free, to prison, or to the electric chair.

Trial by Front Page

Before any formal charge was made, while the surgeon suspect was still living in his parents' home, the emerging Sheppard murder case was selling newspapers all over America. Ohio newspapers, especially in Cleveland, had a bonanza. Their circulations soared as they fanned public opinion to a near lynch-mob frenzy against the most convenient suspect. At least one now ashamed Cleveland reporter recalls that word filtered down from on high "to lay it on."

That is precisely what was done.

One enterprising newspaper led the pack: the *Cleveland Press,* whose front page masthead says it is "Ohio's Largest Daily Newspaper" (it then had about 380,000 daily circulation). *Time* magazine named it as one of the nation's ten leading daily newspapers in its January 10, 1964 issue.

This influential newspaper, whose editorial page displays the lighthouse symbol of the Scripps Howard newspaper chain, illuminated the Sheppard case. It assumed the roles of prosecutor, judge, and jury in trying an unarraigned suspect on its front pages with editorials, many with bold eight-column banner headlines generally reserved for such things as declarations of war. In doing so, to fit its own philosophy in the Sheppard case, it reversed the old Anglo-Saxon common law principle: Sheppard was "guilty until proven innocent." To adapt the motto of the more objective *New York Times,* that of the *Cleveland Press* then was: "All the News Printed to Fit."

On July 16, 12 days after the murder, the *Press* lead editorial entitled *The Finger of Suspicion* lambasted the "tragic mishandling" of the case by authorities, claiming that the prime suspect was being treated too tenderly because of his family and legal connections. This, the journalistic tribunal contended, was "bad for everybody, except the murderer." The next day Cleveland Mayor Anthony J. Celebrezze was quoted as saying that his police department should assume complete command of the Sheppard case.

On July 20 the *Cleveland Press*'s five column headline on its page-one editorial read: *Getting Away with Murder.* The pitch was that the unapprehended murderer should immediately be given "the third degree" by derelict authorities. That evening the Bay Village City Council voted to transfer the investigation from its own small police department to the Cleveland Police Department's Homicide Squad and appropriated $5,000 for expenses.

The following day, on July 21, the *Press* published in its city edition a front-page editorial across the top of its eight columns. Above its masthead was this headline: *Isn't This*

Murder Worth an Inquest? Its later home edition changed the headline to read more demandingly, *Why No Inquest? Do It Now, Dr. Gerber.*

Coroner Gerber promptly ordered a public inquest to start the following morning at 9:00 A.M. It was scheduled to be held in the large gymnasium of the new Normandy Public High School in Bay Village instead of in the less spacious quarters of his Cuyahoga County Coroner's Office. Though an inquest is presumably held to determine the cause of death—which in this case was seemingly known—this turned out to be a Hollywood-type inquest with 57-year-old Dr. Gerber as the star performer. He, too, served as prosecutor, judge, and jury.

The inquest was attended by several hundred boisterous spectators, and it was televised. It ran for three days, July 22, 23, and after the weekend, on Monday, July 26. Catering to the photographers and hostile crowd, which included women carrying infants and men playing hooky from work, policemen frisked suspect Sheppard, his two brothers, and their wives—all of whom had been subpoenaed. Sheppard was interrogated savagely for six hours by Gerber without counsel. The suspect waived his privilege to refuse to testify against himself.

When the inquest began, Coroner Gerber stated that no witness could have counsel. Enraged by the hostile crowd's behavior, Sheppard's newly engaged lawyer, William J. Corrigan, rose and asked the court stenographer to record this behavior. Commanded to sit down and shut up by Gerber, Corrigan refused. Gerber ordered a policeman and a sheriff to eject Corrigan from the gymnasium. The audience roared approval. "What does Sheppard need a lawyer for if he's innocent?" one heckler demanded.

Gerber also issued subpoenas for Sheppard's parents. He likewise ordered seven-year-old Chip to appear at the inquest on Monday morning. No subpoena could be served on the boy because he was out of the state at a Pennsylvania children's camp. Steve and Betty Sheppard drove to the Pennsylvania camp over the weekend and returned with Chip.

However, Corner Gerber had a change of heart. He decided not to put the youngster on the witness stand. Instead, he questioned the boy in his office the following day,

July 27, with Assistant Prosecutor Saul Danaceau and Detective Inspector James McArthur.

The primary purpose and undoubted result of the inquest was to subject Sheppard and his family to public ridicule. Impartial observers dubbed it the "Sheppard Circus." When it had been concluded, several women rushed up and kissed Coroner Gerber.

On July 28 the *Press* asked in a page-one editorial: *Why Don't Police Quiz Top Suspect?* "You can bet your last dollar," this editorial said, "the Sheppard murder would be cleaned up long ago if it had involved 'average people.' . . . Now proved under oath to be a liar, still free to go about his business, shielded by his family, protected by a smart lawyer who has made monkeys of the police and authorities, carrying a gun part of the time . . . Sam Sheppard still hasn't been taken to Headquarters."

The following day the *Press* published a cartoon with a pair of handcuffed hands designated "officials" and "police" under the caption: "Handcuffs on the Wrong People?"

On July 30, the *Press*'s eight-column headline across its entire front page, accompanied by a photo of Sheppard in dark glasses wearing his orthopedic collar, put it bluntly: *Why Isn't Sam Sheppard in Jail?* The final afternoon edition changed the questioning headline to a direct command: *Quit Stalling—Bring Him In.*

The Cleveland Police Department promptly reacted.

At 10:00 P.M. that Friday evening a howling mob stormed the property of Dr. and Mrs. Richard Allen Sheppard, whose home was situated several hundred yards back from the road. Scores of onlookers jammed the large lawn, trampling on the flower beds. The senior Dr. Sheppard ordered them off the premises and the porch, but the crowd just laughed. Dozens of reporters were present, some of whom peered into the windows. Photographers' bulbs continually popped, and even amateur shutterbugs recorded this epic event.

Sheppard's imminent arrest, which had been leaked all over town, was timed for late evening. Some police officials suspected that the alleged culprit was a narcotics addict and that a craving for a "fix" might force him to confess. After three police officers arrived, the suspect was handcuffed in front of his parents in their living room and hustled out into a waiting police car. "Murderer!" shouted some spectators. Dr. Sam protested in vain that he had a right to talk to his lawyer before being arrested.

The manacled prisoner was driven for 50 minutes to the Bay Village City Hall. There he was arraigned before Gershom M. M. Barber, the City Council president. Mayor Houk witnessed the scene but did not preside because of his involvement in the case. A murder warrant was read. Sheppard pleaded: "Not Guilty." Barber ordered him committed to the Cuyahoga County Jail. Despite his demands that he be permitted to telephone his lawyer, Sheppard was chained, arraigned, and compelled to plead in a murder case without counsel before any formal charge was officially made.

Thus was justice served in Cleveland, Ohio, one of the great cities of the free United States, on July 30, 1954.

Seventeen years later *Newsweek* in its August 23, 1971, issue said, "As the Sam Sheppard case showed, we still have a press that can be more concerned with vengeance than justice."

One of the moving forces behind the press verdict was a titan in the Sheppard shadow named Louis Benson Seltzer, the 56-year-old editor of the *Cleveland Press* and editor-in-chief of the Scripps Howard newspapers of Ohio. Born of poor parents, in the city that he loved, Seltzer was an articulate crusader against community corruption. He basked when admirers affectionately characterized him "Mr. Cleveland." Seltzer had edited the *Press* for almost 27 years. Among the public figures who had been elected with the *Press*'s welcome support were Ohio five-time governor Frank Lausche, later Ohio's U.S. Senator, and Cleveland Mayor Anthony J. Celebrezze, later Secretary of Health, Education, and Welfare in President Eisenhower's cabinet. Celebrezze was disrespectfully dubbed "Louie's Mayor" by Cleveland cynics, who insisted that the two maintained a private telephone wire which he denied.

Two years later, in 1956, when Sheppard was in prison seemingly for life, Seltzer published *The Years Were Good,* his autobiography. In this nostalgic memoir, he boasted that he had goaded public officials into prosecuting Sheppard through what he called his "hard-hitting" editorials and that he "would do the same thing over again under the same circumstances." Seltzer wrote: "The newspapers began to lose interest—except one. . . . The *Press* kept the Sheppard murder case in top position on Page One. . . . It was a calculated risk. . . . It was my neck I was sticking out. . . ."

Seltzer described editing as "the endless, sometimes thankless job of keeping at the primary business of living with understanding, and being sympathetic towards all people." The book's jacket said that Seltzer lived by the creed of "love thy neighbor."

Other Cleveland newspapers joined the anti-Sheppard crusade, even if less aggressively. The *Cleveland News* (since purchased by the *Press*), the slogan of which was "A Friend of the Family," deplored that Sheppard, upon the advice of attorney Corrigan, had declined to take both lie detector and truth serum tests at police headquarters. Its impatient July 21 editorial entitled *Time to Bring Bay Slaying into Open* suggested subpoenaing and examining all the principals and witnesses under oath.

Once Cleveland newspapers went on record that Sam Sheppard had killed his wife, they had to maintain momentum. "I don't think our brass later gave a damn whether or not Sam was guilty," recalls one Ohio newsman. "The papers *had* to get a conviction. Even if they were wrong, they had to prove that they were right."

During this newspaper assault Sheppard family members pretended to each other that they had not read the inflammatory newspaper stories. "I used to sneak the papers home and read them privately," recollects Steve. "I did the same thing," adds Richard, "and I assume Mother and Dad did likewise." They all hoped that the others had not read the painful stories. Family friends discreetly refrained from discussing them. One day at a Sheppard family conference lawyer Corrigan threw a batch of hostile newspaper clippings on the coffee table and thundered, "These papers are Sam's enemies—not the court."

In Great Britain, even during trials newspapers are permitted to publish only what is formally disclosed in court. During investigations an accused person is generally identified only as a "man" or "woman." British courts zealously enforce this protection of the right of any suspect or defendant to a fair trial. Newspapers in England have been fined heavily, and offending editors have even gone to prison for violating these safeguards.

In the dank Cuyahoga County Jail during the closing days of 1954, England's justice was meager solace to prisoner Sam Sheppard.

Cooperate, Translated Confess

Behind bars in an isolation cell without a toilet or washbasin, Dr. Sam continued to suffer the Ohio onslaught.

On Saturday, July 31, Sheppard's lawyers and family were denied permission to visit him in the Cuyahoga County Jail. But police and detectives grilled him up until midnight for almost a dozen consecutive hours. They questioned their prisoner intensively, trying to make him confess over the weekend before lawyer Corrigan could have a habeas corpus hearing at 10:00 A.M. on Monday morning. Some of the interrogators exhibited almost a primitive thirst for vengeance.

"They came at me in pairs hour after hour without getting me to change or contradict my story," Sheppard later recalled. "They showed me horror pictures of Marilyn's body, whispered that Chip was not my son, threatened to prosecute members of my family as accomplices, called me and them vile names, insulted our profession, told me that I had disgraced my family and friends. They used the third degree without physical torture, which they knew might boomerang on them. I was not beaten, but physical torture would have been a pleasure in comparison. They came at me with loaded questions such as: 'Why did you kill your wife, Sam?' 'What did she do to you?' 'Why, Sam? Tell us why.' "

Although Captain David Kerr, of the Cleveland Homicide Squad, later denied to newsmen that Dr. Sheppard had been mistreated in jail, the defendant offered testimony during the trial that was never rebutted. "It was like a brain washing behind the Iron Curtain," he said.

Detectives tried to make deals with Sheppard, as did other officials with his family outside the jail. "Now, Doc, why don't you come clean?" one soft-talked him. "You'll feel so much better about it. Just sign this paper that you did it and we'll get you a manslaughter instead of a murder rap, and we can all knock it off."

"How can I confess to something I didn't do?" protested the prisoner.

Another detective tried a more compassionate approach: "Look, Sam, try to think clearly. Lots of guys bump off their wives after a fight. They didn't mean to, but they did. They plead temporary insanity and later go free. We'll send you up to Lima [State Hospital for the Criminally Insane] on a psycho rap. You'll be out in maybe nine months and still be able to practice medicine, water ski, and drive your sports car. The heat will be off you and us. C'mon, Sam. Be sensible."

But Sheppard grimly retorted, "I'd rather go to the chair before I confess to a murder that I didn't commit."

An impatient detective lashed out, "Now, look here, you dirty no good son-of-a-bitch. You killed your wife in cold blood. We know it. You know it. The whole town knows it. For Chrissake, it's been in all the papers. Wake up, you horse's ass! We're going to burn you if you don't confess."

A sympathetic officer strolled by his cell later and asked, "Doc, how can you stand all this?"

"Only because I know that Marilyn is in my corner," the prisoner murmured as he clutched the Bible given to him by his friend Reverend Alan Davis. "Do you think I could ever face Chip if I had killed his mother? Guilt is a matter of conscience, not of law."

A police officer who participated in the grilling later admitted, "I thought Sheppard killed his wife because of the missing T-shirt, folded corduroy jacket, and the desk drawers being pulled out in a phony way. But we were never able to trip him up. We couldn't find anyone else, so we assumed it *had* to be him."

On August 2 at 7:15 P.M. Sheppard was removed from jail and driven by four detectives and sheriffs to the Cleveland City Hospital, where he was given a comprehensive physical and neurological examination by Dr. Spencer Braden, a neurosurgeon consultant of the police department. Dr. George Greene, the Cleveland Police Department medical officer, and other medical associates were present. Sheppard was stripped and X rayed despite his protests. His orthopedic collar was removed, and he was tested for all types of reflexes and reactions.

When lawyer Corrigan heard that Sam had been examined without a court order and that he had not been notified of this move, he was enraged. So were the Sheppard family, who had heard over the radio that Sam had been taken, handcuffed, from the jail and removed to some unspecified place. The prisoner's father drove to the murder home, suspecting that his son was being taken there to reenact the crime and would be shot on the subterfuge that he attempted to escape. Steve suspected that his brother might need medical attention if he ever returned to the jail and rushed there to wait outside with his medical bag. At 11:10 P.M. the prisoner was returned to jail.

The following day, August 3, the *Cleveland News* published two Cleveland Police Department photos of the prisoner in front face and side view. The caption said, "The Bay Village doctor was minus his orthopedic collar and eyeglasses."

On August 16 Sheppard's lawyer persuaded Judge William K. Thomas, of the Common Pleas Court, to release his client on $50,000 bail. "I am not passing on the question of his innocence or guilt," Judge Thomas ruled, "but merely on what evidence has been presented here."

As the ecstatic prisoner started to leave, Chief Jailer Michael Ucello yelled, "You forgot your radio, Sheppard."

"Hold it for me—I'll be back," the departing defendant bitterly replied.

Indeed, on the afternoon of August 17 a grand jury indicted Samuel Sheppard for first-degree murder. Juggling the bag of fruit that his mother had packed for him, Sam was handcuffed, rearrested, and hauled back to the Cuyahoga County Jail, where he spent the rest of the summer.

Most of his time was spent reading books and magazines, writing letters, keeping a diary, and playing cards with other prisoners. He refused to let his mother or Chip visit him even though he missed them. A guard let him telephone Chip once a week for a $10 bribe.

The trial was set for fall, 1954.

The Combatants Square Away

Damon Runyon, who enriched the English language with his quaint prose, once wrote rather simply:

> A big murder trial possesses some of the elements of a sporting event. . . . I find the same popular interest in the murder trial that I find . . . on the eve of a big football game, or a pugilistic encounter, or a baseball series. There is the same conversational speculation on the probable result, only more of it. . . . The trial is a sort of game, the players on the one side the attorneys for the defense, and on the other side the attorneys for the State. The defendant figures in it merely as the prize.

The Sheppard murder trial, which began in the Common Pleas Court of Cuyahoga County, Cleveland, Ohio, on October 18, 1954, and dragged on until December 21, was until then one of the longest continuous trials in American criminal history. It took twice as long as the 1935 Lindbergh kidnapping trial in Flemington, New Jersey, which resulted in the electrocution of Bruno Richard Hauptmann, a German immigrant.

The Sheppard court record filled more than 10,000 pages of trial testimony, bills of exception, and appeal briefs. Despite the transcript's 2 million words, 87 witnesses, and nearly 300 exhibits, the trial left much in limbo. Far more significant questions were raised than were ever answered.

The physical setup of the small courtroom in the grimy old Criminal Courts building was altered for massive press coverage. Reserved seats were scarcer than for a World Series game or a Broadway opening—with no scalpers operating. Judge Edward Blythin personally assigned all of the reserved seats for the trial's duration.

A long temporary table was improvised behind the single counsel table inside the bar. It stretched over the courtroom width, parallel to the bar railing. One end was less than three feet from the jury box. Twenty press representatives, mostly of Cleveland newspapers and the three wire services, were assigned seats at this table by the court.

Directly behind this bar railing there were four rows of benches. The first row was assigned to television and radio news representatives. The second and third rows were for reporters from out-of-town newspapers and magazines, including nationally known byliners such as Dorothy Kilgallen and Bob Considine, as well as a pipe-smoking inspector of Scotland Yard named Robert Fabian, who covered the trial for a newspaper chain and radio network. The fourth row was reserved for important visitors and later witnesses such as members of the Sheppard family.

Marilyn's aunt, Mary Brown, who had been the slain woman's closest female relative, sat with the Sheppard family because she was firmly convinced of Sam's innocence. On the other hand, Marilyn's stepmother, Mrs. Jane Reese, and her father's two sisters, Mrs. Keith Wiegle and Mrs. Henrietta Munn, kept a cool distance. Marilyn's father, Thomas Reese, appeared only to hear the closing arguments of the trial as a spectator. The prosecution did not call him as a witness; perhaps it feared that Reese could not testify that his son-in-law evidenced a killer instinct.

The jurors, who were constantly exposed to the news media, were treated as minor celebrities by the press. Every juror except one testified to having read something about the case in the Cleveland newspaper or to having heard broadcasts or telecasts about Sam Sheppard.

On the second day of the jury selection a discussion by newspaper reporters was broadcast over WHK radio in Cleveland. The participants accused Sheppard's lawyer Corrigan of throwing roadblocks in the prosecution's path and asserted that the osteopath had conceded his guilt by hiring this prominent criminal lawyer. Because of their broadcast Corrigan requested a continuance, but the judge denied the motion.

Before the trial began, it took 17 days to pick a jury out of a *venire facias* of 75 citizens. All of the names and addresses of the prospective jurors were published 30 days before the trial in Cleveland's 3 daily newspapers—*Press, Plain Dealer,* and *News*. This extraordinary procedure enabled the jurors' families and friends and the public-at-large to discuss the pending case freely with them. The potential jurors then received many anonymous telephone calls, letters, and threats from all types of advice givers and assorted cranks—all of which may have interfered with the possibility of a fair trial.

Since extramarital relations were expected to be a bone of contention in Sam's case, the defense tried to keep off the jury any woman involved in a broken marriage. Finally, a jury of seven men and five women was selected. They were not sequestered during the trial but permitted to go home evenings where they could read or hear the daily newspaper, radio, and television reports.

The 12 jurors sworn in on October 28 were: Howard Barrish, a young Republic Steel clerk; James Bird, a railroad station cashier and the only college graduate, elected foreman; Elizabeth Borke, a middle-aged mother; Louise K. Feuchter, a woman in her fifties; Ann Foote, a working mother with five children; Frank J. Kallorits, a young father with two sons; William C. Lamb, a construction company superintendent; James Roger Manning, a real estate salesman; Frank Moravec, a toolmaker; Edmond Verlinger, a hardware store manager; Beatrice Orenstein, a housewife; and Louella Williams, a middle-aged woman and the only black juror.

James Manning, who had been accepted by both the prosecution and defense, shortly afterward had his arrest in 1943 on a morals charge raked over in the Cleveland press. The prosecution was panicky, fearing that the entire jury would have to be dismissed and a new one picked all over again in order to avoid a mistrial. To the prosecution's relief, Manning withdrew at his own request and the first alternate, Jack Hanson, a factory foreman, replaced him. Judge Blythin ruled that this was perfectly legal inasmuch as the jury had not yet heard any testimony.

The jury was a motley group. As juror Mrs. Feuchter told *Dayton Daily News* reporter George Gilbert ten years later: "They didn't want us too smart. They didn't want us too dumb. They wanted us run of the mill and that's what we were—run of the mill."

On the first day of the trial, court was swiftly adjourned by Judge Blythin so that the jury could be transported by bus to inspect the Sheppard murder house. The handcuffed defendant was driven there in a police car. When he saw Chip's teddy bear on the bureau, he wept.

The time of the jury's visit was disclosed so far in advance that hundreds of persons awaited them outside on the roped-off property. Photographers and reporters were the most peripatetic observers. One newspaper publisher rented a helicopter to fly over the house and had its photographer take long-shot pictures of the jurors. One privileged representative of the news media, a pool reporter, was permitted to accompany the jury while it inspected the house. He was a representative of the *Cleveland Press*.

Back in the courtroom, Dr. Sam Sheppard wore a conservative charcoal gray suit, white shirt, knitted dark tie, black shoes, and dark socks. He could have come straight out of central casting as a successful Madison Avenue advertising executive. To some, though, he had a different veneer.

One of the more fair-minded press representatives, *New York Daily News* star reporter Theo Wilson, recalled her impressions of Sheppard 16 years later: "He looked like a big, gawky kid who didn't understand why he—of all people—was accused of murder. He cried a lot when there were references to Marilyn. . . . He wept all through the gruesome display of her autopsy slides. . . . if you did ask him something innocuous [such as] what he ate for lunch, he would answer in that strangely high voice of his: 'A peanut butter sandwich and milk, thank you,' and smile politely. . . ."

The presiding judge, Edward J. Blythin, was a slim, angular man of 70 with a glacial manner. He spoke with the lilt of his native Wales. He came to the United States in 1906, was naturalized in 1911, and received his law degree at Baldwin-Wallace College in Berea, Ohio, in 1916. He became Mayor of Cleveland in 1941 and a judge on the Common Pleas Court of Cuyahoga County in 1948.

When the Sheppard trial opened in October, 1954, Judge Blythin was a candidate for reelection to another six-year term. As the chief jurist in the criminal division, he assigned this important case to himself.

The three prosecutors, all of whom nurtured political ambitions, were tough, competent lawyers.

The chief, John J. Mahon, was a tall, white-haired,

breezy man who, in his 22 years in the prosecutor's office, had acquired a phenomenally successful record for convictions.

Saul D. Danaceau was a short, bald, middle-aged man, a skilled legal tactician.

Thomas C. Parrino, the youngest prosecutor, was an aggressive, ambitious man: his brilliant performance during the trial favorably impressed *Cleveland Press* Editor Louis Seltzer.

The prosecution was understandably overzealous, perhaps because it had no direct evidence. The slain woman's husband was charged with the murder and the state demanded justice; yet the state was unable to deliver to the jury the murder weapon, the method by which the murder was committed, or a clear-cut motive—usually necessary evidence for a murder conviction.

The chief defense counsel, William J. Corrigan, was a short, dynamic, wrinkled man of 68. As a young lawyer, he had been an assistant prosecutor and later chief of the Cuyahoga County Criminal division. He later received a well-earned modest fee from the Sheppard family. He fought doggedly for his client but occasionally over the wrong points. He often failed to pursue some gray areas in which the prosecution was exceedingly vulnerable. Though he scored numerous hits during the trial, his angry outbursts at the prosecution and their witnesses during cross-examination, often irritated the already prejudiced Judge Blythin, who, in turn, reacted punitively. He even shouted at the judge during Coroner Gerber's crucial testimony: "Will you leave me alone and let me ask my questions?" When the press corps laughed at one of his comments, he lashed back, "You—you television men!"

"Corrigan never believed that his client could possibly be convicted solely on circumstantial evidence," a Cleveland attorney later mused. With classic irony he added, "Corrigan tried the case like he was defending a guilty man. Only near the end of the trial was he absolutely convinced that his client was innocent. But then it was too late to switch tactics."

Number two defense counsel was Fred Garmone, a hard-hitting man who often joined Corrigan in difficult criminal cases.

The third defense lawyer was Arthur E. Petersilge, the Sheppard family lawyer and friend. He was the secretary of the Bay View Hospital's board of trustees and the first lawyer to be consulted by the family. As a corporation lawyer he fully realized that defending a client against a murder charge was hardly his forte.

Corrigan's namesake son, William, Jr., who had recently graduated from law school, completed the defense team, serving mainly as a leg man and researcher.

Thus did the lawyers weigh in for Cleveland's heavyweight championship bout. The lines were drawn. The issues were irreconcilable. For many years to come, other lawyers throughout Ohio and other parts of the United States were to throw hooks and jabs at the Sheppard punching bag.

People came from different parts of the United States in a vain attempt to attend the trial. A Pennsylvania barber who was denied entrance picketed the courthouse; a disturbed Michigan woman was ushered away from the courtroom door despite her protests that she had a "message from God."

This was one of the few claims made by neither the prosecution nor defense.

Surgical Instrument

The most damning witness for the State of Ohio against Dr. Sam was another Sam—Dr. Samuel R. Gerber, the Coroner of Cuyahoga County.

A man with both M.D. and law degrees, since 1937 Gerber has been routinely reelected by admiring Clevelanders who deemed him, not without reason, a dedicated public servant. His credentials include being past president of the National Association of County Coroners and co-author of a textbook titled *Criminal Investigation Interrogation*. He has jealously held sway over his well-equipped crime laboratory on the Western Reserve University campus. The proud, often cocky, Gerber bristled whenever his laboratory was irreverently called "a morgue" by Corrigan and other detractors.

Dr. Gerber reached the Sheppard murder house at 8:00 A.M. on July 4, possibly not more than four hours after

Marilyn Sheppard had died. He promptly said to Bay Village Chief of Police John Eaton, "You're going to need some help on this case." After a quick look at the corpse and bedroom and before assessing Sheppard's injuries, he was both suspicious and enraged at what he judged the undue haste with which the slain woman's husband had been hurried to the family osteopathic hospital by his brothers. Smoldering with suspicions, according to his own later accounts, Dr. Gerber rushed to the hospital to question the victim's husband personally.

Dr. Gerber demanded to talk privately with Dr. Sam, who had just emerged from the X-ray room and was still under heavy sedation. Dr. Gerber heard the patient's story of the murder without any witnesses, and he was skeptical of the story.

Though he could find no blood evidence on any part of the patient's body or clothing except a smudge on the left trouser leg, the coroner took all of the clothing that Sam Sheppard had been wearing when he arrived at the hospital—his wet slacks, his shorts, his loafers, his socks, his handkerchief, and his wallet containing a small penknife, an inhaler, three $20 bills, three $1 bills, and Sam's soggy $1,000 check from the Sheppard Clinic.

On the stand Coroner Gerber, prosecution witness for three days, confidently testified that the bloody "imprint" on the pillowcase beneath Marilyn's head was caused by a surgical instrument. He showed gruesome color slides of Marilyn's bludgeoned body, which some of the jurors could only look at sideways if at all. Defendant Sheppard wept behind the screen, unable to view the pictures.

Like a stern schoolmaster, the ebullient Gerber lectured that Marilyn Sheppard was slain by blows on her head with a heavy two-bladed surgical instrument about three inches long with teeth on the end of each blade. This surgical instrument, Gerber testified, contained teeth or claws that made an impression upon the pillow—an unmistakable "blood signature." The prosecution and defense each grabbed the pillowcase, but photographs of it were passed to the jurors over heated overruled defense objections. The bloody bed sheets were likewise spread before the jury.

Coroner Gerber never produced or explained what kind

of surgical instrument was involved, nor did he offer any evidence that the defendant possessed such an instrument.

Before Gerber's bombshell the unknown murder weapon had been sought by the prosecution in vain. At first it hinted that Marilyn was killed with 16-inch steel orthopedic wrenches, which Dr. Sam, as the Bay Village police surgeon, kept in a surgical kit in his car. But these did not jibe with Gerber's pillow print testimony. When tested, the instruments showed no blood. A two-foot iron pipe, hooked iron tire rod, and Sheppard's riding whip found in his garage were also reluctantly ruled out by the prosecution. The bottom of the lake was searched for the murder weapon by a team of divers with a mine detector. Marilyn's missing golf club was likewise rejected by the prosecution since it was doubtful that such a long-handled instrument could have inflicted 35 blows at close quarters.

But Coroner Gerber seemingly had saved the day for the state. No "bushy-haired intruder" could possibly carry a "surgical instrument." Only a doctor would.

Before Gerber was cross-examined by Corrigan, Judge Blythin warily asked the witness, "Do you mean that the impression on the pillow could not have been made by any other instrument?"

"No, sir."

"Could it, indeed, have been made by another instrument?" the judge continued.

"Yes. I meant that the impression could only have been made by an instrument similar to the type of surgical instrument I had in mind," Coroner Gerber explained.

The defense never pinned down Gerber nor got him to retract that the imprint was from a surgical instrument. Instead, it retorted that the alleged pillow imprint was caused by a collection of blood trapped in the rumpled fold between the pillow crease while it was still wet. Or, the defense speculated, the blood imprint could have been caused by a garden tool or some other implement.

Was Coroner Gerber bluffing? Or did he truly believe that such a surgical instrument existed somewhere? His seemingly authoritative testimony about the surgical instrument had a decisive effect upon the lay jury, and it was perhaps the turning point of the trial. Dr. Gerber was never properly cross-examined about it. Had he been, the case of the state of Ohio against Dr. Samuel H. Sheppard might have collapsed.

For some years later Coroner Gerber lectured on legal medicine before professional groups about the Sheppard case. On one occasion, when Gerber was in Boston lecturing and showing his slides, he had a drink with Sheppard's new lawyer, a 29-year-old local attorney named F. Lee Bailey.

"Coroner, just what 'surgical instrument' did you have in mind when you gave your testimony?" Bailey recalls asking.

"You know," replied Gerber, "nobody ever really asked me that!"

"Well, sir, when Sam gets his new trial," shot back Bailey, "I'll ask you that. And you'd better bring that 'surgical instrument' along with you—or get ready to do a little jig for the jury. There hasn't been a surgical instrument like the kind you mentioned since the days of Hippocrates."

MDs vs. Osteopaths

Whether Coroner Gerber's fervent testimony was motivated, even if subconsciously, by latent professional animosity is difficult to determine. The conflict between the orthodox American Medical Association and the osteopathic branches of medicine was a bitter backdrop to the controversial case. Like many M.D.'s, Dr. Gerber probably did not have a lofty regard for osteopaths, who had established themselves strongly in Ohio just as they had in California, and their success in Ohio was largely due to the eminence of the defendant's father.

Dr. Richard Allen Sheppard was a former president, fellow, and life member of the American College of Osteopathic Surgeons and a past president of the American Osteopathic Hospital Association. He settled in Cleveland in 1921 and founded the small downtown Cleveland Osteopathic Hospital—the city's first—when his youngest son Sam was ten years old. In 1948 he moved the hospital to Bay Village, renaming it the Bay View Hospital. Deeply dedicated to his profession, the senior Sheppard found time to lecture at the Los Angeles College of Osteopathy. The

College of Osteopathic Physicians and Surgeons in Los Angeles awarded him an honorary Doctor of Science degree in 1944.

As each of his three sons graduated from the Los Angeles College of Osteopathic Medicine and from the California College of Medicine, he returned to join his father on the staff of Bay View Hospital. The sweetest music to the ears of the proud father was when the hospital intercom operator announced: "Call for Dr. Sheppard"—and he had to wait to hear the appropriate first name. Richard specialized in obstetrics and gynecology; Steve and Sam, in surgery.

Osteopaths, who are often mistakenly confused with more maligned chiropractors, have largely the same medical school training as M.D.s. Their respective medical school curricula are similar. But osteopathic medical students, in addition, study body mechanics and manipulation. Osteopathy is a theory of disease and method of treatment based upon the belief that most diseases are caused by a deformation of some part of the body. Most ailments, according to osteopathy, stem from displaced bones and nerves, which can be helped by manipulative therapy. Osteopaths treat disease by manipulation as well as by conventional medicine and surgery.

On the other hand, the much larger group of conventional—M.D.—physicians in the United States generally practice allopathy. This is a method of treating disease by drugs or other agents that produce effects *different* from those of the disease. Allopathy has also largely absorbed homeopathy, which treats disease in healthy persons by drugs producing symptoms *similar* to those of the disease. Today, in short, there are only two main branches of medicine: allopathy and osteopathy.

Before the jurors were even selected in the Sheppard trial, the backstage bickering between conventional and osteopathic medicine flared. Defense lawyer Corrigan used two of his six preemptory challenges to disqualify prospective jurors who were only vaguely connected with the American Medical Association.

During the trial a defense witness, Dr. Horace Don, a Bay View Hospital intern, testified that he had overheard Coroner Gerber say to police officers in the Sheppard house on the murder morning, "It's evident that the doctor did it. Let's go get a confession." Gerber denied saying this. According to Dr. Sam's autobiography, Dr. Don told him years later in 1953, that Coroner Gerber had said to him: "So you work with the Sheppard boys at Bay View? Some day I'm going to get one of them."

The M.D.-osteopath antagonism seethed to the surface in the testimony over whether the defendant's injuries on the murder day were trivial or faked.

Not trusting Dr. Stephen Sheppard's early morning July 4 statement that his brother probably had suffered a broken neck, Coroner Gerber chose an M.D. to examine Dr. Sam in the Bay View Hospital on that murder afternoon at 2:45 P.M. for forty-five minutes: Dr. Erwin Richard Hexter, a general practitioner in Bay Village, whose job as physician to the football team Dr. Sam had taken over shortly before.

After examining his younger medical competitor, Dr. Hexter reported to Dr. Gerber that the patient's injuries were minor—a black eye, right cheekbone swelling, a red, swollen right temple. Yet Dr. Hexter observed that the patient had difficulty moving his head from side to side, and he noted a right rib blow and a lack of thigh and left abdominal reflexes—which he later said were of no importance. When Dr. Stephen Sheppard heard this diagnosis, he exploded, "It may not mean a thing to Dr. Hexter, but it means a lot to me. Absence of reflex in the human body is a big red warning signal. It could be a brain concussion." Steve was likewise incensed that Dr. Hexter had failed to write his diagnosis on the hospital chart, as is customary.

The aroused Sheppard family that night decided to call in one of Ohio's outstanding M.D. neurosurgeons: Dr. Charles Elkins, chief neurologist at Cleveland City Hospital.

Dr. Elkins examined Sheppard at 8:00 P.M. on the evening of July 4 at the Bay View Hospital. After studying the X rays he determined that the patient had seemingly suffered a spinal cord bruise and a probable fractured neck in the second cervical vertebra area. He said that a particle of bone seemed to have been separated from this vertebra, possibly as a result of a blow on the back of the neck. Dr. Elkins also noted, on this first examination, painful spasms in the patient's neck, which he was certain could not have been feigned. Dr. Elkins wrote on the hospital chart on July 4 that the patient "was suffering from a cerebral concussion."

After examining Sheppard again on the following two days, July 5 and 6, Dr. Elkins added that the patient had suffered a spinal cord contusion and concussion but that no surgery was required because the damage would eventually heal.

Dr. Elkins testified to all this without fee or subpoena during the trial as a defense witness. Under cross-examination he testified that Sheppard could not have faked the loss of certain reflexes.

Dr. Spencer Braden, the police department neurologist who examined the defendant on August 2, was not summoned by the prosecution as a witness. His findings were never revealed, presumably because they corroborated the testimony of Dr. Elkins on the seriousness of Sheppard's injuries. Instead, the state argued that the defendant had injured himself falling or jumping off the rock jetty near his lakeside home.

Although osteopathy may not have been "respectable" in othodox medical circles in Cleveland in 1954, today organized medicine is trying to take it over, as it did homeopathy. In California the medical society has largely absorbed the osteopaths, enabling many to use an M.D. degree in their practices instead of a D.O. (Doctor of Osteopathy).

The would-be nationwide takeover by the American Medical Association has been traditionally resisted by the 13,000-member American Osteopathic Association despite osteopathic members who contend that they need to join local AMA-affiliated bodies to secure hospital staff privileges. A former osteopathic president, Dr. Marion E. Coy, declared, "I am proud of my D.O. degree, and I don't need any M.D. or XYZ at the end of it, either."

Ironically, when President Nixon lived in New York, his personal physician was osteopath Dr. W. Kenneth Riland who has long been personal physician of the Rockefeller family, including Vice President Nelson Rockefeller.

In late 1954 in Ohio an M.D. mused over his Scotch, "If Sam Sheppard had been a member of our local medical society, instead of being an osteopath, he would never have been arraigned, much less indicted or tried."

Blood Will Not Tell

The blood evidence—or lack of it—stumped both the prosecution and defense.

In such a gory crime a murderer is generally soaked in his victim's blood. Laboratory tests show that even repeated washing or dry cleaning will not remove blood evidence from garments.

Yet the only blood found on Sheppard was a single splotch on the knee of one trouser leg. The defense insisted that this resulted from his leaning on the blood-spattered bed to check his wife's pulse after returning from the lake.

"If Sam had been the murderer, he would have splattered blood all over his trousers," thundered Corrigan.

Prosecutor Mahon charged that after murdering his wife Sheppard rushed down the steps and jumped into the lake in an attempt to wash away the blood on his clothes with cold water. At first, speculated Mahon, the defendant tried to drown himself in the lake, but he changed his mind after being refreshed by the cold water. He then planned his alibi.

"Isn't cold water better than hot water in washing away blood?" Mahon demanded of the defendant.

"I am certainly no authority," Dr. Sam quietly answered. "I never tried."

Before Sheppard was arrested, three months before the trial began, Cleveland Detective Inspector James McArthur was quoted in the July 26 newspapers as saying that "scientific tests at the Sheppard home have definitely established that the killer washed off a trail of blood from the murder bedroom to the downstairs section." No such evidence was produced by the state at the trial.

Actually, there was little blood in the house outside the murder room, and most of that blood had soaked into Marilyn's mattress and bed clothing. There were spots on all four walls from the blood that had spurted from the blows but no spots on the ceiling and no blood on the floor. The bloodstains on all four of the murder bedroom walls were virtually ignored by the prosecution and defense.

Coroner Gerber speculated, "Somebody mopped up a lot of blood from the stairway and in the first-floor rooms before Mayor Houk was telephoned. Who had time enough to do that except Dr. Sam?"

The prosecution charged, without proof, that the blood spots found throughout the house were Sheppard's. But the defense claimed that prosecution witnesses could not swear whether the blood in the basement was animal or human. Eleanora Helms, the Sheppard maid, testified that in April, 1954, the family's female Irish setter Koko was in heat and had dropped blood throughout the house and garage.

Henry E. Dombrowski, a Cleveland Police Department chemist, testified that while working in the murder house, he and his assistants had sprayed most of the house with liquid Luminol, which glows when it reacts to blood. They then circled the resultant spots with chalk. These spots were later cotton-swabbed with Benzidine, which produces a strong blue-green color when it contacts with blood.

"Isn't it a fact that you get the same reaction from a great many other things?" Corrigan asked on cross-examination.

"Yes, you get it from some things."

"What things?"

"Certain vegetables, such as carrots and radishes."

When questioned further, Dombrowski admitted that tomatoes, cherries, berries, apples, limes, and even horseradish produces a similar blue-green color.

"Didn't anyone tell you there was a dog in the house and that the animal dropped blood since March?" Corrigan continued.

"No, sir. I heard it some time in September after I had completed the examination."

"Why didn't you examine the floor in Marilyn's bedroom for blood?"

"It was our opinion from the appearance of that room that it would have added nothing to the investigation," Dombrowski replied. "We knew that the blood was there from our experience with blood."

The prosecution's top blood witness was Mary Cowan, chief medical technologist in Coroner Gerber's office for fifteen years. She testified on November 29 that she had found six human blood spots in the downstairs and basement of the murder house, but she could not type them as either Sam's blood, Group A, or Marilyn's, Group O with an M factor. The state argued, nevertheless, that these seven spots were Sheppard's "blood trail."

Cowan likewise tried to type what appeared to be blood on Marilyn's and Sam's wristwatches—the latter having stopped at 4:15 A.M. But here, too, she conceded that her findings were not definite. The bloodstain on Sheppard's trousers was likewise inconclusive, she admitted. Cowan's important card containing her findings of the blood found on Marilyn's wristwatch—which showed not only Marilyn's and Sam's but a *third* blood factor—strangely disappeared during the trial. It reappeared when the case was reviewed a year later by the Ohio Supreme Court.

Actually, the entire blood evidence was so confusing that it is doubtful whether the jurors understood it fully. Even the judge, prosecution, and defense seemed to have difficulty in following the trail of the blood testimony.

Paul Holmes, who covered the 1954 trial for the *Chicago Tribune* and later in 1961 published a pioneer book about the case, wrote me in January, 1964: "I shudder at what a good cross-examiner could have made of the state's blood evidence. It got by solely on the defense legal staff's ineptness, ignorance and senility."

Sheppard's missing T-shirt, which he was wearing when he fell asleep on the couch, was likewise one of the trial's great mysteries. He was barechested when the Houks arrived on the murder morning.

The prosecution claimed that the defendant took off his T-shirt and disposed of it after the murder because it was blood-stained. Ten days after the slaying Bay Village policeman Cyril M. Lipaj found a bloodless, torn T-shirt, size 42-44 large, hooked on a pier wire near the Sheppard beach. Though it was introduced as an exhibit in court, neither the prosecution nor defense requested that it be displayed before the jury. The state's theory was that the shirt "obviously" wasn't the defendant's because it was too large.

Corrigan blandly asked his client, "Is this your shirt?"

"It certainly could be. I don't know."

Neither Corrigan nor the prosecution asked the defendant to try it on in front of the jury. One stubborn question persisted in objective listeners' minds: if Sheppard had killed his wife and faked a burglary, as the prosecution contended, why didn't he put on another clean T-shirt before telephoning Mayor Houk?

Another T-shirt was reputedly found later on the beach near the Sheppard home underwater. It was given an intensive laboratory test by authorities. No blood was found on it. "*That* was *my* T-shirt," Sam Sheppard insisted to me in July, 1964. "But it had no blood on it, so the authorities said it wasn't mine. It was a medium-size Hanes T-shirt, which I always wore, as they damn well knew from my other ones."

"What really happened to your T-shirt?" I asked Sheppard.

"Frankly, I don't know. It must have been ripped off in my struggle on the beach before I was knocked out. Maybe the intruder took my T-shirt to replace his own bloody shirt when he was leaving."

The blood trail led nowhere.

Mystery and Miscellany

Many other objects were inadequately assessed during the trial. Some have puzzled serious crime students ever since.

Two fragments of Marilyn's teeth were found on her murder bed while she was being transferred to the stretcher. Another tooth chip was later discovered on her bedroom floor. Were these tooth chips broken off when she was bludgeoned to death? If so, why did they not lodge in her mouth or throat? The prosecution offered no explanation. The defense claimed that the position of these tooth fragments indicated that Marilyn had bitten her assailant and that her teeth had chipped when she struggled with her murderer. Her husband had no tooth marks or blemishes on his hands.

Coroner Gerber, who found the two tooth fragments on the bed before the victim was removed, testified, "At the time I did not know whether they came from Marilyn's teeth. I attempted to determine whether her teeth had been chipped but discovered that rigor mortis had set in and that it would be difficult to open her jaws."

Dr. Stephen Sheppard testified that when he saw Marilyn's body before Coroner Gerber arrived, her mouth was partly open. The defendant's brother also charged that the authorities had altered the position of Marilyn's body on her bed before photographing it.

Other puzzling items found on the murder bedroom floor, which matched nothing in the house or Dr. Sam, included a small piece of red leather, a chip of a woman's nail polish that was different from the type Marilyn used, and fiber scrapings under her fingernails. Mary Cowan testified that she had found wool threads in microscopic scrapings of two of the fingers.

Neither the prosecution nor the defense offered explanations for any of the other objects. They were never even photographed and were shown to the jury only in an envelope and small test tube at Corrigan's insistence.

The state broadly argued: Why didn't the "bushy-haired" intruder, if indeed there was one, kill Dr. Sam rather than risk letting the only possible identifying witness remain alive? Why didn't the defendant grab a poker from the fireplace when chasing the alleged intruder or intruders? Why didn't he turn on the lights when he heard his wife scream? Why didn't he telephone the police immediately before chasing this so-called intruder?

The defense claimed that if any doctor had really wanted to kill his wife, he wouldn't have done it so crudely. He knew more sophisticated methods—with drugs, for example. Moreover, a strong man like Sam Sheppard would never have needed 35 blows to kill a woman. The defense hinted that the blows indicated that someone—possibly a woman—wanted to disfigure Marilyn.

Other conflicting claims and unanswered questions fouled up the testimony. Why were there no fingerprints in the house? Did Sheppard or his brothers wipe them off, as the prosecutor suggested? Or did a bushy-haired criminal do so? Why were a woman's footprints on the beach not investigated by the police? How did Sheppard's small green cloth bag get on the grassy hill before it was found there by Mayor Houk's 16-year-old son Larry? Were the contents of

Dr. Sam's medical bag dumped on the living room floor by him or by an intruder looking for dope? Who smashed Sam's athletic trophies? If he was lying on the beach with waves washing over him, why wasn't there sand in his hair? Why didn't an intruder take the money in a kitchen teacup and the two rings from Marilyn's fingers, including a diamond ring? Marilyn's wristwatch, with a seemingly blood-encrusted band, was found in the downstairs den. How did it get there? The prosecution charged that the blood had dried while she was still wearing the watch and that her husband had removed it and tossed it on the den floor to pretend a burglary.

There was no evidence of forcible entry.

What about the corduroy jacket in which Sam had fallen asleep? Was it crumpled on the den floor, as Steve testified, when he first arrived? Or was it neatly folded on the den couch on the murder morning, as the police charged. If so, *who* folded it? Sam? Marilyn—before she went upstairs, taking it off her husband when he was sleeping on the couch? Or was it later folded by one of the many persons tramping through the house on that murder morning, perhaps some neatness-prone female?

Was the front door locked on the murder evening? Don and Nancy Ahern, the Sheppard's guests, did not recall whether Marilyn had locked the front door after them, but they assumed that she had not because it was not customary for the Sheppards to lock their doors, testified the maid and Dr. Lester Hoversten, a house guest who had arrived three days before the murder for a visit.

A friend and college classmate of Sam, Hoversten, a prosecution witness, was under suspicion until he produced his alibi: on Saturday afternoon he had gone to Kent, Ohio, for a holiday weekend.

Dr. Horace M. Don, a former intern at the Bay View Hospital, testified as a defense witness that the Sheppards left their Lake Road door open. When asked whether the defendant was a light or heavy sleeper, he replied, "He was very difficult to wake up. Sometimes we had a hard time getting him up."

Corrigan charged that the autopsy of Marilyn's body made by Deputy Coroner Lester Adelson was incompetent because the state had already decided that her husband was the murderer. Marilyn was not examined to see if she had been raped, yet her pajama tops pulled up over her breasts and her legs spread over the bottom of her bed indicated a sexual assault. Bay Village Sergeant Hubach testified, "Dr. Sam says he pulled the sheet up to her waist because Marilyn always was a modest girl." Marilyn's head was shaved immediately so that no traces of metal or the nature of the murder weapon could be found. No toxicological examination of her stomach contents was made.

Dr. Richard Sheppard, Sam's oldest brother, was one of the calmest defense witnesses. He was even restrained when he firmly denied Mayor Houk's testimony that he had asked on the murder morning whether Sam had anything to do with it. "I am positive that I never said such a thing," Richard testified. "I could not have because it never entered my mind that my brother could have killed his wife or anyone else."

Dr. Steve, in contrast, was a hostile witness because of what he considered to be the outrageous treatment of his younger brother. His indignation caused him to contradict himself several times under cross-examination.

When Steve first went through the house on the murder morning, he noticed the butt of a regular Lucky Strike cigarette floating in the toilet bowl of the upstairs bathroom. Marilyn rarely smoked during her pregnancy and then only a filter type. Sam smoked a pipe.

"Don't touch anything," cautioned Bay Village Sergeant Jay Hubach. "We want to preserve everything as evidence."

Was this evidence of an intruder in the murder house? The butt was either taken out of the bowl or flushed away. It was never mentioned by the prosecution during the trial.

Before the trial Dr. Steve had suggested to police several possible suspects who were "very interested" in pretty young Marilyn as a woman. He hinted that some of their interest might have exceeded family friendship or neighborliness and that some of their alibis might not be as airtight as they seemed. During the trial Detective Schottke testified that on July 10 even the defendant had told police that his wife had at least three potential lovers and that she was extremely jealous of his female professional contacts, as are many physicians' wives.

Steve testified that Marilyn had told him that Houk annoyed her for two years with his attentions. Infuriated, Houk threatened to punch the witness in the nose. This seeming aspersion upon the slain woman's virtue prompted Mayor Houk to testify, "Marilyn was the purest girl I ever knew." Yet Houk was on such friendly terms with the Sheppard family that "When Marilyn was ill and alone, he used to go up to her bedroom to see her," testified Eleanora Helms, the Sheppards' maid.

Houk, a fatigued, worried-looking man, suffered severe strain before the trial and was a painfully halting witness against his former friend. His replies were slow and studied. Fearful of uttering the wrong words, sometimes he took as long as half a minute before answering a simple yes or no. His replies were often studded with "I don't remember," "I can't recall," or "I couldn't be sure." "Whether he was unnerved by the maelstrom of July 4 or haunted by some terrifying secret fear, he was obviously a shaken soul," reported Dorothy Kilgallen.

Three weeks after the murder, recalled Houk, he had "urged Sam to confess if he had done it."

"I couldn't have done it, Spen," Sam protested, according to Houk.

Houk's wife Esther, another prosecution witness, was far more composed. She testified acidly that the defendant had once told her that head injuries in car accidents were easy to fake because they were difficult to prove or disprove. Though Mrs. Houk's testimony was antagonistic to Sheppard, some of it indicated some truth in what skeptics deemed an incredible intruder story. Esther Houk recalled that on the murder morning, she had noticed a puddle of water on the porch and wet footprints on the uncarpeted first to second floor stairs. If these weren't faked after the crime, they seemed to corroborate the defendant's claim that after he had recovered on the beach, he had returned to the house and gone upstairs to check his wife's condition. Esther Houk also quoted Sheppard as saying bitterly in the den, "And I laughed at Steve for the way he keeps his house locked up."

Two defense witnesses, unknown to each other, who drove past the Sheppard home around the time of the murder, testified that they had seen a tall "bushy-haired man" wearing a white shirt lurking outside the Sheppard home. Both said that they had reported this to the Bay Village police.

Leo Stawicki, of Cuyahoga Heights, revealed that he was returning from a Port Clinton fishing trip with his two brothers between 2:25 and 2:30 A.M. "When I ride, I take a pretty good look," he said. "I had my window down and my bright lights on. When I first seen him, I seen him about a hundred feet ahead of me. I was looking right at him. . . . He looked kind of suspicious to me. That's what kind of got me. I mentioned it to one of my brothers. . . . I passed him on the side of the road, 12 or 15 feet from my car. . . . I had the road to myself. . . . I couldn't forget the place on account of the trees there. I know trees. . . . I worked in a lumber camp. . . . There were some hemlocks and some soft maples. . . . I drove along at about 30 or 35 miles an hour. . . . He was about 6 feet tall, and his hair was standing up."

Confronted with defendant Sam Sheppard, Stawicki was asked by Corrigan, "Is this the man you saw?"

Stawicki replied, "No, he ain't got enough hair on his head."

Richard Knitter, of Sheffield Lake, who was returning with his wife and niece from a Cleveland movie, testified that he observed a suspicious-looking man at 3:50 A.M. standing about a hundred feet from the Sheppard home between the Houk and Ahern houses. The man was "very ugly and his hair was bushy on top." When he drove past, the man was about a foot from his car. He recalled remarking to his wife, "How would you like to meet that guy in the dark?" When cross-examined he added, "I didn't see anybody else on the road that night."

Bay Village Police Chief Eaton, a prosecution witness, corroborated that his department had taken a statement from a motorist who stated that about the murder time on the Sheppard property near a tree, his bright lights had spotted a man "in a white shirt." This motorist was not identified by Eaton. His police department, he said, had released the man without investigating this information further.

The *Cleveland Press* wasn't silent during the trial.

On October 28, as the trial was warming up, the *Press,*

over the full top half of its front page, published an editorial with this bold banner headline: *But Who Will Speak for Marilyn?* Understandably, it infuriated the Sheppard family. "Goddammit, we and Marilyn's family speak for her, not Louie Seltzer!" exploded Steve.

A month later, shortly before the defense was heard, the newspaper printed a streamer headline: *Sam Called a "Jekyll-Hyde" by Marilyn, Cousin to Testify.* The story began: "Two days before her death, murdered Marilyn Sheppard told friends that her accused husband, Dr. Samuel H. Sheppard, was 'a Dr. Jekyll and Mr. Hyde.' " It continued to report that the prosecution had a "bombshell witness"—Thomas Weigle, 26, Marilyn's first cousin—"on tap who will testify to Dr. Sam's display of fiery temper—countering the defense claim that the defendant is a gentle physician with an even disposition."

This "bombshell witness" did *not* testify. After this story was published, the defense made motions for change of venue, continuance, and mistrial, but they were denied.

Some national publications and commentators joined the festivities. *Time* magazine called the osteopathic defendant, the "Romeo of the Rubbing Table" and his secret girl friend, "an orthopedic wench." On November 19 Bob Considine, ordinarily most compassionate, in a radio broadcast heard over radio station WHK in Cleveland, compared Sheppard to Alger Hiss. Rejecting a defense request that the jury be polled on how many heard this broadcast, Judge Blythin said, "We can't stop people from listening. It's a matter of free speech."

When the trial was in the seventh of its nine weeks, Walter Winchell breathlessly told America in a report heard over WEL television and WJW radio in Cleveland that a woman arrested for robbery in New York had confessed that she was Sheppard's mistress and had borne him an illegitimate child.

Sheppard assured his lawyer, "This is the first time I ever heard of this woman." The defense asked that the jury be polled about this inflammatory Winchell report on the only occasion that the jury was questioned about the trial's publicity. Two jurors admitted in open court that they had heard it.

"Would that have any effect upon your judgment," Judge Blythin asked.

"No," both replied.

One juror, Elizabeth Borke, was apparently so confused by some of the testimony that she asked Corrigan while Sheppard was on the stand, "May I ask a question?"

"Sure, go ahead," agreed the defendant's lawyer.

The prosecution rose in protest. Juror Borke directed her request to the court: "Judge, may I ask a question?"

Solemnly, Judge Blythin intoned, "The law does not permit it."

Outside the courtroom another juror said, "It's more fun going bowling or reading a sex magazine than being on this jury."

But the sex was soon to come.

Guilty of Adultery

Indeed, sex spiced the climax of the 1954 Sheppard trial. Dr. Sam's infidelity turned the trial into a sex spectacle.

Even before the flamboyant July inquest the surgeon was becoming known as an All-American Sex Boy—the Errol Flynn of Osteopathy. Seeking a motive for why Sheppard might have killed his wife, authorities pursued a growing variety of rumors about Sheppard's extracurricular marital activities.

A former patient of Dr. Sam—his skillful suturing had spared her from face scars after an automobile accident—was among the first named. One day when the woman and her husband chanced to meet the Sheppards at a vacation resort, she had walked in the woods with Sheppard for an hour. Though both denied that "anything happened," when she returned, her husband slapped her face. Their friendship with the Sheppards was terminated.

A happily married wife of a baseball pitcher was described by the press as the "sixth woman in Dr. Sam's life." On the afternoon that her husband read about it in the newspaper he blew a decisive game in the second inning. The next day the *Cleveland Press*, possibly to avert a libel suit, published a big photograph of the pretty woman on page one saying that she had been mistaken for another woman. No apology. Just a caption correction.

A Los Angeles woman whom Dr. Sam had known when he was living there in 1950 was also dubbed one of his numerous "other women." Cleveland detectives tracked her down in Detroit. They flew there to interrogate her. The woman denied having engaged in illicit intercourse with Sheppard. She consented to take a lie detector test, which the disappointed detectives later agreed exonerated her.

Then, in a court of law, with the threat of the electric chair hanging over him, Dr. Sam faced the real "other woman" in his life.

The *femme fatale* who dramatically appeared near the trial's end on December 1 as the state's final and star witness was Susan Hayes. A slim, suntanned woman of 24, she looked more like a wholesome, fun-loving college girl than the inamorata in a murder case.

Susan Hayes had been hired at the Bay View Hospital in 1948 when she was 18 and had since become an exceptionally competent laboratory technician. She was extremely popular with both physicians and patients. She had first met Dr. Sam when he returned in late 1951 to Ohio with Marilyn and Chip.

At the July inquest Sheppard denied having engaged in sexual relations with her, but first he conferred with his lawyer, William J. Corrigan.

"She wouldn't dare tell on you," the experienced attorney assured his client.

"Well, I'm not sure," demurred Sam. "Gee, I don't want to hurt Susan, but I'd like to tell the truth at the inquest."

"If you do, they'll clobber you. Forget it, son."

At the inquest Coroner Gerber goaded the young surgeon into being a kiss-and-tell boy.

"Did you sleep in the same bedroom with Susan Hayes?"

"No."

"At no time?"

"Absolutely not."

"Not during any time in California?"

"Not at any time."

What the still unarraigned suspect did not then know was that two weeks earlier, shortly after Marilyn's murder, Susan Hayes had been questioned in the Los Angeles District Attorney's office. The young lady admitted that she and Dr. Sam had been good friends, that he was an excellent surgeon and a most considerate boss but had *never* been her lover.

Cleveland policemen, who were already building their case against the slain Marilyn's husband, were far from satisfied with this report. They embarked on a California fishing expedition.

In mid-July Assistant Prosecutor Thomas Parrino and Detective Robert Schottke, accompanied by *Cleveland Press* reporter James Vail, flew to Los Angeles to grill Miss Hayes. The interrogation took place until nearly midnight in the offices of the Los Angeles Chief of Police. She repeated the story she had told in the district attorney's office. But Parrino and Schottke didn't buy it, so they did more legwork, retracing Dr. Sam's March, 1954, California trip.

They returned to question Miss Hayes again at police headquarters. Parrino greeted her, "We've already talked to Dr. and Mrs. Miller in Glendale. They told us everything."

The frightened girl was persuaded to sign a statement in which she confessed her sexual intimacies with Sam Sheppard and to fly back to Cleveland with her interrogators to testify against him. She was placed in seclusion, at first for a week at a Cleveland hotel with a policewoman to protect her and later at her parents' Rocky River home.

Was police "heat" put upon the terrified girl to secure her cooperation? After all, adultery is legally a felony in Ohio, for which a culprit can be not only arrested but extradited. Or was she merely promised immunity from prosecution if she voluntarily appeared as a state's witness? Whether there would have been reprisals against her if she had refused to sign the statement and testify is doubtful.

On the witness stand her crisp figure appeared willowy and demure in her black woolen dress and her prim white Peter Pan collar, which seems to be standard wardrobe for females in murder trials. She wore little or no makeup that day. Her luminous dark eyes avoided those of her former lover, who stared at her impersonally, his facial muscles twitching.

Though ordinarily vivacious, she listlessly dished out the appetizing morsels to be devoured later by voracious newspaper readers. Marilyn's alleged rival, according to the state, testified that her year and a half liaison with Dr. Sam began in December, 1952, when she was working at the Bay View Hospital. She often saw her lover on Friday evenings when he drove her home from the hospital. Their affair continued when she quit the hospital in January, 1953, to work in a downtown Cleveland laboratory for six months.

Prosecutor Parrino guided her through her direct testimony.

"When you returned to the Bay View Hospital in August, 1953, until February, 1954, did you have intimate relations with Dr. Sam Sheppard during that time?"

"Yes."

"Where did the acts take place?"

"In his auto and in his apartment above the Sheppard Clinic."

When Sam and Marilyn first settled in Cleveland in 1951, they had rented an apartment in Rocky River. Susan Hayes lived just a block away. Nearly every working morning she would walk over to catch a ride to the hospital. The girl would frequently open the garage door and sit in the car while waiting for Dr. Sam to emerge. Marilyn would sometimes yell, "Sam isn't ready yet, Sue. You'll be late for work if you wait for him."

"That's all right. I'd rather be late than ride those awful buses."

On evenings when she worked late at the hospital with Sam, she would often say, "Doctor, would you please drive me home? Though she had seemingly fallen in love with Dr. Sam, to him the affair was merely a married man's physical arrangement. "I love Marilyn and Chip and can never leave them," he told the heartbroken Susan.

At his thirtieth birthday party at his home on December 29, 1953, Susan crashed it with her mother and a friend, according to Sam. He also claimed that Marilyn knew about his affair with Susan. Though it naturally made her unhappy, Marilyn had once said to Sam, "My father had a mistress ever since I was a little girl."

Susan Hayes moved to California in February, 1954, and Sam and Marilyn flew there a month later. They stayed at the ranch of Dr. and Mrs. Randall Chapman in Monterey, where Marilyn's child was conceived. Several days later Dr. Sam and Dr. Chapman drove down to Los Angeles to attend an osteopathic convention.

The roving husband telephoned Susan Hayes. He took her to dinner at the Glendale home of Dr. and Mrs. Arthur Miller. Many other osteopaths were playing poker there later that evening.

Parrino coaxed the facts out of his reluctant witness.

"Where did you stay that night?"

"At the Millers'."

"Where did Dr. Sam Sheppard stay?"

"At the Millers."

"Did you share the same room?"

"Yes."

"The same bed?"

"Yes."

"Did you have intimate relations?"

"Yes."

"For what period of time did you remain at the Miller residence?"

"About seven days."

Frugal Dr. Sam figured that this was an easy way to save a hotel or motel bill—where he would have had greater secrecy in his tryst. Had he done this, he might never have been convicted or even indicted. He had previously had sexual relations with Susan in his parked car, at the Sheppard Clinic, and even once in the home of Susan's parents when they were away. Dr. and Mrs. Miller were good friends, but they hardly could be expected to lie about the incident in a murder case.

During their stay at the Miller home Sam and Susan drove to San Diego to attend a wedding. Susan left her watch in a gas station bathroom. Sam promptly purchased another one for her for $50 and wrote the gas station proprietor to mail the found watch to him in Bay Village, which was done. When Dr. Sam returned to Bay Village, he attempted to put the watch expenditure on his expense account in order to deduct it from his income tax return. Marilyn one day found the sales slip.

Parrino wanted the jury to know what happened after Dr. Sam returned to Ohio. He jogged the memory of his witness.

Q: After Sam Sheppard left California, did you write letters to one another?
A: Yes.
Q: How many?
A: About four.
Q: Who started the correspondence?
A: Dr. Sheppard wrote to me first.
Q: Was there any profession of love in these letters?
A: No.
Q: Was the subject of divorce ever discussed?
A: Yes.
Q: Recall an instance?
A: Yes, in the early part of 1953.
Q: What did he say?
A: Well, he said that he loved his wife very much, but not as a wife, and he was thinking of getting a divorce.
Q: Anything else?
A: He wasn't sure his father would approve.
Q: He mentioned the subject again?
A: Later in November, 1953, at Bay View Hospital.
Q: Did the subject come up on other occasions?
A: It was never discussed, but it was mentioned.

Corrigan did not cross-examine the state's uncomfortable star witness. Assistant Defense Counsel Garmone was brief and even gallant, yet he threw a final sleeper question.

"Miss Hayes, in all your activities with Dr. Sheppard, were you always aware that he was a married man?"

"Yes, sir," she murmured almost inaudibly.

"Thank you. That's all. No further questions."

The defendant's other woman was dismissed. After she had completed her testimony, the state of Ohio rested its case against Dr. Samuel Sheppard.

The day after Susan Hayes testified, columnist Dorothy Kilgallen wrote that Susan's account of the affair hardly seemed one of undying passion. Sam read this story in jail. He promptly sent writer Kilgallen an oral message via his brother Richard: "Dorothy, you hit the nail on the head. Our affair was purely physical. We weren't emotionally involved. The watch I gave Susan didn't mean a thing to me."

The defense naturally tried to persuade the judge to

throw the case out for lack of evidence. But Judge Blythin ruled otherwise.

The *Cleveland Press*'s six-column headline that evening was *Susan Says Sam Loved Her,* with this subhead: *Tells of Their Trysts, His Desire for Divorce.*

Dr. Sam's "desire" for a divorce was testified to earlier by another state witness, Nancy Ahern, dinner companion on the murder eve: "Mrs. Sheppard always seemed very much in love with her husband, but I was never sure about Dr. Sam."

Then Mrs. Ahern came up with this twister: Marilyn had told her that she (Marilyn) had been told by Dr. Chapman (when Marilyn visited him in California) that Dr. Chapman had been told by Sam that he (Sam) was thinking about a divorce!

This "double hearsay" gossip was admitted as evidence by Judge Blythin over vigorous defense protests.

Why wasn't Dr. Chapman, who was living in California and available, invited by the State or defense to give *direct* testimony. The State may have feared that since he was a friend of Sheppard's, he might contradict Nancy Ahern's testimony. On the other hand, Defense Attorney Corrigan may have reasoned that it was not his job to refute hearsay, which any higher court would throw out. He was busy enough refuting what he deemed *proper* evidence.

Corrigan may have had another sticky reason. Dr. Chapman, who was then maritally embroiled himself, had privately told Marilyn, according to Sam, about the Susan Hayes Los Angeles interlude and had assured Marilyn that he would persuade Sam to be a "good boy"—if Marilyn would urge her Sheppard in-laws to invite him as a full partner in their Ohio practice.

Dr. Lester Hoversten, another fair-weather friend of Sheppard, testified for the state that Dr. Sam had once discussed with him a possible divorce from Marilyn. Sam had been best man at Hoversten's wedding and was even a character witness for him, over Marilyn's objections, when Hoversten divorced his wife in a Cleveland court. Sam insisted that it was Hoversten's—not Sam's—divorce that was discussed.

The *Cleveland Press*, in the finest tradition of yellow journalism, had previously published on July 16 a picture story of a 23-year-old woman who claimed that she had met a woman on a public beach who resembled Marilyn Sheppard and had told her about contemplating a divorce. As far as is known, Marilyn had never gone to a public beach during her marriage.

When Dr. Sam took the witness stand himself from December 9 to 14, he swore that he had never really loved Susan. He contended that it was Susan—not he—who had suggested a divorce, quoting Susan as saying, "Other men divorce their wives—why can't you?" He admitted having lied at the inquest. But he did so, he insisted, to protect Susan's name rather than his skin.

The prosecution asked whether he had engaged in extramarital intercourse with any women other than Susan Hayes. Yes, the defendant admitted. But he refused to name any names.

"I always told my wife about my affairs with other women," Dr. Sam claimed with amazing candor. "I didn't want her to hear about them from other people."

Sheppard disputed Prosecutor Mahon's description of his admitted infidelity as a "continuous thing." He insisted that both Susan and he realized their affair was finished after he left Los Angeles. His real roots were with Marilyn. As his attorney had pointed out, he had bought and put their Lake Road home in Marilyn's name and had taken out two $20,000 insurance policies on his life naming Marilyn as the sole beneficiary.

When Marilyn and he returned to Bay Village from California, Sheppard testified, they had agreed to make a fresh start. Sam testified that Marilyn had lost her "sexual aggressiveness" after the birth of Chip. They both recognized this, and Marilyn was trying to overcome her mental block about sex. Richard and Steve had reported that Marilyn had asked them how to make her intercourse less painful.

Ironically, after Marilyn's murder, a rumor had buzzed around Bay Village and Cleveland that Dr. Sam was sterile. It was widely whispered that he had slain Marilyn in fury because he was not the father of her expected child. Similarly, it was rumored that Chip was not Dr. Sam's child. Even at the inquest, these rumors were publicly explored.

In his summation Corrigan, a devout Roman Catholic,

argued that the defendant had no compelling reason to murder his wife, contending, "He certainly didn't have to kill his wife to get Susan Hayes. She was available whenever he wanted her."

The state never directly charged that Susan Hayes was the motive for a premeditated murder. In Ohio the state does not have to prove or establish a motive in a murder case. However, it was implied that the defendant wanted his wife out of the way so that he could marry Susan. The prosecution strongly suggested that any man who had lied about infidelity could also lie about killing his wife.

Motive or no motive, this stubborn fact was clear beyond any reasonable doubt to the jury, the state of Ohio, and the world: Sam Sheppard was guilty of adultery.

Verdict

The prosecution and defense were each allowed five hours for closing arguments in the tempestuous trial's ninth week.

The prosecution asked the jury to return a verdict of murder in the first degree. It did not specifically demand the death penalty, but that would have been mandatory if the jury did not recommend clemency. Murder and adultery were closely linked by the state, and this hit the defendant's confessed lie about his infidelity with triphammer force.

In his nearly two-and-one-half-hour summation, Prosecutor Parrino reminded the jury, "We're not dealing with something insignificant here, ladies and gentlemen. We're dealing with murder. If the defendant would lie under oath to protect the name of a lady, how many lies would he utter to protect his own life?" Sheppard was portrayed as a cold-blooded murderer, adulterer, and perjurer.

Prosecutors Mahon and Parrino thundered that this admitted perjurer's "bushy-haired intruder" story was a lie. Why didn't he get to his wife's aid quicker? How could he possibly sleep through the slaughter taking place upstairs? How could such a strong, athletic man be knocked unconscious so readily? Why didn't the dog bark? Why didn't the defendant yell when he chased the alleged killer down to the beach? After his so-called assault, how could he dial

Mayor Houk's telephone number? Why did he refuse the relaxing whiskey which Esther Houk offered him?

These and other puzzling though unanswered questions were drummed into the jurors' minds by one of the cleverest prosecutions in American criminal history. Lacking direct evidence, the prosecution built its case upon speculation.

Danaceau seemed to be asking for a manslaughter conviction when he reasoned: "Sam may have been awake. He may have walked up to the bedroom. Perhaps there were some recriminations over these other women, some arguments, some fight. When men are terribly angry, they sometimes do things they wouldn't otherwise do."

The defense summation to the jury was begun by Arthur E. Petersilge, the Sheppard family corporation lawyer. His voice was restrained. His approach was as reasoned and controlled as if he had been presenting a business brief.

"Five and one-half months after the murder of Marilyn Sheppard, the state does not know *how* she was killed, with *what* weapon she was killed, or *why* she was killed. Yet on the basis of this flimsy evidence, the state is asking you to send Sam Sheppard to the electric chair."

Defense Counsel Garmone ungallantly likened Susan Hayes to Mary Magdalene. He challenged anyone without sin to cast the first stone.

Attempting to prove that Sam and Marilyn were a happily married couple, Corrigan rhetorically inquired, "Is sex the only thing in a marriage? Is it the only thing in a love between a man and a woman?"

Melodramatically raising his client's hands, the lawyer declaimed: "These are the hands the state would have you believe killed Marilyn Sheppard. Look at these hands, these hands that just a few hours before had worked with skill and devotion to save the life of a child."

Corrigan then returned to his client's adultery, which he knew was weighing heavily upon the minds of the moralistic Ohio jurors: "Sheppard wandered from the path of rectitude. That didn't prove he didn't love his wife, his home, or his family. Sam Sheppard succumbed to sex, the strongest lure in the human body, as you and I know. I, too, would lie under oath if I were asked to confess to some private sin intended only for the ears of a confessor." He paused. His voice softened to almost a whisper. "We are approaching the Christmas season, when God came down to earth to set man free and establish on earth the principle of freedom. Unless we American lawyers and we American jurors do our part in maintaining that freedom in this case, we have failed in our duties."

Eloquent though he was, Corrigan was only a bush league Clarence Darrow. He failed to hammer home the big gaps in the state's case, such as the unproduced and unidentified surgical instrument, the blood discrepancies, the unidentified tooth chip, nail polish, and fragment of leather found near Marilyn's bed, and the admission by the judge of obviously inadmissible evidence.

It was time for the judge to speak.

Judge Blythin was relieved that the testimony had been concluded. It had been a grueling trial for him and had strained his patience and drained his energies. He was a man of character, a judicial precisionist who firmly believed in the American constitutional guarantees. He prided himself on always conducting fair trials without judicial error, even for defendants who were obviously guilty. He had worked long and hard on this complex case and was anxious that there be a speedy verdict with no hung jury.

The judge's carefully prepared, hour-long instructions to the jury on December 17 were verbose and technical. They may have confused some of the lawyers, not to mention many of the laymen jurors.

On the difference between direct and indirect (circumstantial) evidence, however, he was more clear. He offered this folksy example almost like an anecdote from *The Reader's Digest* which the judge read regularly:

> Let us assume that I had on a certain day a very fine cherry tree in my yard. The family happens to be away on that day, and when I return about five o'clock in the evening I find my cherry tree chopped down. I proceed to investigate and first make inquiry of my next-door neighbor, Mr. Smith. I ask him if he saw any stranger doing anything in my yard that day.

He replies: "Yes, I saw George Washington chop it down with an ax." That would be direct evidence because Mr. Smith is relying on his own sense of sight and states what he himself saw with his own eyes. For that reason he is able to give direct evidence that George Washington chopped down that cherry tree.

Let us consider now a case of circumstantial evidence in the same connection. Assume that on inquiry of Mr. Smith, my neighbor, he, in answer to my question, says that he did not see anyone chopping down my tree. I then ask him: "Did you see anyone about my place today?" He replies: "Yes, I saw George Washington walk along your driveway from the yard to the street with an ax on his shoulder."

Here is evidence of a fact which does not directly prove who chopped down my cherry tree but which permits a natural and fair inference that George Washington was in my yard with an ax, which, combined with the fact that my tree was chopped down, would constitute very definitely a piece of circumstantial evidence to be weighed in consideration of a charge against George Washington involving the act of chopping down that tree.

This colorful anecdote indicated to many impartial observers in the tense courtroom that Judge Blythin was saying indirectly—or circumstantially—that the defendant was guilty. One waggish newspaperman later quipped, "I'm offering even money that the jury returns with a verdict convicting George Washington of first degree murder."

Before he dismissed the jurors late that afternoon, Judge Blythin instructed them to return with one of these five possible verdicts:

1. Guilty of murder in the first degree (penalty: death in the electric chair);

2. Guilty of murder in the first degree with a recommendation for clemency (life imprisonment without parole);

3. Guilty of murder in the second degree (intentional but unpremeditated murder, calling for life imprisonment but with parole eligibility after ten years);

4. Guilty of manslaughter (penalty: one to twenty years, with parole eligibility after one year);
5. Not guilty.

The defendant was handcuffed and hauled back to his cell on the fourth floor of the Criminal Court building.

The jury retired to begin deliberations on Friday morning, December 17, at ten o'clock. From there the jurors were escorted out to lunch and later to dinner. Still no verdict. That evening they were taken to the Hotel Carter about a mile away to sleep, having been instructed beforehand by Judge Blythin to bring overnight bags.

Every time the jury convened, recessed, went to lunch or dinner or returned to their room to deliberate, the handcuffed defendant received an elevator ride from the fourth floor down to the first floor courtroom. "I felt like a yo-yo," he later quipped. The judge was not legally permitted to address the jury without the defendant being present.

Long before their deliberations began, some members of the jury had seemingly already made up their minds. At least they had expressed prejudice against the defendant. During Dr. Sam's testimony one juror told friends that he was irritated by the pompous manner in which the osteopathic surgeon threw around his extensive medical vocabulary. While the trial was still in progress, another juror, who consented to have photographs of his family and home taken by an enterprising member of the press, voiced skepticism about Sheppard's "bushy-haired intruder" story.

Late one evening midway during the trial—before any defense testimony had been heard—Dr. Stephen Sheppard received a strange telephone call. It was from a woman who reported that at dinner that night in a downtown Cleveland restaurant she had overheard one female juror talking about the case to friends and saying that Sam was guilty. The defendant's zealously loyal brother made a date with the telephoner to meet him in the courtroom the next morning to identify this juror. She did. Steve reported this to Corrigan. But the Sheppard attorney, who had infinitely more experience with juries than the defendant's brother, said, "What's the point of objecting? The judge won't sustain our objection, and the entire jury might only get mad at Sam."

While sequestered in their hotel for five days, the jurors were permitted to make regular unmonitored telephone calls to anyone they chose. The calls presumably were made to their families, but they could have been to anyone else—even to those hell-bent on putting Sam Sheppard in the electric chair. The complaisant bailiff allowed the jurors to come to his own hotel room and dial the unsupervised calls from his phone, as he later admitted after his action was exposed. The activity was a clear violation of a specific Ohio statute. The bailiff had been sworn to prevent the jurors from communicating with any outside persons.

The jury was out for five days. It was one of the longest deliberations in a twentieth-century criminal trial. In the Lindbergh trial, where the evidence was likewise circumstantial, the jury was out only 11 hours. Corrigan began to worry; he suspected from long experience that acquittals were generally quicker.

Shortly after four o'clock on the afternoon of Tuesday, December 21, 1954, the buzzer rang sharply several times in the courtroom. The prosecution and defense attorneys and the press moved into position. The jury had reached a verdict.

The defendant was brought down from his upstairs cell in this building, and his handcuffs were removed in the courtroom. Corrigan did not like the look on the jurors' faces as they entered the room. They avoided the chief defense counsel's piercing blue eyes. He placed his arm on his tense client's shoulder as if he expected the worst and said, "Steady yourself, Sam. I don't think the verdict's good. They're going to convict you."

Judge Blythin, with the verdict in his hands, repressed a small smile as he brushed his robes with his bony fingers. The judge began reading, "We, the jury, being duly empaneled and sworn, do find the defendant, Samuel H. Sheppard, not guilty of murder in the first degree." The seated prisoner showed no outward emotion, but a shriek of joy emanated from his family and friends in the rear of the courtroom.

Ignoring this breach of courtroom protocol, Judge Blythin continued reading: "But we find him guilty of murder in the second degree"—intentional but not premeditated murder.

There were stunned gasps in the small courtroom, which was jammed to capacity. Several newsmen attempted to rush out to their telephones, but guards prevented anyone from departing until the judge had adjourned court. The jury was polled. As the clerk read all of the jurors' names, Judge Blythin asked each one, "Is this your verdict?" All twelve solemnly replied yes.

The judge then intoned, "Samuel Sheppard, will you please step forward?" The inference was that Judge Blythin planned to pass sentence upon the convicted man then.

"Why sentence him now," Corrigan protested, "before I file a motion for a new trial?"

Judge Blythin pretended not to hear the defense attorney.

"Oh, go ahead," snapped Corrigan. "It's indicative of the entire trial."

The prisoner rose and walked to the bench with Corrigan at his side. He stood silent and erect, outwardly composed. Asked if he had anything to say before sentence was pronounced, he answered with quiet dignity, "I'd like to say, sir, that I am not guilty. I feel there have been facts presented to this court that definitely prove that I could not have performed this crime."

Corrigan again pleaded that sentencing be delayed until his motion for a new trial could be made. Many judges, in serious cases, refrain from immediate sentencing. The defense counsel's request was again denied. In a low, firm voice, Judge Blythin said to the convicted man standing before him: "It is the judgment of this court that you be taken to the Ohio penitentiary, there to remain for the rest of your natural life."

The prisoner was manacled and escorted out of the courtroom by two deputies.

Stunned and speechless, Corrigan finally found his voice, "I object to how this court has conducted this entire trial." The objection was overruled. Seeking an outlet from his highly charged emotions, Corrigan walked over and attempted to speak to a juror. Judge Blythin reproved him for this. The defense counsel shouted, "I have a right to talk to jurors in this courtroom." He continued to do so. Judge Blythin commanded the court stenographer, "Please let the record show that Mr. Corrigan talked to a juror while court was in session after the court had ordered him to desist."

Corrigan apologized and wearily returned to his seat. Judge Blythin thanked the jurors for their patience and diligence and discharged them. He kept everyone else in the courtroom until the jurors had filed out under guarded protection.

The verdict was flashed around the world within minutes.

Reaction was mixed.

When an ordinarily mild-mannered Detroit grandmother heard the news, she exclaimed to her daughter, "Good!" But when informed that the verdict was second degree, she deplored, "They shoulda hung him! He did it!"

On the other hand, a New York City cab driver philosophized, "They proved that Sam had a little action on the side. Who doesn't? They said Sam didn't get along with his wife. Who does? For *this* he's guilty of murder? Maybe he killed his wife because she made blueberry pie that night when he told her he wanted apple?"

The press, too, had divided feelings over the verdict. Many out-of-town newsmen and women, who were generally more objective in their trial reporting than the Cleveland press, suspected that Sheppard might have been guilty but that the state certainly did not prove it. Margaret Parton, who covered the trial for the *New York Herald Tribune,* later reflected, "No two people who sat through the trial saw it in quite the same light."

One newspaper woman was enraged by the verdict. Dorothy Kilgallen, who represented the *New York Journal American* and King Features Syndicate, a crime reporter for 30 years before achieving nationwide prominence as a Broadway columnist and television panelist, wrote, "The prosecutors for the State of Ohio did not prove he [Sam Sheppard] was guilty any more than they proved there are pin-headed men on Mars. Astounding is the word for the verdict! I heard the same evidence that the jury heard . . . I could not have convicted him of anything except possibly negligence in not locking his front door. . . . It is the first time I have ever been scared by the jury system . . . and I mean scared. . . ." Her syndicated column was dropped from the Cleveland newspaper the next day.

On the jury's first informal poll, it was later learned, half had voted for acquittal. The male jurors seemed to think that he was guilty, but the women had strong reasonable doubts. Eighteen ballots were necessary to reach a verdict, indicating that some speculation, hunches, and compromises influenced it. The jurors who later talked about their deliberations admitted that collectively they had never considered sending the defendant to the electric chair for premeditated first-degree murder. The weary jurors were understandably anxious to return home for some last-minute Christmas shopping. The snow was on the ground and the Yuletide merriment was in the air.

Objective students of the case later agreed that the state mainly had proved two things against Dr. Samuel Sheppard: (1) he was in the house at the time of the murder, and (2) he had been unfaithful to his wife as recently as four months before the murder.

"They found him guilty of adultery but convicted him of murder," concluded Joseph Frank, a New York attorney who studied the proceedings. "If you did that to every unfaithful husband or wife, there wouldn't be enough jails to hold them. The jury said Sheppard was guilty because he was there."

Yet this conclusion of the jury and state of Ohio is understandable. What precisely happened between 12:30 A.M., when Marilyn closed the door on her guests, and 5:50 A.M., when her husband telephoned Mayor Houk, is still a mystery.

On the day after his conviction Sheppard agreed to be interviewed in jail by Paul Holmes, whose objective reporting of the case in the *Chicago Tribune* had impressed him. Holmes, a laconic, methodical man, had been a member of the *Chicago Tribune* staff since 1941. Before that, he had been city editor and executive editor of the *Milwaukee Sentinel*. He was also a member of the State Bar of Wisconsin. The case haunted him. In August 1961, he published *The Sheppard Murder Case*, a brilliant book, which revived the dormant case.

Two years later, in August, 1963, Holmes told me an anecdote that he had not published in his book—about why he could never visit prisoner Sheppard in jail after the conviction.

Defense attorney Corrigan refused to permit his client to be interviewed by the Chicago journalist-lawyer, who had probed deeper than any press member covering the trial.

"But here is a note from your client saying that he wants to see me," remarked the puzzled Holmes. "Why can't you let me talk to him?"

Sam Sheppard's lawyer glared a moment; then he shot back, "Do you want them to bury me?"

Aftermath

The trial did not end the Sheppard case. There were many strange, bitter, even tragic sequels.

Judge Edward Blythin was overwhelmingly reelected to a six-year term on his Common Pleas bench on November 4, but he never lived to fill it.

In that same election Chief Prosecutor John J. Mahon won a seat on the court and became a conferee of Judge Blythin on January 5, 1955. A widower of 69, Mahon married Gertrude Bauer, his assistant, shortly after the trial ended.

The other two prosecutors were similarly elevated to local judgeships in part because of the vast publicity they had received during the trial.

Saul Danaceau was elected to the Common Pleas bench in 1956. He served there until his death in 1965.

Thomas Parrino ascended to the bench earlier. In the fall of 1955, when an incumbent Cleveland municipal judge suddenly died, the *Cleveland Press* boosted young Thomas Parrino for the post.

Susan Hayes married a television editor in Hollywood and is now the mother of several children. Though she has since shunned the press, she reportedly told a friend not long after the verdict, "I still can't believe that Sam did it. But I hope that I never hear of the Sheppard case again."

J. Spencer Houk, whose health was impaired during the investigation and trial, left politics and sold his butcher shop. He became an automobile salesman. Houk was divorced in 1962 and has since remarried.

Esther Houk, his former wife, became a telephone operator in a suburban Cleveland shopping center.

Their son Larry, who worshipped Sam Sheppard, is now an M.D. with a general practice elsewhere.

One of the jurors, a lifelong Clevelander, moved to a distant state, presumably to avoid the abuse that he had to endure after the controversial trial. He said that even strangers on the bus, who believed that Sheppard was innocent, heckled him. Another juror committed suicide. So did one of the tormented witnesses.

Bar Association officials deplored this "trial by newspaper." The American Bar Association, in its semimonthly newsletter, the *Coordinator*, on November 1, 1954, warned against "creating a circus of the Sheppard trial. If the coverage continues in the same sensational vein of the opening days, it could set the cause of courtroom photography back twenty years. . . ." Other bar organs cited the warning of the late U.S. Supreme Court Justice Robert H. Jackson that excessive publicity during the accusation and trial of criminal suspects was "one of the worst menaces of American justice."

Edwin M. Otterbourg, ex-president of New York County Lawyers Association, addressed the Prosecuting Attorneys Association of Ohio during the Sheppard trial, on December 11, 1954. His speech, published in the January, 1955, *Bulletin of the Cuyahoga Bar Association,* warned:

> The newspaper articles contain predictions of forthcoming testimony long before it is offered in court, and some of them print testimony which was stricken out at the trial by the Court. Personal likes and dislikes are highlighted by constant characterization of both testimony and witnesses; thus, certain testimony is characterized as being "most damaging," and other as being "shaky" or being "gingerly" and "unwillingly" given. Even in an account of the trial, it has been reported that copies of certain exhibits have been mailed out by the district attorney's office and to whom and for what purpose.

Even segments of newspaperdom denounced the press treatment of the Sheppard case. The *Asheville Citizen,* in North Carolina, on December 23, 1954, compared it to William Randolph Hearst's classic cablegram to his Cuba correspondent in 1898: "You furnish the pictures, and I'll furnish the war." The *Toledo Blade* editorialized on December 22, 1954, ". . . the press must ask itself if its freedom, carried to excess, doesn't interfere with the conduct of free trials. . . . One of the papers, which virtually demanded the arrest of Dr. Sheppard, almost had a vested interest in his conviction. . . ." Later, the *Blade*'s associate editor, John M. Harrison, in the October 15, 1955, *Saturday Review* added, "Almost from the moment Marilyn Sheppard's body was found, the press took over the roles of detective, sheriff, prosecutor, judge, and jury."

In December, 1954, the Newspaper Institute of America called the Sheppard press coverage, "a disgrace to American journalism and brought back all the traditions of yellow journalism." Agreeing with this charge, editor Robert U. Brown, in the December 4, 1954, issue of *Editor and Publisher*, the trade publication of the Fourth Estate, had one qualification: ". . . the guilty parties are a small minority of the daily newspapers and confined almost exclusively to some, but not all, of the large metropolitan cities." In a posttrial panel conducted by the American Society of Newspaper Editors, 10 of the 14 editors said that the Sheppard case was the most overplayed story of 1954, as *Hartford Courant* Editor Herbert Brucker reported in the March, 1955, *Connecticut Bar Journal.*

Newsweek magazine, in a January 3, 1955, press column titled *Disgraceful,* stated: "After Dr. Sam's trial began in mid-October, one third to one half of the nation's newspapers were front-paging daily developments. . . . The night of the verdict the [Cleveland] *Press* sold 30,000 extra papers."

Newspapers have to live. But so do people. Or do they?

A Mother and a Father

In 1954 Dr. Sam's mother, Ethel Niles Sheppard, was a tiny, silver-haired woman of 64. Before her marriage she had taught Latin and English in a small town Indiana high school near her rural birthplace.

After her youngest son was first taken away in handcuffs in her living room, she was never the same person. Her world crumbled. An idealistic, retiring, religious woman, she had been sheltered from the outside world first by her educational environment and later by her protective husband. In her litany of life, goodness and truth always prevailed in the end. Mrs. Sheppard was ill-equipped to face the public furor following her daughter-in-law's murder. She had always wanted a beautiful, lovable daughter, and Marilyn filled that niche.

When her son privately confessed to her and her husband his infidelity to Marilyn shortly before the newspaper reports about Susan Hayes in mid-July, Ethel Sheppard's puritannical values were outraged.

"Sam, how could you have done such a terrible thing?" she exclaimed, more in anguish than in censure. "Don't you remember the Seventh Commandment: Thou Shalt Not Commit Adultery?"

"Mother, I know what I did was wrong . . . it was inexcusable . . . I hate myself." Sobbing, her youngest son buried his head in his hands.

His father, a lifelong member of the Methodist Church, stood erect and stonily silent. What could he add to what his wife had already said?

The only time that Ethel Sheppard emerged publicly in her son's case was several days later. She was subpoenaed to testify at Coroner Gerber's inquest. Sam's mother answered questions quietly and completely, her manner proud and proper. She shielded her inner feelings from the morbid throng.

After her testimony a ghoulish local newsman telephoned her several mornings, sometimes as early as 6:30 A.M., inquiring "And how are you feeling *today*, Mrs. Sheppard?"

Thereafter she left the receiver off the hook and withdrew even more. Wearied in spirit, she was sapped of her physical and mental strength. She spent her days sitting at her desk writing in her private journal.

The day after her youngest son was arrested she wrote a long letter to him, which she handed to her son Stephen to deliver in jail.

"This envelope is unsealed," she told Steve, "so you may read what it contains if you wish, but after that, get it to Sam. When he has read it, he is to give it back to you so you can destroy it. That is all I have to say."

Steve did as he was told except that he did not destroy the letter after Sam had read and returned it. Instead, ten years later in *My Brother's Keeper*, his book written with Paul Holmes, he published it. The salutation was, "My son, my Sam, my dearest one." This is an excerpt from the letter:

> You have not been perfect—especially as a husband, but there are reasons for that which we both know. I make no excuses for your infidelity to Marilyn and I know that you ask no quarter on that account. But let me say this and then bring it to an end—you have been a good son, a loving and considerate and kind and decent person since the first day you were born.
>
> Don't let what is happening to you now twist you into a bitter, hateful, vengeful human being but try to take in your stride whatever may come your way, realizing that God put you there for reasons known only to Him and that He will deliver you when they have served His purposes, whatever they may be. . . . Until you send for me, I will respect your wish that we not see one another.

When the trial was less than half over, shortly after Coroner Gerber had completed his "surgical instrument" testimony and before the defense had been heard, Ethel Sheppard was in a virtual state of shock. On the evening of November 19, she burned her private journal and swallowed an overdose of Tuinal sleeping pills. She was rushed to the Bay View Hospital, and her stomach pumped. Officially, she was treated for "a mild stroke." The suicide attempt was never revealed to Sam, Corrigan, or, of course, the press.

Ethel Sheppard was seemingly on the road to recovery when her husband was hospitalized for what appeared to be pleurisy on December 23, two days after their son's conviction. Rather than let her spend Christmas alone in her large house, Steve and Betty Sheppard persuaded her to stay at their Rocky River home. They gave her their master bedroom. Despite the brave attempts on everyone's part, the holiday season was hardly joyous.

Seventeen days after her son's conviction, on the cold Friday morning of January 7, 1955, Ethel Sheppard wrote a brief note to her son Steve, who was at the hospital. Betty was out shopping. The note did not mention her youngest son. It read: "Dear Steve: I just can't go on. . . . I'm sorry. Thanks for everything, Mother."

The retiring woman, who loathed violence and feared firearms, picked up her son's revolver from his drawer. She locked her bedroom door and swiftly ended her life with a bullet in her brain.

Steve rushed home from the hospital after Betty telephoned. He cried. "I should have known. I should have known." He telephoned the Rocky River Police Department and requested the answering officer to notify the Coroner of Cuyahoga County. "I don't think I could bear ever talking to Sam Gerber again," he murmured. He then rushed to the jail to inform Sam and to the hospital to tell his father before they heard the tragic news on the radio or elsewhere.

Judge Harry Hanna, presiding jurist of the Common Pleas Court, with Judge Blythin's concurrence, permitted prisoner Sheppard to leave the Cuyahoga County jail for several hours to attend his mother's funeral on Monday afternoon, January 10. Handcuffed to two guards, he was driven to the Saxton Funeral Home, in Lakewood. Though the inside chapel services were allegedly private, outside an estimated 3,000 persons, including newsmen, photographers, and rubberneckers, crowded the area roped off by police. Reverend Alfred C. Kreke, the Sheppard family friend who had delivered the eulogy at Marilyn's funeral, performed the service. At the end of the services the deceased woman's three sons approached the open casket to pray. But there was an intruder, a deputy handcuffed to her youngest son—an unusual occurrence at a loved one's casket for even the deadliest criminal.

On the drive to the Sunset Memorial Park Cemetery, in North Olmstead, curiosity seekers hid behind shrubs, climbed fences, and craned their necks to peek into the mourners' cars. At the open grave of his mother her child stood pale and silent, his head bowed, manacled to a pair of deputies.

On the return trip the bereaved prisoner requested permission to stop briefly at the Bay View Hospital to visit his sick father. The elder Sheppard was too ill to attend his wife's funeral. Permission was denied. The prisoner and two deputies drove back to the jail.

Dr. Sheppard, Sr., had always been highly esteemed by his slain daughter-in-law. Marilyn had often said, "A little bit of God walks with Dad Sheppard wherever he goes." The dignified man had lived an abstemious life and had seemingly been in good health before his daughter-in-law's tragic death. But he began to age as his son's trial progressed. His formerly springy movements slowed. Like his wife, he felt his life was finished, even though he never doubted Sam's innocence. After his youngest son's conviction he said to his older two sons, "You boys must always be proud of Sam, never ashamed, because we all know that he did not kill Marilyn."

Richard and Steve persuaded their father to leave their Bay View Hospital for supplementary tests at the noted Cleveland Clinic. There the diagnosis was cancer of the stomach. Dad Sheppard asked to be returned to his beloved Bay View Hospital. He was brought back on January 14.

On the evening of January 18, 11 days after the death of his wife, Dr. Richard Allen Sheppard died of a hemorrhaging gastric ulcer at the age of 64. An autopsy performed by Dr. Virgil Hawes revealed that death resulted from internal bleeding after a huge gastric ulcer had eaten into his bloodstream. His two eldest sons were convinced the ulcer had been induced by constant worry since Marilyn's murder. He left combined holdings worth $272,078, which was not as "wealthy" as popularly believed.

The senior Sheppard's funeral on January 20 was another carnival. His youngest son again stood handcuffed at the casket. The prisoner watched his father follow his mother to the grave.

Immediately after his father's funeral prisoner Sheppard was transferred to a bare "suicide cell" without a toilet or washbasin. There, with a bright bulb shining inside, a guard patrolled the cell outside to insure that the inmate did not try to take his own life.

Within 11 days, less than a month after his conviction, a dejected doctor had lost both of his parents. In less than seven months he had also lost his wife and his freedom. As he paced his cell, he mused bitterly, "Injustice pulled the trigger on my mother and killed my father. Some people in Ohio wish I *would* kill myself because they're sick of my face and my case."

But Sam Sheppard wanted to live very much—regardless of what awaited him.

3

THE PRISON

DR. SAM was transferred to a regular cell with other prisoners in the Cuyahoga County Jail.

According to some penologists, more rapes are committed inside big county jails than in the communities outside. County Prisoner Sheppard was shocked to learn of two instances of violent homosexuality by "jockers" who preyed upon young, innocent boys. In the first case six hardened criminals raped a sixteen-year-old youth, a first time offender who was awaiting trial. The second instance concerned a veteran felon who performed sodomy upon a seventeen-year-old inmate.

"Both of these boys were so badly injured that they had to be sent to the Cleveland City Hospital for rectal repair," Dr. Sam later explained. "I reported this, which was the reason for the referrals."

Prisoner 98860

Prison was beginning to feel like Sam's normal home. His Bay Village house, whose ownership was listed in Marilyn's name, was turned over with his consent to a real estate agent to sell to obtain funds for legal costs. Shortly after the house was placed on the market, in June, 1955, it was purchased by a Cleveland attorney who has lived there ever since with his family.

The year that Dr. Sam had spent in the county jail did not count as "time served" should he ever apply for parole. According to the Ohio statute on his life sentence of second-degree murder, he was required to serve ten years in the penitentiary before parole eligibility.

Even more important to him, he felt restless and rotting in the wasteful grabbag county jail while his legal battle continued. "I hadn't seen the sunlight in a year, and I had bedbug bites all over my body and face," he recalled. At the Ohio State Penitentiary in Columbus, he could at least try to settle down into some constructive life and program, including regular exercise, while waiting for some distant judicial gods in black robes to free him, he reasoned. He formally requested to be transferred there.

On the evening of July 19 Sam was suddenly thrown into solitary for no apparent reason. "It was just a farewell kick in the teeth from Cleveland authorities," he mused bitterly.

The next morning he was transported 150 miles south to enter the Ohio Penitentiary in downtown Columbus, built in 1834. Prisoners were taken there usually at 5:00 A.M. in a van dubbed the "Blue Goose"—so named because the grimy vehicle once sported a blue-gray color. But Dr. Sam left later, at 8:00 A.M., in an automobile, handcuffed to another prisoner, to oblige local newsmen and photographers, who could trail after him in other cars. The press cars often pulled alongside at red lights to enable the newspaper and television cameramen to snap closeups.

"Smile, Mr. Sheppard!" coaxed one photographer. Dr. Sam felt like punching the insulting creature.

On the ride down on Route 71 prisoner Sheppard stared into space. He drank in the free world scenery. It might be his last look for a long time.

"Sam, the newspapermen are going to ask me what we talked about during the ride," said one of the guards. "What shall I say to them?"

"Tell them they are sending an innocent man to prison and that the people responsible damn well know it."

They finally arrived at the penitentiary, and Sam heard the steel gates clang behind him.

Like the other prisoners, he was searched from ear to anus to insure that he had smuggled in no contraband. He was assigned his number—98860—given two pairs of prison trousers and two shirts, and marched down to the mess hall for chow. He was shocked to observe that the white prisoners marched in front of the black ones.

"Hey, Sam, tell us about that broad you were shacked up with," a fellow convict greeted him in the chow line.

The new prisoner controlled his anger and softly answered, "Son, there are some things that a gentleman does not discuss in public."

Another convict heckled, "Sam, I'll bet that schlong of yours has seen a lot of action!" A third contributed to the merriment by adding, "Man, he must have gotten his end wet a lot!"

The prisoners laughed, and the newcomer smiled. The convicts, with their penchant for swift character assessment, appraised him as an okay guy and a welcome addition. The Doc was keeping his mouth shut and his eyes open.

Sheppard quickly proved popular with fellow inmates largely because of his lack of pretension. "Sam never made like a big shot," recalls one. "He was just one of us mugs." Some, though, considered him "a dumb cluck" because he later shelled out money from his four dollars a month prison earnings to fellow convicts with hard luck stories who claimed to need it for cigarettes or to pay off gambling debts.

"I could never really become 'one of the boys,' " Sam later told me. "I could not speak the language of the professional criminal. I had no bank robberies to reminisce about. But I found that with care I could tread the middle line, and I did. I was known as a 'loner' and 'a solid square.' This meant that while I did not join prison society as a full-fledged member, I nonetheless was not a danger to my fellow inmates. I would not join in their activities, but they knew I wouldn't squeal on them."

Dr. Sam quickly learned to trust the simple hoodlums and the thieves most. Too many intelligent prisoners, he found, who were often imprisoned for rape or child molesting around schools, turned out to be finks, informers, or prison punks. Inmates called them "the bad asses" and "motherfuckers"—terms which at first shocked Sam's sensitive nature.

The homosexuals, whom he shunned, bothered him most. "If you were hungry, would you eat garbage?" he asked himself. Yet the language and shamelessness of the "queens" and the "jockers," who comprised about half of the penitentiary population, revolted him.

One day a highly articulate middle-aged homosexual approached him, saying, "Sam, I've had my eye on you ever since you came here. Have you ever been screwed in the ass? It's great for your prostate gland. You're a doctor—you should know. I once screwed a cow and even blew another guy in church. If you want to think about that, Sam, just let me jerk you off meanwhile. I can do it in the movie when the lights are out. Everybody does on Jack Night. I'll do the pitching. You can just do the catching."

Sam Sheppard's face reddened. He felt like grabbing the man by the neck, but he feared that he would kill if he did. Certainly, he would be thrown into solitary indefinitely. Smoldering with fury, he restrained himself and walked away without answering the man.

He did, however, give vent to his emotions when an immature, frightened 20-year-old youth named Steve, whom he had befriended, told him that a husky Negro had threatened to attack him sexually and would use a gas pipe or hammer from the carpenter shop to do so. Sam approached the would-be molester and asked if this was true.

"Damn right, man! So what?"

Sheppard recalled, "He was too large and well built for me to take on an equal basis, and he was younger than I was. So I sucker-punched him and used karate. He dropped like a bag of cement."

Steve was never bothered by the bully after that.

Nearly 14 years later, on July 8, 1969, when he testified before the United States Senate Subcommittee to Investigate Juvenile Delinquency, Sheppard said, "One of the classic problems involved the so-called homosexual 'Madams.' These are inmates in charge of the hospital or some other office in the institution. They are highly valued positions. Many men aspire to them. Those who get the jobs often get them because of homosexual favors. I have seen a homosexual warden allow his love partner to more or less run the prison. This reflects on the quality of the staff that is in charge of correctional institutions and illustrates their inadequacy and weakness. . . . It sets the atmosphere in penal institutions. . . . The teacher does not have the opportunity. Yet the homosexual who works for the deputy warden gets everything."

To preserve his body and heterosexuality Sheppard plunged into a vigorous exercise program.

"I did calisthetics until I was exhausted," he recollected. "Sometimes I did 500 pushups a day. Most of all I enjoyed practicing weight-lifting whenever I could."

A natural athlete since boyhood, Sheppard participated in nearly all prison sports. He played guard on the basketball team. He played baseball. He was chief trainer of the football squad, dubbed the Hurricanes. He wrestled and refereed wrestling bouts in the prison courtyard.

To preserve his soul, with inner fortitude he resisted the prison dehumanization and brutality masquerading as "treatment." He evolved a philosophic defense against the psychological pressure he experienced living with three other prisoners in a seven-foot square cell; the inability to use the seatless toilet except in his cellmates' sight; the occasional solitary confinement without clothing in the bedless unheated "hole," where men were forced to wallow in their own excrement. He also learned to withstand the needless insults from the sadistic guards, the agony of loneliness, the forever clanging bells, the slow, sleepless hours during the long nights.

The only way to avenge Marilyn and his parents, he rationalized, was to sustain his life, with some positive direction.

"I thought a great deal of my family," he recalled later. "I thought of Marilyn as she was in life. I kept her picture in my cell throughout my ten years in prison, just as I did Chip's. I reminisced about the happy years of our marriage when we really led the best of lives."

Prisoner 98860 respected Warden Ralph Arvis, whom he found a tough yet fair administrator, but he had mixed feelings about Deputy Warden Ernest Maxwell. Inmates dubbed the Ohio Penitentiary "Maxwell's House."

Shortly after Dr. Sam arrived, Maxwell asked, "How old are you, Sheppard?"

"Thirty-one."

"Well, you'll only be forty-one when you get out. That's not too old."

"Maybe I'll get out earlier, on parole."

"Maybe, if you keep your nose clean and your people on the outside don't yell too loud. Stay away from the trouble-makers inside here. Don't listen to them. Just obey all the rules. Read the rule book in your cell carefully. We got a place for rule breakers here. And it don't have no Beautyrest mattress."

The deputy warden paused before continuing: "For the first six months, you'll work in the mill or some cell-block job. After that you can work in the hospital, if you want."

Stiffening, Sheppard retorted, "I don't want to work in the hospital."

Maxwell's face reddened at this uncooperative remark.

"It just might be too hard on me to be around surgery and not be able to perform it," explained Dr. Sam. "Frankly, I'd rather work in the coal pile."

"That's just for niggers."

"I don't mind. How about the recreation department?"

Instead, Sheppard was assigned to teach auto mechanics in the vocational school because he was a car buff and knew physics. He was transferred to another cell with three other teachers, who helped to stimulate his mind. For teaching he received "good time" parole credit and was given an extra shirt with a special stripe. Later, he taught five International Correspondence School subjects to fellow convicts: physics, chemistry, physiology, biology, and public health.

One day early in 1956 a classification officer casually asked him, "Sheppard, do you know anything about anesthesia?"

"How could I have been a neurosurgeon if I didn't?" Dr. Sam irritably replied.

"Well, we got a spot open in the hospital for a male nurse who knows anesthesia and surgery."

Prisoner 98860 was reluctant to leave teaching. His deep inner hurt at not having been able to do any medical work for a year and a half caused him anguish. But he thought of his father's and brothers' as well as his own dedication to their profession.

"If I can be more useful in the hospital, I'll be glad to work there," he mumbled.

After Sheppard was assigned to the prison hospital as a male nurse, Warden Arvis explained to the surprised press, "We needed qualified personnel in the hospital. Dr. Sheppard is certainly qualified. Should I let him be a blacksmith instead? He won't perform any operations, though."

Dr. Sam's duties as a male nurse, for which he earned one dollar for a 60-hour week on 24-hour emergency call, included more than administering anesthesia. "We used every form of anesthesia," he recollected. "We even used the poison that African natives use in their blow-gun darts, which paralyzes a patient in readiness for an operation."

The new male nurse likewise took temperatures, checked pulses, made beds, folded linen, prepared surgical packs, and mopped up after operations. He began reading general medical journals ravenously in the prison library and the more specialized ones sent to him by his friend Dr. Arthur Miller. His youthful enthusiasm for sports cars gradually was replaced by a deeper interest in medicine. Increasingly, fellow convicts and prison employees began to call him "Doc."

One of the dividends of his promotion was a move into the hospital dormitory. There 98860 had a single bed, a bedside table, supplementary meals and a 24-hour hospital pass.

All of the visiting surgeons except one soon requested that he assist them during their surgery. His favorite was Dr. Roy E. Swenson, of Columbus, a partner of a physician who had been his father's roommate in medical school. Other prison surgeons "consulted" him before performing their operations. This was the most satisfying aspect of his entire incarceration. It again made him feel like a doctor, not just a prisoner, especially when he was unofficially put in command of the postoperative division after the regular physicians had left for the day.

One evening after a surgeon who had performed a routine appendectomy had left, the patient's heart stopped. He was dead after emerging from the anesthetic. Dr. Sam immediately applied external cardiac resuscitation. In three minutes he had restored a heartbeat, and an hour later the patient was conscious.

Despite such successes, Sheppard's hospital labor wasn't without its problems. Once when a prisoner named Cassidy was brought in dying after being stabbed in the chest nine times, a prison bureaucrat said to Sheppard, "This rat's not worth a damn. Keep him alive long enough just so the guys who stabbed him won't have a first-degree murder rap. But let him die right afterward because he deserves it." The bureaucrat walked out of the hospital muttering, "Retribution, Sheppard."

"This was an insult to my medical oath," Dr. Sam later mused. "We saved Cassidy. I even got a Christmas card from him when he was out of prison saying, 'Thanks for everything, chum.' "

Another bureaucrat in the prison powerhouse once asked Dr. Sam to "plant" a syringe containing a drug in a prisoner's mattress. A guard would then "find" it, and the "culprit" would be thrown into the "hole."

"I wouldn't even do that to you, you bastard," Sheppard said to the would-be conspirator. "If you want to frame this man, go plant your own goddamn syringe."

Dr. Sam's biggest hospital headaches were the male nurses who stole the morphine and other drugs. Narcotics were often purchased by "jockers" who used them as bait to lure young men into homosexual activity.

Various tricks were used by corrupt male nurses to steal drugs. Sometimes they squirted the drug into bottle caps and then removed the caps after their shifts. Other times they would drain it out of a bottle with a syringe and replace it with colored water from another syringe. On still other occasions, a thief nurse would fill a syringe with distilled water and conceal it under a towel. Another syringe, containing the drug that a patient needed, would be placed on top of this towel. The crook would then stealthily switch these syringes, keeping the one that had "the good shit."

Dr. Sam was infuriated when he discovered these ploys, not just for the shameless thievery but because the patient would be cheated out of necessary medication. He slugged two crooked male nurses he caught in the act but never squealed on them. Needing an outlet to communicate his sense of outrage, he wrote to his brother Richard about it, but his censored letter never left the penitentiary.

Faced with such an adversary, Sheppard's hospital enemies retaliated. With the help of a prison official involved in the corruption, Dr. Sam was suddenly transferred to the print shop, where he sorted colored paper and typed and was a timekeeper.

Several months later, in April, 1957, a visiting neurosurgeon requested Sheppard's assistance in a delicate brain surgery operation. Sam was reassigned to the prison hospital after Warden Arvis had ferreted out the truth behind his transfer.

Thereafter, Dr. Sam plunged himself into even more strenuous medical work. He toiled long hours during the prison's 1957 flu epidemic. He donated as much blood as permitted—once every two months—during the Red Cross nurses' monthly visits.

During the two-month 1959 Sloan Kettering Cancer Research project in the prison under the direction of Dr. Chester M. Southam, Associate Professor of Medicine at Cornell, the disbarred osteopathic neurosurgeon was the first convict to volunteer for the live cancer cell injections—the first time that this experiment had been attempted on human guinea pigs. Sheppard's arm was injected with thousands of live cancer cells; years later he developed a phobia about having contracted cancer as a result of the experiment.

"Trying to be a big shot with that cancer crap," sneered one convict.

Dr. Sam stared hard but answered his heckler softly, "Next time they ask for volunteers, why don't you try it yourself."

Twenty convicts followed him. The experiment was widely publicized as an important contribution to cancer research.

Visitors to the Ohio Penitentiary invariably asked about Dr. Sam. He rarely discussed his case, and when he did so he spoke without bitterness. He merely said that he was innocent and would one day be vindicated.

On June 3, 1960, the *Cleveland Press* published exclusive prison photographs of Prisoner 98860. "After more than five years in the Ohio Penitentiary," it reported, "Dr. Samuel H. Sheppard retains the dubious distinction of being the best known American behind bars."

A Family Goes on Living

Outside prison bars Sheppard's family strove to keep their lives and careers from being destroyed. Nearly everyone in Bay Village knew a member of the family or someone close to it.

The family's Bay Village Hospital received so many telephone calls that an extra switchboard operator had to be hired to handle them. "After Sam's conviction," recalls Dr. Stephen Sheppard, "we didn't know what would happen to the hospital. But the sick people kept coming, more than ever. We think this was a testimonial to their faith in Sam and the Sheppard family."

The family's loyalty and unswerving belief in Sam's innocence was reminiscent of the Kennedy clan's devotion to each other. The Sheppards drained their family savings to help defray Sam's legal costs. Richard and Steve put aside one-third of their professional earnings for their prisoner brother in accordance with their father's wishes.

Yet no member of the immediate Sheppard family was immune from attack. The Sheppard children often ran home from school sobbing at how they had been slandered by classmates in school or on the way home. Their parents were invariably gaped at. Even worse, they received many anonymous letters and crank telephone calls at all hours of the day and night. Profanity and character assassination abounded over the invisible wires.

Dr. Richard Sheppard and his wife Dorothy remember some of the other taunts.

"They often came from motorists who stopped in front of our home," recalled Richard. "Some of them yelled: 'Sam's a dirty killer.' Many of these tormentors were women. That wasn't all. One morning we found a path of bloodstains leading from our house to the garage, and we called police. Then we found out that some nut had put animal blood there to scare us."

Dr. Steve, his wife, and their two young daughters Janet and Carol were likewise horrified one day when red paint was spattered all over their front pavement, driveway, and steps by an anonymous vandal.

Steve suffered the most frequent abuse because he was

the most vocal and powerful personality in the Sheppard family. A silver-haired, well-tailored dynamo with a Man of Distinction appearance, he often appears arrogant to strangers. Yet beneath his smooth, hard-hitting facade lies an extraordinarily compassionate human being. His headstrong indignation at injustice often interferes with his cooler judgment, yet when Stephen speaks, which is often, the words are to the point, honest. Sam always listened to Steve more than to anyone else.

Steve attended Washington-Jefferson College in Pennsylvania, Hanover College in Indiana, and Western Reserve University in Cleveland. He received his D.O. degree from the Los Angeles College of Osteopathic Physicians and Surgeons in 1944 and later his M.D. from the California College of Medicine. He was certified in general surgery by the American Osteopathic Association in late 1954—during Sam's trial.

After the trial a doctor friend reported to Steve some new information about the murder morning, which he had heard from a patient. Steve quickly confronted the source, a television station employee, and asked, "Why didn't you go to the authorities with these facts during the trial? It might have influenced the jury's thinking."

"Frankly, Doc," he apologized, "I didn't want to get involved. I was afraid of the publicity. It was a risk that I couldn't take."

Dr. Stephen Sheppard sighed and shook his head at how his brother's controversial case had fomented fear throughout Ohio. "I wonder how many other decent citizens who knew something were afraid to come forward," he mused.

I first met Steve while his younger brother was still in prison. At the time he said, with deep feeling, "The jury guessed that Sam was guilty. But if Sam is guilty, *I'd* like to know about it. I'd *want* my brother to stay in jail. If he were really guilty, it would be entirely different and a lot easier on all of us on the outside." Steve paused and reflected, "My mother and father might still be alive. I would have left this goddamn Cleveland area years ago and set up my practice somewhere else. We would have all folded up and quit. That's what the cops tried to get Richard and me to do—put pressure on Sam to confess. But because I *know* that Sam did not kill Marilyn, I *had* to stay here and raise my kids. . . ."

During his younger brother's incarceration Steve was Sam's strongest supporter psychologically and financially—and in virtually every other way. Steve lived in Sam's shadow outside prison walls. Steve wrote Sam at least weekly, and he drove monthly the 150 miles from his Rocky River home to the Columbus penitentiary to visit him. Steve even wrote a verbose, unproduced, unpublished play about his brother's conviction, titled *The Case*.

Steve constantly tried to cheer his brother's spirits with laughter. Steve sent him a corny joke published in a newspaper column about a nervous man walking up to a policeman and confessing, "I just shot my boss, knifed my best friend, dynamited a building, robbed a bank, and raped 12 salesgirls."

"You want to turn yourself in?" asked the cop.

"No. I want you to direct me to a publisher. I think I got a best seller in me."

Steve and Betty took Chip into their home and reared him as a member of the family. "Why does my Daddy have to stay in jail?" he asked them one day. "He didn't kill Mommy. I'll be a lawyer when I grow up so I can get Daddy out of jail."

Unkind classmates often pointed to Chip and said behind his back: "That's the kid whose father killed his mother." One day he overheard a kid loudly say, "His father's a jailbird." Young Sam walked over to him, clenched his fists, and said, "Shut up or I'll smash you!" The boy shut up.

Classmates and teachers always called the boy Chip to avoid the formal name of his convict father. One morning he stood up in class and announced: "My name is Sam Sheppard. I'm proud of that name. Everybody please call me that."

When Prisoner 98860 heard about this incident on Steve's monthly visit, he burst into tears and said, "This is the proudest moment of my life. But I'll never have a chance to go fishing with him, teach him how to box or wrestle, or tell him about the birds and the bees."

From his finger Sam removed a black onyx cameo ring sent him by an admirer who strongly believed in his innocence. It pictured a two-headed eagle and bore the Latin inscription *Vincit Qui Patitur* (He Who Endures, Conquers). "Steve, please give this to young Sam," he instructed. Thereafter, his letters to his son closed with the initials of this Latin motto.

The convict father at first refused to permit his son to visit him. "I'm dying to see him, but I don't want his picture in the paper or stories about his visiting me," he explained simply.

But the boy wrote to his Dad regularly and never failed to send him a Father's Day card or a new pipe as a birthday present.

The day after Sheppard's conviction Marilyn's father, Tom Reese, and his second wife Jane telephoned Steve and demanded immediate custody of Chip. Steve patiently explained that Marilyn had written a will five months before her tragic death and had named him as Chip's legal guardian in case anything happened to her and Sam, who were soon to fly to California together. Brother Richard was Marilyn's second choice of guardian if anything happened to Steve. Moreover, Sam wanted him to be his son's guardian, Steve added.

Several months later Marilyn's aunt Mrs. Henrietta Munn and her husband Worth made the same request, a matter that was reported in the press since they had filed a suit in the Cuyahoga County Probate Court. A hearing was set for August 3, 1955.

"I felt so helpless and tortured, and I knew that Marilyn would be ashamed of the Munns for this," said Sam.

After the court was advised of Marilyn's will, the Munns were informed that unless they could show cause that Stephen and Betty Sheppard were incompetent or financially unable to provide for the boy, they had no case. The would-be litigants were told privately that a custody battle would be harmful to the boy. When they decided not to pursue the action, Sam Sheppard and his immediate family were tremendously relieved. In his prison cell a man convicted of second-degree murder wrote to a friend, "Many people live a long and so-called full life without ever having one real brother, sister, or true friend. I am indeed a rich man to have Chip, Steve, Richard, Betty, Dorothy, and others who have stood firm in their faith and knowledge of my innocence. In finding out how wonderful they all are, my life has taken on an entirely new meaning."

4

THE APPEALS

INDEED, the Sheppard murder case would soon take on a new meaning.

The day after Dr. Sam's conviction, Bay Village Police Chief Eaton returned the keys of the murder house to Sheppard through lawyer Corrigan.

The prosecution had held the keys for nearly five months and had barred the defense from inspecting the house when it had impounded the premises, almost from the day of the murder. Corrigan had attempted to secure a court order releasing the house, but Judge Blythin had denied the request and Corrigan had never pursued the matter in a civil suit.

By contrast, the prosecution had leisurely searched the house for "proof" of Sheppard's guilt for months before and during the trial. The state had admitted in the trial that the blood spatters in the murder bedroom revealed nothing about the killer or about how the blows were struck. It charged, nonetheless, that the foul deed was committed by an up and down chopping motion, with, for example, a surgical instrument.

Now that it legally possessed the keys, the defense was belatedly enabled to study the murder house.

Kirk Kicks Up

Corrigan swiftly invited an outside expert, the late Dr. Paul Leland Kirk, one of America's most distinguished criminologists, to conduct an independent study of all the physical evidence connected with the murder. Dr. Kirk stipulated that he would make an entirely objective investigation of all physical evidence "without bias to the state of Ohio or to the defendant."

Kirk was a professor of criminalistics in the School of Criminology and founder of the criminalistics department at the University of California in Berkeley. Kirk had trained police and crime laboratory technicians throughout America and aided countless police departments in solving hundreds of crimes by means of blood detection and other methods. His textbook *Crime Investigation: Physical Evidence and the Police Laboratory* is studied wherever criminology is taught and is a standard reference volume for law enforcement agencies throughout the world. International scientific societies had honored him, and one admirer had even dubbed him "better than Sherlock Holmes."

Dr. Kirk's academic education included a Bachelor of Arts degree with highest honors from Ohio State University in 1924, a Master of Sciences degree in chemistry from the University of Pittsburgh in 1925, and a Ph.D. in biochemistry from the University of California in 1927.

Sparking a movement toward truly scientific crime detection based upon physical evidence, he founded crime laboratories in Chicago, St. Louis, and several other cities. Many federal and state courts welcomed his authoritative testimony.

On January 22, 1955, Kirk began, in Bay Village, investigating many aspects of Marilyn's murder that Cleveland authorities had seemingly neglected. He studied the exhibits in the prosecution's possession. He analyzed the blood on the murder bedroom walls. He meticulously vacuumed the carpets with a special sweeper he had developed. He probed the ticking on Marilyn's bed. No infinitesimally small object, whether a flake of dust, single hair, or pinch of sand, was too inconsequential for his trained eye.

"It is virtually impossible for a person to commit a crime

without leaving a microscopic clue," Dr. Kirk once wrote. "Every crime has a pattern all its own."

Criminologist Kirk took a sample of Sam Sheppard's blood and all of the new evidence he had unearthed in the murder house back to California, where he studied it in his laboratory.

In April, 1955, Dr. Kirk completed a 10,000-word affidavit. Among its main findings were the following:

1. Chemical analysis revealed a large unexplained spot of human blood on the wardrobe door of the murder bedroom that matched neither Sheppard's blood specimens (Group A) nor Marilyn's (Group O with an M factor). This indicates that the blood must have been splattered there by a *third person* who was in the room—the murderer—perhaps when the individual's hand was bitten by Marilyn.

2. The ceiling did not contain a single spot of blood. However, if the blows had been struck vertically, the ceiling would have been stained as much as any wall. Only horizontal swings could have confined the blood marks to the walls.

3. Before she died, Marilyn had, in all likelihood, bitten her murderer ferociously on the hand or fingers, and this mark would have been noticeable on the murder morning. (Sheppard bore no bite marks.) "The murderer had a definitely injured hand or finger on July 4, 1954," the report stated.

4. Marilyn's killer was *left-handed*. (Sheppard is right-handed.) Dr. Kirk based this conclusion on the position of her body, the force and backswing of the murderer's blows, and the pattern of bloodstains on the wall.

5. The murder weapon was not more than one foot long. Dr. Kirk suggested that the flared front edge of a heavy red-lacquered flashlight, which was perhaps brought into the room for another purpose, had been used to inflict the fatal wounds. It was definitely *not* a "blunt surgical instrument." The so-called nail polish found in the murder bedroom was probably red lacquer used to coat small objects and could conceivably be chips from the weapon. It was entirely possible that the defendant was struck on the

back of the neck by the same weapon used to kill Marilyn Sheppard.

6. The crime started as a sex attack, not as a murder, which was indicated by the fact that Marilyn's pajama top had been pulled up over her head and her pajama bottoms down. Her murder appeared to be the result of a sexual assault, not by her husband but by someone else.

7. The tooth chips from Marilyn's broken medial incisor found under her bed had been pulled loose when the murderer's hand was jerked away, perhaps after it had been put over her mouth to stifle her screams. She had no bruises on her mouth. "The teeth were found outside her mouth, not inside or in her throat as would be expected if broken by an external blow," reported Dr. Kirk. The angle of the break indicated that Marilyn's broken tooth had resulted from an outward pull rather than a downward blow.

8. The four-inch tear in Sheppard's trousers indicated corroboration of his story. It is physically impossible for a person to rip his trouser pocket *downward* when removing a key chain because the only hand movement possible without extreme contortion is *upward* and *outward.* A downward tear is likely when someone else rips the pocket on a prone body.

9. Microscopic study revealed that neither Sheppard's belt nor the seams of his shoes showed any blood, but bloodstains can never be completely removed from leather.

10. The two tablespoons of sand found in Sheppard's trousers pockets could only have gotten there by his lying in the water for at least an hour.

As a result of these findings, Kirk came to some conclusions about other aspects of the crime:

1. If Sheppard had removed his T-shirt because it was bloody, he would surely have put on another one to cover the loss of the first.

2. After commission of the crime the attacker faked a clumsy attempt to indicate that a burglary had been committed. The defendant's account was vague. It is not a story that might be expected of an intelligent person who was faking the account. The method and clumsiness of the

removal of the watch and key chain from the defendant's pocket appears to be the work of another person. The defendant's watch could not have been in the lake after the murder; the water must have been under the crystal previously.

3. It is not reasonable to believe that the defendant would deliberately break his own and his wife's athletic trophies. It is consistent only for someone who hated the Sheppards or who was jealous of their athletic abilities.

4. It cannot be conceived that the injuries to the defendant were self-inflicted. A person fully aware of the danger associated with a blow to the back of the neck, such as a doctor, would never risk it. It is equally ridiculous to assume that these injuries were sustained in falling from the landing platform at the beach since that type of fall would inflict many abrasions, bruises, and secondary injuries to the limbs.

5. Careful appraisal of the technical evidence presented by the prosecution shows it to be worthless as proof of the guilt or innocence of the defendant.

After submitting this affidavit, which is now considered a classic in modern crime detection, Dr. Kirk was even more certain of the validity of his findings. Eight and a half years later, on October 10, 1963, he wrote to me: "My belief in Dr. Sheppard's innocence is based upon solid facts and study of the physical evidence, which I have corroborated further since the affidavit."

Privately, Kirk added that he strongly suspected the identity of Marilyn's murderer, but he did not have sufficient proof to establish conclusively the individual's guilt. "I never agree to testify until I'm damn sure of my conclusions," he remarked.

When Corrigan showed Dr. Kirk's report to his client, Sheppard expected the prison gates to swing open, proclaiming his innocence. "I only wish Mother and Dad were alive to read it," he said.

After reading Dr. Kirk's findings, impartial lawyers who had been puzzled by the perplexing case became convinced that Sheppard had never been proved guilty beyond reasonable doubt and that, if anything, Sam was innocent. After all, Kirk's was the only scientific study ever made of the murder bedroom. "If the jury had this evidence before it retired, it would have had to acquit Sheppard," speculated one Ohio attorney.

Those who had convicted Dr. Samuel Sheppard, however, had contrary opinions of the Kirk affidavit. They characterized it as "a good college thesis . . . far-fetched, unconvincing . . . an opus of fantasies . . . shockingly negligent and slipshod . . . parroted theories . . . self-serving declarations, speculations, arguments, conclusions, and misstatements and misrepresentations of facts."

To all this Dr. Kirk succinctly said, "I don't think any of them wanted the facts."

Ohio Courts Say Nay

The new Kirk facts were swiftly presented to Judge Blythin's court in an attempt to secure a retrial. Corrigan and Sheppard's other defense lawyers deemed these facts more revealing than any offered by the prosecution—or even themselves—during the stormy trial.

Four months earlier, on January 3, 1955, Judge Blythin had overruled Corrigan's routine motion for a new trial. When rejecting this motion, Judge Blythin wrote a verbose opinion, which seemed more an attempt to purge his soul of his inner torment over the case. Among the astonishingly unjudicial lines committed to paper by Judge Blythin was this statement: ". . . what actually was involved was a mere mystery—a 'whodunit'."

Now on May 4, 1955, Judge Blythin again heard a defense motion for a new trial—this time based upon the newly discovered Kirk evidence. Dr. Kirk offered to come to Cleveland to testify on his findings, but the court did not consent to this. Instead, six days later Judge Blythin again spurned the Sheppard retrial appeal on the grounds that the Kirk affidavit had arrived too late, and, besides, it was mere conjecture on Kirk's part.

Corrigan promptly appealed Judge Blythin's decision to the Ohio Court of Appeals for the Eighth District, a three-judge tribunal that sat in Cleveland and handled Cuyahoga County appeals.

On July 20, 1955, Court of Appeals Judges Joy Seth Hurd, Julius M. Kovachy, and Lee E. Skeel unanimously affirmed Sheppard's conviction and five days later rejected his motion for a new trial based on the Kirk evidence, which should, they said, have been presented during the trial. Commenting upon what he termed a "reasonable request for inspection of the premises," Judge Kovachy wrote: ". . . it is inconceivable that a formal application to the presiding judge in the criminal branch of the Common Pleas Court would not have been granted."

Corrigan's next step was to approach the Ohio Supreme Court. He confidently expected to win on appeal if it agreed to hear the case because the seven judges, who convened in Columbus, hailed from all over the state and weren't, Corrigan felt, Cleveland-brainwashed. On January 1, 1956, Ohio's highest court consented to review the case—a minor Sheppard triumph.

After this decision was announced, Warden Arvis permitted Prisoner 98860 to hold a press conference—the first time an inmate was permitted to do so in Ohio penitentiary history—but photographers were banned, as was any discussion of the case.

To Corrigan's annoyance, Dr. Sam at that time added, at his brothers' urging, a prominent politico lawyer to his defense team, Paul M. Herbert, former lieutenant-governor of Ohio, who wrote a 40-page supplement to the more than 500-page brief prepared by Corrigan and Sheppard's other attorneys.

Chief Justice Carl V. Weygandt disqualified himself from the case on the grounds that his son Richard was law director of Bay Village, handpicking his replacement.

Oral arguments were heard on April 17, 1956, by the seven justices: James Finley Bell, William Lincoln Hart, John M. Mathias, Charles W. Montgomery (the Weygandt replacement), James Garfield Stewart, Kingsley A. Taft, and Charles B. Zimmerman. Prisoner Sheppard did not appear in court. He busied himself with his hospital chores at the penitentiary.

In reviewing the case the Ohio Supreme Court did not choose to discuss or pass upon the Kirk evidence. The justices confined themselves to the trial record.

The late Justice Kingsley A. Taft asked Assistant Prosecutor Saul Danaceau, "What about the argument that there was no blood on the defendant's trousers?"

"We don't even know if he was wearing trousers at the time," was the reply.

Ohio's loftiest court deliberated the case for nearly a month and a half. On May 31, 1956, it upheld the lower Court of Appeals denial, affirming Sheppard's conviction by a five-to-two vote. The case inspired the jurists to lordship of language and amazing unjudicial candor.

The majority five-judge opinion, written by Justice Bell, contained this astounding lead sentence summary of Dr. Sam's notoriety: "Mystery and murder, society, sex, and suspense were combined in this case in such a manner as to intrigue and captivate the public fancy to a degree perhaps unparalleled in recent annals." This majority opinion went on to deplore the "... circulation-conscious editors who catered to the insatiable interest of the American public. ... In this atmosphere of a 'Roman holiday' for the news media, Sam Sheppard stood trial for his life." Despite this admission, the five judges ruled against Dr. Sam.

The two-man minority opinion, written by Justice Kingsley Taft, was probably the strongest judicial dissent on a defendant's guilt in Ohio criminal history. Legal scholars do not recall any more eloquent disagreement with the majority opinion in a murder case by sitting judges elsewhere in the United States.

The minority opinion charged that Sheppard should be immediately granted a new trial because of 29 prejudicial errors in the record. They included Judge Blythin's admission of inadmissible "clearly hearsay" evidence about Dr. Sam's alleged desire for a divorce; Judge Blythin's misleading and legally erroneous George Washington-cherry tree analogy to the jury about circumstantial evidence; and the illegal telephone calls made by the jurors during their deliberations.

Justice Taft's dissent contained one sentence that was reminiscent of the spirit of U.S. Supreme Court Justice Oliver Wendell Holmes: "Although ... defendant did philander, a philanderer may have propensities for peacefulness." The opinion then went on soberly to say: "If defendant did have these propensities for peacefulness, as this evidence indicates, such evidence would be evidence of a circumstance tending to indicate that the defendant did not commit the crime of violence involved in the instant case."

The Taft-Hart dissent went so far as to suggest, in legal language, that the prosecution itself had introduced evidence indicating Sheppard's innocence. In simpler language, these two dissenting justices were saying: In a land where every man is considered innocent until proven guilty beyond any reasonable doubt, Dr. Sheppard should never have been convicted and should not remain behind bars.

Felix Frankfurter Counsels

Dr. Sam's only legal road seemingly led to Washington, D.C., to the highest court in the land.

Corrigan speedily appealed to the Supreme Court to reverse his client's conviction. The venerable attorney personally delivered his emotional 68-page petition to the nation's top tribunal in late August in the hope that the justices would consider it for the fall, 1956, term, which was scheduled to open in October. This petition recounted the adverse Ohio court rulings and contained an appendix of photocopies of many of the *Cleveland Press* headlines, editorials, news stories, and photographs to illustrate the publicity aspect of the trial. It also foreshadowed the free press-fair trial theme, which was to flare even more in the next decade and a half.

The Sheppard petition sought what lawyers call a writ of *certiorari,* a request for the high court to review the rulings of the lower Ohio courts in the case. The petition contended that these courts had denied Sheppard due process of law as guaranteed by the fourteenth amendment.

The U.S. Supreme Court can decide whether or not to grant any one of the thousands of appeals for *certiorari.* At least four of the nine justices must consent to hear or review a case before *certiorari* is bestowed, and each jurist's vote is secret.

On November 14, 1956, the U.S. Supreme Court announced its decision. It declined to grant *certiorari* and to review the controversial Sheppard case.

Dr. Sam was crestfallen when he heard the news on his radio in his prison hospital dormitory. He later learned from his attorneys that *certiorari* was denied because only three of the required four justices had voted for it. One of the justices who had voted against it was Justice Hugo

Black, who did so solely on the grounds that he was an absolutist on "freedom of the press."

Ironically, one of the three justices who voted to review the case was a jurist who generally opposed *certiorari* as a needless burden upon the court: the late Justice Felix Frankfurter, who deemed himself the most legally learned man on the court. Justice Frankfurter's unusual interest in the Sheppard case stemmed from two deepening convictions: (1) his belief that something must be done to curb prejudicial pretrial publicity, such as modeling our press system after Great Britain's; and (2) his belief in all types of judicial restraint.

Justice Frankfurter chose the Sheppard case, out of the thousands of cases reaching the Supreme Court, to write an extraordinary memorandum to accompany the full court's denial of *certiorari*. In his memorandum Frankfurter indicated astonishment that the Supreme Court of Ohio could possibly believe that any fair trial could be conducted in an inflamed atmosphere such as that which surrounded the Sheppard case.

Justice Frankfurter wrote cryptically:

> Such denial of his [Sheppard's] petition in no wise implies that this court approves the decision of the Supreme Court of Ohio. It means only that for one reason or another this case did not commend itself to at least four members of the court as falling within those considerations which should lead this court to exercise its discretion in reviewing a lower court's decision.
>
> For reasons that have often been explained, the court does not give the grounds for denying the petitions for *certiorari* in the normally more than one thousand cases each year in which petitions are denied. It has also been explained that not even the positions of the various justices in such cases are matters of public concern. The rare cases in which an individual position is noted leave unillumined the function of the certiorari system, and do not reveal the position of all the members of the court.

The Frankfurter memorandum gave pause to many of Dr. Sam's legal and judicial opponents in Ohio. They tried to read between the lines, as did Sheppard's attorneys. Inspired, Corrigan again petitioned the U.S. Supreme Court to reconsider its decision to review the case, but on December 19 the court again spurned a *certiorari* appeal—without a memorandum.

Soon it would be Christmas—Dr. Sam's third behind bars. "I'm going to fight your case until I die," vowed Corrigan when he visited his client. But there didn't seem much that the disappointed attorney could do. Of course, there was always the possibility of parole—in eight years.

Meanwhile, many law school professors throughout the United States had begun lecturing on Sheppard *v.* Ohio. Some interpreted Frankfurter's *sub silento* words as meaning that Dr. Sam had not exhausted his legal remedies; he could still seek relief in federal courts possibly on constitutional grounds, such as a habeas corpus petition. In any case, the puzzling Frankfurter memorandum planted the seeds for the future Sheppard legal flowering before the Supreme Court.

But it was a decade later. In the interim, heartening as the Frankfurter memorandum was, it seemed like the end of his legal road to Sam Sheppard.

Court of Last Resort

Suddenly a flicker of hope sparked. Another court—a nonlegal one—appeared on the dimming Sheppard horizon. It was the Court of Last Resort, a nonprofit organization formed in 1948 by the late Erle Stanley Gardner, the world-famed mystery writer who created lawyer Perry Mason, and Harry Steeger, then publisher of *Argosy* magazine.

The purpose of this impartial Court of Last Resort was to investigate objectively, after all legal appeals had been exhausted, the cases of seemingly innocent persons convicted of crimes. This unique court was highly respected by many governors, judges, prosecutors, and defense lawyers who often sought its free, public-spirited services to correct conceivable miscarriages of justice. It had succeeded in securing many pardons and paroles. "If any of these poor bastards are innocent, we try to spring them," explained Gene Lowall, director of investigations. The court's small nucleus consisted of criminology experts who contributed their time and talents and even paid their own expenses. Their findings were regularly published in *Argosy*.

Shortly after Dr. Sam was convicted, in early January, 1955, a Sheppard sympathizer asked the Court of Last Resort to take up the case. But since Dr. Sam had not yet drained all his possible legal remedies, the request was declined.

Then on February 12, 1957, two months after the U.S. Supreme Court refused to review the case, Steve Sheppard wrote the following letter to the Court of Last Resort, and the letter was published in the June, 1957, *Argosy*:

> My brother, Dr. Samuel H. Sheppard, who was convicted of murdering his wife, is innocent. I ask you to investigate this case and have your board of experts fairly and fearlessly call the turns as they see them. If you will do so, we'll meet you more than halfway.
>
> Before my brother Sam was tried, the authorities wanted to give all of us polygraph [lie detector] examinations to be conducted by the police or by someone selected by them, with no one else present. Under those circumstances the lawyers representing Dr. Sam didn't want any of us to submit to polygraph examination. None of us have ever had any fear of any interrogation conducted by a thoroughly trained, competent, and impartial technician; and if you will designate one or more such experts who have no connection whatsoever with either our family or the prosecution, we agree to take lie detector tests at such times and places as you may direct.
>
> We give you permission to present your conclusions and to publish the facts in the case as you see them. We agree not to file any claim for libel, defamation of character, or damages of any sort so that you can feel free to express your conclusions in the columns of the magazine.
>
> If there is anything else you want from me or the family of Dr. Sam Sheppard, just let us know.
>
> Let's get the cards on the table face up.
>
> Yours,
> Stephen A. Sheppard

We agree to the terms of the above letter, join in the request and in the letter.
Richard N. Sheppard
Dorothy A. Sheppard
Betty M. Sheppard

After studying Steve's request with his colleagues and conferring with Ohio authorities by telephone, Erle Stanley Gardner, a nonpracticing attorney, suggested that the Court of Last Resort investigate the Sheppard murder case. The investigators arranged to administer lie detector tests to the four Sheppards without public fanfare. Gardner cautioned the Sheppards that it was impossible to beat the machine. With microscopic accuracy, the polygraph registers the changes in blood pressure, respiration, pulse, skin resistance, drug usage, and emotional disturbances of persons taking the tests.

"I warned them," recalled Gardner, "that if they helped to conceal any evidence or knew of any attempt, the interrogators would quickly find this out, and they should therefore refuse to take the tests."

Dr. Sam's family decided to go ahead, realizing that if they failed the tests they would not only damage their brother's case but risk prosecution themselves as accessories to Marilyn's murder.

On May 4, 1957, Steve, Richard, Betty, and Dorothy Sheppard went to Chicago to undergo comprehensive lie detector examinations at the laboratory of John E. Reid, co-author of *Lie Detection and Criminal Interrogation.* The other members of the team of independent, internationally recognized polygraph experts who conducted the tests were C. B. Hansom, past president of the Academy for Scientific Interrogation; Dr. LeMoyne Snyder, a doctor of medicine, a doctor of law, and author of *Homicide Investigation*; and Alex Gregory, the official polygraph examiner of the Court of Last Resort, who had made it virtually his life work to study the instrument. "The chances of four people fooling this group of scientific interrogators is mathematically infinitesimal," concluded Erle Stanley Gardner.

The Sheppard brothers and their wives passed the elaborate tests thoroughly. The experiment clearly showed that none had any guilt or knowledge of the crime. Gardner, who wrote a monthly *Argosy* article on the case during most of 1957, reported in the September issue: "These experts are unanimous in their opinion that Dr. Stephen Sheppard, Dr. Richard Sheppard, and the wives of these men do not have anything to do with any cover up or with removal of any evidence; they never heard Dr. Sam Sheppard say anything that would indicate his guilt; and they are individually and collectively sincere in their belief that Dr. Sam is innocent."

When Sheppard foes in Ohio heard these results, they lambasted the Court of Last Resort as a group of "busybodies" interested primarily in promoting the circulation of *Argosy*. Gardner retorted, "We are interested in improving the administration of justice, not the circulation of any magazine. Outside of Harry Steeger, there isn't a member of our group who has any financial interest in *Argosy*. I have never received a penny for any of my Court of Last Resort writings in *Argosy*. In fact, at one time I turned down an offer from a magazine involving some 75 thousand dollars a year because it would have meant commitments which would interfere with the work I was trying to do with the Court of Last Resort and my writings in *Argosy*."

Gardner urged the magazine's readers to write to Ohio Governor C. William O'Neill to permit the Court of Last Resort to administer a lie detector test to Dr. Sam in prison, which Sam was eager to take. On July 19, 1957, Governor O'Neill, who had been the state's attorney general during the Sheppard trial, wired the Court of Last Resort that he would allow this test in the Ohio State Penitentiary. "I was on cloud nine," recalled Prisoner 98860.

The governor's telegram resulted in a wave of protest among Ohio's anti-Sheppard forces. Until then Ohio authorities had steadfastly refused to allow any lie detector test of Sheppard behind bars despite offers by independent polygraph experts. During the 1954 murder investigation the *Cleveland Press* had assailed Sheppard for "refusing" to take a lie detector test on the advice of his lawyer Corrigan, who argued that it couldn't be unbiased if conducted by Cleveland police officials in such a frenzied atmosphere. Sheppard, however, had volunteered, "I'll take any test you want if impartial experts from outside Ohio give it. What's the use of being 'tested' by people who are convinced that I'm guilty before they start?" His offer was rejected.

Bay Village Mayor J. Spencer Houk, a prosecution witness, had taken a lie detector test, which Cleveland Detective-Inspector James McArthur was quoted as saying showed several discrepancies. Yet the results of the test were illegally admitted as trial testimony, giving rise to an inference that Houk was telling the truth and that Sheppard was not.

All hell suddenly broke loose on the case. Shortly after the Sheppard brothers' and their wives' polygraph clearance, Donald Wedler, a 23-year-old Florida convict, confessed to Sheriff Rodney B. Thursby, in DeLand, Florida, that he was the "bushy-haired intruder" who had killed Marilyn Sheppard. He said that on the evening of July 3, 1954, he was in Cleveland, took a shot of heroin, stole a car, drove to residential Bay Village, entered a house, saw a man sleeping on the couch, went upstairs, and when a woman awoke, he hit her with an eight-inch iron pipe. On the way downstairs he slugged the man with this pipe, dumped out the contents of an open bag, ran down to the beach, and after a struggle there with the pursuing man, hurled the pipe into the lake.

Erle Stanley Gardner immediately wired Sheriff Thursby, offering to give a lie detector test to this alleged confessor. The offer was accepted. Alex Gregory rushed to Florida, administered the test, and concluded that Wedler either murdered Marilyn or sincerely believed that he did. The next day Gardner flew to Florida and found some discrepancies in Wedler's story. He promptly notified Governor O'Neill that Wedler's confession should not be accepted until there was more conclusive evidence and that the convict should be given a psychiatric examination.

Coroner Gerber flew to Florida with Detective McArthur and Sheriff Yettra. After questioning Wedler for several hours they branded his "confession" a complete hoax.

There is little doubt that, as a result, pressure on Governor O'Neill to cancel Sheppard's scheduled prison lie detector test was renewed. In any case, on July 22 the governor withdrew his permission, explaining that the test would be permitted only if Wedler's confession was verified.

Judge Blythin joined the protesting chorus. He wired Ohio Attorney General William B. Saxbe (later U.S. Senator and U.S. Attorney General): "To come in as a Court of Last Resort after the Ohio and United States Supreme Courts have acted is to place itself above those courts."

Deeply hurt, Gardner announced that the Court of Last Resort had no alternative but to withdraw from the case. "We will fold our tents like the Arabs and *noisily* steal away," he informed the press. When the italicized adverb was reported as *quietly*, Gardner quipped, "Perhaps that was the unkindest cut of all."

Nevertheless, Erle Stanley Gardner could not get the Sheppard case out of his mind. Nearly seven years later, in February, 1964, he wrote to me: "I have been cussed heartily in Ohio because of my interest in the Sheppard case. The Court of Last Resort took quite a lot of abuse. The strange thing is that no one on the Court of Last Resort ever announced a belief that Dr. Sheppard was innocent. They did state that they felt the case should be investigated thoroughly; and we did give our opinion that the two brothers and their wives had absolutely no knowledge that would indicate Dr. Sam was guilty. Nor had they done anything to obscure evidence. This statement was predicated upon a series of polygraph tests which were so carefully conducted, and under such safeguards, that the conclusions established were either the truth or else we had better throw all of our polygraphs in the ocean and forget about them."

As the Court of Last Resort withdrew, lawyer Corrigan journeyed to Florida and secured a "confession" from Wedler. However, because Cleveland authorities considered Wedler a fake, this was a worthless document, and Sheppard had to console himself with the thought that his real Court of Last Resort now was the American people.

William J. Corrigan died at the age of 75 in August, 1961. Dr. Sam's disheartened attorney went to his grave with a deepening conviction of his client's innocence. Sheppard now had no lawyer, but he didn't seem to need one. He would theoretically remain behind bars for the rest of his life unless paroled in 1964. The case was seemingly dead.

5

THE LAWYER

F. Lee Bailey was a brash, energetic Boston barrister of twenty-eight crowded years. He had been in law practice merely nine months when he happened to be in Chicago in August, 1961, lecturing at the Keeler Polygraph Institute.

The relatively unknown lawyer received a telephone call from Paul Holmes, the *Chicago Tribune* crime reporter whose *Sheppard Murder Case,* recently published, had profoundly moved Lee Bailey. Would Bailey be interested in trying to get a lie detector test for Sam Sheppard, Holmes asked?

The idea intrigued the young criminal lawyer. His automobile sported New Hampshire license plates that spelled out TRIAL, and this not-very-proper, in the conventional vein, Bostonian had begun to envision himself as a Great Defender in the Clarence Darrow tradition. Even Bailey's detractors—and there were many of them—conceded that he possessed virtually all of the qualities needed by any first rate criminal lawyer: imagination, intelligence, courage, stamina, diligence, and a flaming sense of justice. He had a lightning-fast mind, a trigger tongue, and a phenomenal memory. Thinking in paragraphs rather than sentences, he could take in dozens of typed pages with a glance. In court and in his increasingly numerous speaking engagements, Bailey never used notes.

"You miss too much if you do," he insisted. "You're either prepared for a trial or you aren't. Any lawyer who tries a case without complete preparation is as guilty of malpractice as a surgeon who sticks his hand in a tubful of bacteria and then operates without gloves. Most lawyers are chicken in the guts department, especially in murder cases. They consider criminal cases dirty business and don't want to soil their hands. But many corporate and other lawyers secretly would like to try one murder case before they die."

Enter Brash Barrister Bailey

Bailey's talent as a lie detection—not as a legal—expert led him to the seemingly hopeless Sheppard case. Boston critics wisecracked that he was "wired for sound" with electronic devices. "Kick his briefcase," quipped one, "you'll do two thousand dollars worth of damage." Bailey assumed that his phone was being tapped. He had recording equipment not only in his office and home but in his car and later in his boat and airplane.

On November 17, 1961, when flying back from California to Boston, Bailey stopped at the Cleveland airport, planning to spend an hour talking to Steve Sheppard. Instead, he spent the night assessing the complex case at Steve's home. In the morning, he was driven to Marion to the medium-security correctional institution to which Dr. Sam had been transferred in January, 1961, for good behavior.

Sam Sheppard and Lee Bailey had an immediate rapport. After their first handshake the lawyer believed in the prisoner.

"I'll take the case without fee," swiftly said Bailey. "I'll charge you a whopping fee later but help you earn the money to pay for it."

"That's a deal," agreed the prisoner. "I'll work ten years for you to pay it if you can get me out. I'm not sure you can, but if you're willing to try, I'm with you."

When Bailey returned to Boston, he was teased by a legal colleague. "You must be getting a fat fee for taking this dead Sheppard case."

"I haven't got a dime yet and don't expect to for a long time," Bailey cockily snapped. "In fact, I expect to spend a lot of my own money in trips to Ohio, long distance calls, briefs, and whatnot. But I promise you one thing: I intend to walk this innocent guy out. Come around to see me in a couple of years, and if you can't afford a drink, maybe I'll buy you one."

The man who catapulted to fame on the Sheppard case never started out to be a lawyer.

A Depression child, F. Lee Bailey was born on June 10, 1933, in Waltham, Massachusetts, of English-German ancestry. His energetic mother, Grace, and his father, William, who at the time of his son's birth was working for Uncle Sam's WPA (Work Progress Administration), separated and later divorced.

The youth won a scholarship to prep school, Kimball Union Academy in Meriden, New Hampshire, where, among other things, he excelled in hockey despite being small for his age. Once his teachers thought he was cheating in math because there was no indication in the margin of his papers that he had worked out the answers. He was cleared when no other student had the correct answers. At his June, 1952, commencement exercises he was awarded first prize in a speaking contest and commended for his excellent narrative poem.

Winning a scholarship to Harvard, F. Lee Bailey majored in English and planned to become a writer. But he decided not to because, "I couldn't stand sitting and listening to other persons' stories, and besides, what the hell did I have to tell people when I was 19?"

A lawyer's autobiography had a profound influence upon his choice of career. After reading *The Art of Advocacy*, by Lloyd Paul Stryker, a New York criminal lawyer who pleaded for a return of his vanishing profession, the young Bailey decided this was for him. "That book changed my life," he says. "It fired me up."

At the end of his sophomore year Bailey left Harvard to enter the U.S. Naval Flight Training program. He switched to the marines and became a jet fighter pilot, based with a fighter squadron of the Cherry Point Air Station in North

Carolina. When his unit's chief legal officer was killed in a plane crash, 21-year-old Lieutenant Bailey—lacking even a college degree—became the staff legal officer of a 2,000-man unit. He recalls volunteering to serve as a defense counsel on every possible court martial "to learn a little law." Lieutenant Bailey especially enjoyed needling the brass when saving marines from the brig. Away from the base he haunted local police courts, defending marines who had brushes with the civilian law. In the evening he read ravenously.

Discharged from the marines as a captain in 1956, Bailey reentered Harvard in the spring of 1957, attended its summer school, and then persuaded Boston University to accept his marine legal experience in lieu of insufficient undergraduate credits and to admit him to law school in September.

At Boston University he supplemented his textbook studies by moonlighting: he started a private detective agency called Investigative Associates, which did lucrative research for trial attorneys. "A good investigator is more important than a good lawyer in a criminal case," he insisted. "The difference between good and bad cross-examination is solid pretrial investigation." Bailey graduated at the top of his class in June, 1960, and won three competitive awards, including one for writing the best legal brief in a nationwide contest.

At 27 he got his legal baptism when he defended a young auto mechanic who was accused of the murder of his wife. Pointing to the district attorney, Bailey shouted at the jury, "Here is a man trying to put my client in the electric chair for something he didn't do—just to get reelected!" Bailey's client was acquitted, and the D.A. never forgave him.

Heartened by this first victory, Bailey decided to specialize in criminal law. He won an acquittal for a psychiatrist charged with assaulting a patient and for a man accused of raping a girl.

Bailey's courtroom demeanor was unpredictable. Once when a detective witness testified for the prosecution that a murder defendant couldn't possibly have fired a gun "accidentally" with the safety catch on, Bailey, toying with the revolver, innocently asked, "You mean like this?" The witness nodded. Bailey raised the gun, pointed it at the detective, pulled the trigger. When the firing pin clicked and struck an empty chamber, the jury gasped. This stunt so unnerved the detective that his testimony was discredited, and Bailey won another case. Several days earlier Bailey had done his homework by visiting a firearms factory manufacturing a gun with a "false" safe position.

In Boston legal circles Bailey came to be known as a "gimmick lawyer" who employed all sorts of tricks and recording devices. He learned them not only with Investigative Associates but at the Backster School of Lie Detection in New York and the Keeler Polygraph Institute in Chicago, which brought him into the Sheppard case.

A month after taking over the Sheppard case Bailey strolled into the *Cleveland Press* office of editor Louis B. Seltzer. Dr. Sam's new attorney suggested, "How about giving my client a break for a change?" When Seltzer grunted scornfully, Bailey's lip curled, and he unleashed his verbal daggers. "You know, Mr. Seltzer," he began, "I intend to get Sam Sheppard out of jail if it's the last thing I do. Every day I'm getting stronger, and you're getting weaker and older. By all the mortality tables I'm going to outlive you—and get you. And if you die before I do, I'll get your image." The editor rushed the young lawyer out the door.

Bailey has never regretted this incident, which is one of his most poignant memories of the Sheppard case.

"I have balls of brass," Bailey has been heard to say. Yet he once said to me, "My indignation of the outrage toward Sam Sheppard sometimes flavored my own handling of the case when cool advocacy might have served better."

Judges and lawyers were beginning to take note of the impetuous attorney. In Boston, Bailey predicted, "The Sheppard case will rank with the Sacco and Vanzetti and Dreyfus cases as a monumental miscarriage of justice to the everlasting shame of those who convicted him. No matter how efficient our system of justice is, it isn't perfect. Jurors and judges aren't omniscient. To admit that a mistake was made is difficult but certainly not dishonorable."

Through his creative stewardship of the Sheppard case

F. Lee Bailey burst into national and even worldwide headlines.

"How did you become famous overnight?" he was once asked.

"Because my client, Dr. Sam Sheppard, was famous," he retorted not altogether untruthfully.

The Forgotten Governor

Thus the wheels of justice, which had come to a halt, began to grind again for Dr. Sam.

When Bailey first assumed the legal reins, what struck him most about the case was its bizarre aspect: the crime, the trial, the appeals, and all the aftermaths. "Everything about it was bizarre," he recalls. "The more I learned, the madder I got," he said.

Two days after he met his controversial client in prison Bailey wrote Ohio Governor Michael V. DiSalle, on November 20, 1961, asking for an appointment to discuss the case.

Governor DiSalle, then nearing completion of the third year of his four-year term, was an amiable man. A sensitive individual, Governor DiSalle had recently undergone considerable anguish in commuting the death sentence of a woman convicted of murder. He knew that any involvement in the Sheppard case would subject him to even greater emotional torment and would incur the ire of many Ohioans should he seek reelection. After pondering Bailey's interview request for several days DiSalle graciously declined, saying, "The Sheppard case is more properly a matter to be handled by the Ohio Pardon and Parole Commission" and that he hoped that Bailey would understand his delicate position.

Bailey promptly fired back a letter saying that he wasn't interested in pardon, parole, clemency, or commutation of his client's sentence "since this carries with it a strong connotation of forgiveness where there is nothing to forgive." His client was innocent, and he wanted to discuss bringing outside experts into the prison to prove it.

DiSalle replied a week later at greater length, saying in part, "It is assumed from your letter that you seek the opportunity of conducting a polygraph examination of Mr.

Sheppard at the Ohio Penitentiary or another suitable facility. There are approximately 4,400 inmates. . . . To permit one polygraph examination would require us in good faith to permit similar examinations to each and every one of the other inmates. . . ."

The soul-searching tone of the governor's reply inspired Bailey to write an eloquent answer on December 19, 1961, shortly before Christmas, saying in part:

> Well over 90 percent of your inmates have been incarcerated following pleas of guilty and thus would not be in a position to ask for or benefit by a polygraph test. . . . I assume that your experience and familiarity with the polygraph are less than extensive. . . . You are unable to say whether the polygraph is accurate. I know that it is, and will prove the fact if necessary. . . . If he [Sheppard] is not guilty, I will find some means to get him out despite any and all statutes and all constitutional provisions which seem to operate against him. . . .
>
> Within a few years Dr. Sheppard will be free, and will have his polygraph test, bathed in the public eye. If he passes, the reflection thus cast upon the state and its officialdom for standing in the way can hardly be flattering. . . .
>
> Nothing which I have outlined is likely to impose any unusual burden upon the correctional authorities or the executive department; all expenses will be borne by my client, and none by the state of Ohio. . . . I am greatly disappointed that you do not see fit to grant me an opportunity to be heard personally. . . .
>
> I know that you are very busy. But I cannot believe that you are so busy that an innocent man should suffer his destruction without your consideration and deep concern. If this man, who once occupied a position in society no less respectable than yours or mine, has been wronged because the societal system misfired in its aim for justice, his only hope at this point rests upon two men: you and I. I represent him and will go the limit so long as I believe he is innocent; you, as Chief Executive of Ohio, own him, and you have the power to permit me to proceed. . . .

I ask once again that you reconsider my request for an interview. There is no other person in the state to whom I can turn unless you grant some subordinate the power to permit that which I have asked. I am told that you are a lawyer, and I rely upon you, as a lawyer, to feel something deep within which, although we revere the consistency and historical solidity of the law, makes us recoil when injustice stares us in the face.

Bailey enclosed a photostat of a letter he had received the day before from George F. McGrath, Massachusetts Commissioner of Correction, to Massachusetts Governor John A. Volpe, in which a prison polygraph lie detector test had been permitted on another Bailey client. The client had failed the test.

Governor DiSalle's reply to Bailey, dated December 26, 1961, said:

If I were to engage in a long reply to your letter, I could not add any more to what already has been said. Without question, Dr. Sheppard was found guilty by a court. I would have no right to intervene in this matter unless there was evidence that was not present at that time indicating his innocence.

I will not comply with your request to have Dr. Sheppard examined as you suggested. I am happy to have your letter detailing the experience of the Commonwealth of Massachusetts, but as much as I regret it, I am not going to establish the precedent in Ohio, especially in a case involving a circumstance occurring six years ago.

If you would like to discuss the matter, you may discuss it with my Legal Assistant, Mr. David Purkey, who handles all pardon and parole matters.

The disappointed Bailey had wanted a team of the nation's leading polygraph experts to give Dr. Sam an objective lie detector test in the presence of prison authorities. To the Boston attorney the polygraph is a valuable investigatory tool, not a sinister third-degree machine. He feels that it should have the same legal and social acceptance enjoyed by the X-ray camera, radar machine, or cardiograph.

Bailey had hoped to supplement the lie detector with an examination of his client under medical hypnosis by outside experts, as had recently been permitted on a California prisoner. Dr. William J. Bryan, executive director of the American Institute of Hypnosis in Los Angeles, author of *Legal Aspects of Hypnosis,* had filed an affidavit saying that Sam Sheppard might still be suffering from "traumatic amnesia" as a result of his head injuries. He believed that through medical hypnotism, which he had successfully used on many criminal defendants, Sheppard's subconscious memory might be sufficiently restored to jog repressed events so that he could clearly identify Marilyn's murderer or murderers.

Dr. Sam had been given a sneak, unscientific "truth serum test," called narcointerrogation, in the Ohio Penitentiary hospital in 1956, when he was in deep anesthesia after a hemorrhoids operation. A hospital orderly, a hardened criminal incarcerated for armed robbery, was alone in the room with the unconscious patient. He figured this was a golden opportunity to use any "admission" under a drug to blackmail Sheppard later. This unscrupulous convict injected a heavy dosage of sodium pentathol into Sam's veins with a hypodermic needle and demanded to know, "Why did you kill your wife?"

"Oh, no! I couldn't do it and face Chip," Sam blurted out. "But I'll get who did it!"

Another prisoner, Richard Nolan, a medical technician who was in for a lesser offense, strolled in as Sheppard made his astonishing remark. The convict who had administered the sodium pentathol immediately tried to make Nolan a confederate. Nolan refused to coöperate, though he did at first keep silent.

Later, as a rehabilitated member of society, working in an Illinois hospital—Nolan was paroled in 1963—his conscience troubled him. When Sam was later released from prison, Nolan told the story to Dr. Sam and me. "Too bad Governor DiSalle never heard this," I said.

After Governor DiSalle, Correction Commissioner Maury Koblentz, and the Marion warden had rejected Bailey's request to give Sheppard lie detector, medical hypnosis, and "truth serum" tests, the aroused attorney appealed their decisions to the Ohio Supreme Court. To overrule these officials he sought a writ of *mandamus*. A year later, on December 27, 1962, the state's highest court refused to order the tests, saying, in effect, in an unjudicial decision that ignored the California precedent, "This is something for the warden to determine."

By this time Sheppard was inured to legal defeats. He vowed, "The first thing I'm going to do if I am ever released is to take a lie detector test! If I pass, as I am sure I will, it will help me to face the outside world. After that I want to be questioned under medical hypnosis. There may be answers to some questions in my subconscious mind."

When Governor DiSalle ran for reelection, the *Cleveland Press,* which had supported him in 1958, switched to Republican nominee James A. Rhodes, who decisively defeated DiSalle in November, 1962. During his two months as a lame-duck governor DiSalle's conscience continued to trouble him. On December 20, 1962, shortly before leaving office, he received a moving letter from Paul Holmes, urging him to pardon an innocent man. "Sheppard was convicted in a caricature of a trial, and his conviction was sanctioned by judicial sycophants," wrote Holmes.

On his last day in office, January 14, 1963, Governor DiSalle considered freeing convict Sam Sheppard. But when word of this got back to Ohio's kingmakers, the governor was reputedly informed that if he did, he was through in Ohio politics.

Two years after Dr. Sam was released from prison, ex-Governor DiSalle, who was practicing law in Washington, met F. Lee Bailey at the Overseas Press Club in New York. With his talent for the jugular, Bailey couldn't resist teasing. "Mike, if you had done what I said, you would have been remembered in history as the man who freed Sam Sheppard. Now you're just a forgotten governor of Ohio."

Mike DiSalle forced a smile. I spilled my drink, laughing.

Parole or Habeas Corpus?

Freeing and exonerating Sam Sheppard became an all-consuming crusade for F. Lee Bailey.

The Boston attorney had no faith that any Ohio court or body would parole or vindicate his client. Steve had already petitioned the new Ohio governor, James Rhodes, to pardon his brother or commute Sam's ten-year sentence to a reduced manslaughter charge, which would clear the way for immediate parole. Bailey reluctantly pleaded this appeal in a public hearing on January 29, 1963, before the Ohio Pardon and Parole Commission in Columbus. During this plea for executive clemency, Bailey cited Dr. Sam's exemplary prison record, and with amazing candor he said, "Frankly, I prefer that my client remain in prison so I can litigate and clearly prove his innocence. If he is freed on parole, the question of his guilt becomes moot. But I'm his attorney, not his soul. He is requesting commutation of his sentence."

Gertrude Mahon, the widow of the chief prosecutor in Sheppard's conviction, vehemently opposed the appeal as a representative of the Cuyahoga County prosecutor's office. Coroner Gerber sat silently during the proceedings. Dr. Sam was not allowed to attend.

If his pardon or commutation appeal was successful, Sheppard planned, with Ohio authorities' approval, to start a one-man clinic in India. The precedent was the case of the late Nathan Leopold, Chicago thrill killer of the 1920s, who was paroled to do laboratory research in Puerto Rico. India was selected not only because it was a medically needy area but because Dr. Sam's father had wanted to establish such a clinic there fifteen years earlier. The elder Sheppard believed that young American doctors could train Indians and secure experience in studying diseases that are more prevalent in India than in the United States.

However, two days after the commutation hearing on January 31 the parole board unanimously voted against Sheppard, partly because of the flamboyant entrance into the hearing of Ariane Tebbenjohanns, the widely publicized "new woman" in Dr. Sam's life. The commission cited the prisoner's "misconduct"—three demerits for oversleeping. Sheppard, who was known to prison guards as a sound sleeper, had overslept three times in eight and a half years. Governor Rhodes upheld his board's ruling the following day when he officially denied clemency.

Because of the growing public furor outside prison, punitive action was taken against Dr. Sam. Five days later, at 4:00 A.M., February 5, 1963, at the orders of Commissioner of Corrections Maury C. Koblentz, Sheppard was awakened, handcuffed, chained, and hauled back from the Marion, Ohio, prison to the antiquated Ohio penitentiary in Columbus, where he was thrown into solitary confinement. His honor status was forfeited, and he was given a demerit for "oversleeping." The transfer was planned so as to incarcerate Sheppard before 6:00 A.M. to avoid his being seen by any of the regular prison reporters, who did not generally arrive until later.

As an ex-prisoner, Sheppard testified about the incident six years later, on July 8, 1969, to the U.S. Senate Subcommittee to Investigate Juvenile Delinquency:

> I was placed in the "hole" . . . to discourage me from communicating with my attorney, brothers and future wife. I was approached by Mr. Koblentz and asked to disassociate myself from these people who were trying to help me. I was promised parole if I did. Koblentz told me that if I didn't get rid of this "blond bitch," as he called her (she was not my wife at the time but she had been approved on my mailing list), and my "damned brother," as he called him, and that "SOB Bailey," . . . he would bury me indefinitely.
>
> I naturally refused. Whereupon, I was chained with leg chains, hand chains, chains around the neck and I don't know where else. I was then given the treatment . . . being placed between two doors for six days. There was no food. There was no light and little air, and I felt I would suffocate. I couldn't sleep. I was allowed to wear my shorts, shoes, and socks. I had no toilet privileges and just stood in my own excrement.
>
> After six days they removed me from the doors, and Koblentz asked me if I had changed my mind. I made a rather unfortunate comment about Mr. Koblentz's heritage, whereupon I was placed between the doors for three more days. When I came out, my ankles had swollen so large the shoe strings had split on my shoes. I spent a total of nine days in the "hole" simply because I wouldn't call off Bailey, Steve, and Ariane. . . . During this time I was beaten

on four occasions with rubber hoses. I can show you the scars on my back, Senator.

Corrections Commissioner Koblentz asked Steve Sheppard to come to Columbus for a chat. Sam's brother did so three days after the "hole" punishment, and Koblentz warned Steve to stop all the publicity. Otherwise, he said, his brother would never make parole. When Steve reported this message to Sam on his next visit, Dr. Sam exploded, "Keep building a fire under those bastards! It's the only way I'll ever get out. Steve, you know I could have gotten off with six months nearly nine years ago if I was willing to lie and say that I killed Marilyn."

Several days later, on February 13, 1963, Marilyn's father, Thomas Reese, at age 62, killed himself with a shotgun, in his Cleveland motel room. He was living alone, having separated from his second wife Jane. Tom Reese was never the same man after his daughter's murder. He refused to testify at the trial, disassociated himself from his son-in-law and the Sheppard family, and had declined to say anything publicly about the verdict. The coroner's office did not release the full text of his suicide note, reporting only that Reese had written, "I am sick of everything. Goodbye." His death precipitated a slew of rehash newspaper stories about his daughter's murder and sordid speculation about the new woman in Sheppard's life.

Sam Sheppard asked permission to attend his father-in-law's funeral. The request was denied, according to Commissioner Koblentz, because Reese had not been a blood relative.

The state of Ohio allows time off for "good behavior," which Sheppard had earned by teaching and doing hospital work. Dr. Sam would become eligible for parole when he had served ten years in prison; the six months spent in Cuyahoga County Jail did not count.

Politics frequently influences parole. In practice, few uniform standards apply to questions of parole. Parole often depends upon who talks to whom and when. "Parole granted" are the two most beautiful words in the English language to the 200,000 inmates now incarcerated in America's prisons; "Parole denied," two of the most crushing. More than sixty years ago Winston Churchill said,

"The mood and temper of the public with regard to the treatment of crime and criminals is one of the most unfailing tests of the civilization of any country."

"They won't let Sam Sheppard out until they absolutely have to," observed an Ohio lawyer. "Some people would rather let an innocent man rot in prison rather than admit that they made a mistake. The forces that put him in prison are hell-bent on keeping him there."

Even if Sheppard was paroled, he would still have to live out his life as a convicted murderer. He would no longer be permitted to practice medicine. Dr. Sam's license was revoked after his 1954 conviction and suspended indefinitely on April 2, 1957.

Alexander H. Martin, Jr., a Columbus, Ohio, lawyer who was working on the Sheppard defense team without fee, pitched strongly for parole and squabbled with Bailey over the direction of legal strategy. Shortly thereafter, Martin, whose father was one of Ohio's first black attorneys, partly as a result of his differences with Bailey, suddenly withdrew from the complex case.

Seeking a new judicial viewpoint, Bailey had decided: "The hell with parole and the state courts. Let's go into the federal courts and try for habeas corpus and fight the case on its errors of law and disregard the fact of Sam's innocence." It was a bold throw of the legal dice. Bailey would go for broke in the federal courts on habeas corpus, as Supreme Court Justice Felix Frankfurter had hinted seven years earlier.

The writ of habeas corpus—often called the Great Writ—is a constitutional rampart against illegal imprisonment. If granted, it requires that the body of a person be brought before a judge or court for investigation of restraint of this person's confinement without due process of law. Habeas corpus is a long-shot civil suit used for prisoners who have exhausted all other legal remedies and seek legal relief on the grounds that they have been deprived of their constitutional rights.

Corrigan had tried for habeas corpus in state courts, but Ohio Supreme Court Justice Weygandt denied his application on September 5, 1960, and the petition was dismissed on May 5, 1961.

Bailey hired three Harvard Law School students for

nearly two months to read all the trial testimony and briefs and prepare research material for his federal habeas corpus appeal. Bailey became so engrossed in this undertaking that he began using "Habeas" as his cable address.

Bailey was aided by two similarly unpaid Ohio attorneys: Benjamin L. Clark, of Columbus, and Russell A. Sherman, of Elyria.

On April 11, 1963, Bailey filed a habeas corpus petition in the United States District Court for the Southern District of Ohio. It was Sheppard's thirteenth legal bid for freedom and the first time his case would be heard in a federal rather than a state or local court. Federal Judge Mel G. Underwood in Columbus stalled on the petition, presumably because it was too hot a political potato. However, in December he assigned the case to Judge Carl A. Weinman, the no-nonsense chief jurist for the Southern District of Ohio, who swiftly called a pretrial conference on January 17, 1964. Ohio Attorney General William B. Saxbe's two able assistants, David Kessler and John Cianflona, represented the state.

In 22 explosive charges the 29-page Bailey petition contended that Sheppard's fundamental rights had been denied him by the trial judge, prosecution, jurors, court officers, and press before, during, and after the trial. The petition claimed that many "errors of law" had been made during the trial. It insisted that defendant Sheppard was arrested and arraigned without counsel even though he had one. It accused two court bailiffs of permitting jurors to make unmonitored private telephone calls while deliberating their verdict. It denounced the police and prosecution for "suppression . . . of relevant, material, and substantial evidence" and seizing the Sheppard home before and during the trial without permitting it to be searched by the defense for proof of his innocence. It lambasted the trial judge for permitting "double hearsay" evidence to be admitted and for allowing two police officers to offer inadmissible lie detector testimony.

If Judge Weinman agreed with any *one* of these 22 contentions, Sam Sheppard would be released outright or retried.

The unique aspect of the blistering habeas corpus appeal lay in the fact that it plainly named those who allegedly helped to deprive Sheppard of a fair trial. The petition clearly connected the conviction with hostile "trial by newspaper . . . specifically to the perverted power of the *Cleveland Press* . . ." It charged that during the 26 days before Sheppard was arrested, perhaps because of inadequate evidence:

> . . . Louis B. Seltzer [editor] caused to be printed in the said *Cleveland Press,* deliberately and with malice toward petitioner [Sheppard], articles and editorials implicating petitioner as the murderer and criticizing enforcement officials for failing to arrest him; and creating in the public mind the thought that petitioner had murdered his wife . . . mass hysteria and mass hostility . . . was continued and intensified . . . until petitioner's conviction . . . with a total disregard for the ends of justice . . . Seltzer and . . . *Cleveland Press* had a substantial pecuniary interest in causing petitioner to be convicted, in order to preclude or diminish the possibility of civil action . . . for substantial damages for defamation of petitioner's character.

Not unmindful of this extraordinary legal blast at it, the *Cleveland Press* ominously warned, in September, 1963, "If the court here releases Sheppard on a writ of habeas corpus and he is retried and again convicted, he could be sentenced to death in the electric chair."

Bailey's timing was a stroke of luck or genius. Three recent landmark United States Supreme Court decisions, starting in March, 1963, tremendously broadened habeas corpus law for convicted criminals and laid down a new set of guidelines for lower courts. The opinions in *Gideon v. Wainwright, Fay v. Noia,* and *Townsend v. Sain*—and others to follow—virtually ordered federal courts to reexamine prior state convictions to ensure that defendants' constitutional rights had not been denied during their trials. These Warren Court decisions enlarging defendants' rights literally instructed federal judges to reassess state court decisions and trial records more critically instead of ducking or rubber-stamping them, as many had done in the past.

"I knew that school was out when I read those opinions," said Bailey.

Suddenly, as Sheppard's habeas corpus petition moved into high gear, another bizarre turn of events occurred. Unexpected, seemingly generous recommendations for Dr. Sam's immediate release on parole by reducing his sentence to manslaughter swept the state of Ohio. It was almost as if some contrite Ohioans had read Bernard Shaw's irreverent words: "We have been punishing ever since Jesus told us not to; and I defy anyone to make out a convincing case for believing that the world has been any better than it would have been if there never had been a judge, a prison, or a gallows in all that time."

Out of the blue, Coroner Gerber wrote to Attorney General Saxbe on February 24, 1964. He told the press that he had said:

> No one could have an honest basis for criticizing Governor Rhodes if he should parole Sam Sheppard at this time, if the parole board should so recommend. I have always felt that justice would have been served if the jury had rendered a verdict of guilty of manslaughter in the first degree. My recommendation for parole of Sam Sheppard at this time should in no way be interpreted to suggest that I have any doubts as to his guilt in causing the death of his wife. However, in my long experience in the investigation of homicides, I have come to recognize the futility of life imprisonment for persons such as Sam Sheppard. Up until the time of the homicidal act, he was a respected and apparently responsible citizen. The homicidal act was the result of a spur-of-the-moment incident. Punishment should not be vindictive.

The *Cleveland Press* reported in a page-one headline: *Gerber Urges Dr. Sam Parole.* The following day the newspaper published a lead editorial titled *Sam Gerber's Judgment*, applauding the coroner's wisdom. It did not specifically mention Gerber's illuminating manslaughter remark, but the tone was of complete agreement with Gerber. The editorial said, "Now Dr. Gerber again enters this contentious and disputed case, again demonstrating knowledge and courage . . . penal and parole officials should match his objectivity . . . if they find an imminent parole is called for, then they should parole him [Sheppard]."

Some *Press* readers with long memories wondered why the coroner and newspaper had not indicated at the time of the motion for a new trial that Sheppard should have been tried for manslaughter, not first-degree murder. George Gilbert, a *Dayton Daily News* reporter, asked *Cleveland Press* editor Seltzer to amplify, but Seltzer demurred. "I'm not talking about the Sheppard case. This thing has gotten fantastic," Seltzer said.

Other figures involved in Sheppard's conviction now urged parole, saying that he was never guilty of anything more than manslaughter and that he had served his time for that.

Cleveland Police Chief Frank Story, who had recently retired, was quoted, "I was and am convinced that Dr. Sheppard was only guilty of manslaughter."

Ohio Penitentiary Warden Ernest L. Maxwell said Sheppard was a good inmate and ready for parole. "He never caused us any trouble outside of a few minor infractions of the rules," he reportedly said. The warden explained that Sheppard's teaching credits made him eligible for parole in October, 1964, nine months earlier than the required ten years.

Bay Village Police Lieutenant Fred Drenkham was quoted, "Sam is a model prisoner. It seems senseless to keep him. He has served his time." Drenkham added that he was convinced of Sheppard's guilt because "we can't come up with anyone else."

Homicide Detective Patrick Gareau agreed with Gerber, saying, "I never thought he was guilty of anything more than manslaughter. If the prison and parole officials feel he has been rehabilitated, he should be released. Sam apparently doesn't represent any threat to society, and from what I hear, he has been rehabilitated."

The parole pitch of the sudden forgive-and-forget chorus drew a caustic response from Sheppard's articulate lawyer.

"The authorities are now on the run," snapped Bailey. "They tried to rush through the parole to beat the habeas corpus decision. They want Sam paroled and discharged from state custody to kill our habeas action. They're worried that the trial's legal errors, including their own, set forth in our petition are so blatant and numerous that a new trial is practically certain. They want Sam to live out his life as an ex-convict instead of as a doctor, and to protect themselves from damage suits. Some people are deathly afraid that Sam is innocent and that heads will roll if this is ever discovered. Until now, they have violently opposed every attempt of Sam's to be paroled. The same people who now want to give Sam a friendly pat on the head and let bygones be bygones once nearly put him in the electric chair. But their sudden concern is nine and a half years too late."

A conspicuous objector to paroling Dr. Sam was Gertrude Mahon. "Why all this fuss about Sheppard?" the prosecutor's widow said. "He murdered his wife. The jury returned a fair verdict. There's nothing wrong with circumstantial evidence. It's used all the time in courts of law. Who, may I ask, ever sees a crime being committed?"

Meanwhile, the object of this speculation was itching to get out of prison by parole, habeas corpus, or any other legal method. One day the prison chaplain assured Dr. Sam that if he wanted to be paroled, all that he had to do was to make a request of the parole board. Prisoner 98860 impulsively scribbled a three-line note to the board, saying, somewhat sarcastically, that if they wanted to parole him that badly, go ahead and do it. When the board received his less than respectful communication, it could hardly save face by paroling him.

When Bailey heard of this unadvised note, he flew to Columbus to see his client. In a sense, he was playing Russian roulette with his client's freedom. If Sheppard accepted parole, the habeas corpus petition was dead, as was any possible lawsuit against those who had imprisoned Dr. Sam. It was a painful visit for Bailey. He urged Sam to be patient and to remain in jail a little longer, until there was a ruling on his habeas corpus petition so that a fight could be made for complete clearance and a new trial, if necessary.

"Sam, do you want to spend the rest of your life as a doctor or as a paroled convicted murderer?" Bailey asked.

"Are you absolutely sure that I'm getting out on habeas?" Sam responded.

"In this business I can't guarantee anything. But I guarantee you this, Sam. I think I know what Judge Weinman is thinking. He's a very decent judge who knows the law, and he is honest. No honest man could possibly refuse you a writ of habeas."

Dr. Sam agreed to go along, but the parole question soon became academic. On Friday, March 13, 1954, the Ohio Pardon and Parole Board voted unanimously to deny the premature parole of Sam Sheppard, which it was scheduled to consider formally in October. It ruled that Sheppard must "continue to serve his sentence until he becomes eligible for parole consideration after expiration of his minimum sentence."

Several days later, the *Saturday Evening Post* whimsically rejected an article that it had assigned me about the case. "We bounced your piece, Jack," an editor confided, "because we don't believe Sheppard will *ever* get out of prison. He's guilty as hell! So why should we give that prick and his lawyer any publicity?"

In the Ohio Penitentiary Dr. Sam couldn't help wondering if he would not suffer a far greater debacle. His flame of hope still burned, but it had flickered and died often. He approached his fortieth birthday in prison, teaching, reading, wondering, and waiting. If a lawyer's confidence could open prison doors, he was a free man. But most Ohioans believed that the habeas corpus petition would fail, that no retrial would ever be held, and that Bailey was just making his by now customary big noise.

But another big gun was now coming to Sam Sheppard's defense.

6

THE WOMAN

A STRIKING 25-year-old woman was flipping through a German picture magazine while waiting in her dentist's office in Düsseldorf, Germany, in mid-December, 1954.

Her perceptive eyes fixed upon the photograph of a handsome American who was on trial 4,300 miles away for killing his wife, allegedly because he loved another woman. The article presented a series of questions: "Is this man the killer?" "Does he have a Jekyll-Hyde personality?" "Was the Cleveland community prejudiced because of his wealth?"

By the time she had finished reading the article, she was shaking with fury. She could not believe that the doctor was a murderer. She felt that because he was so successful at age 30, people were jealous of him, just as classmates had resented her when as a child she was driven to school in a chauffeured automobile. The man seemed to her a victim of the "justice" she knew and hated when growing up in Nazi Germany.

That afternoon she said to her mother, "He's innocent. I feel it. I can tell by looking at him. How could this happen in America? Isn't American justice supposed to be the best in the world?"

That evening she prattled on about the case to her husband Olaf, a young steel company heir and industrialist.

"Forget it. There's nothing you can do about it," he said.

But Ariane Tebbenjohanns could not forget the Sheppard murder case, and her inability to put it out of her mind changed her life.

A week later, when she read about Dr. Sam's conviction, she wanted to write to him immediately to express her outrage at the verdict. But she demurred because of a sensitive reserve beneath her outspoken and ostentatious exterior.

The Riviera Reader

Three months later, Ariane took a month's winter vacation with her husband on the French Riviera. There they became friendly with a vacationing physician and his wife who lived in New Haven, Connecticut. Naturally, Ariane brought up the Sheppard case, having read everything she could secure about it in German, English, and French publications (she was also fluent in Italian). The American couple expressed a belief that someone else had killed Marilyn.

"Well, why don't you do something about it?" demanded Ariane, who was becoming obsessed with the innocence of a faraway prisoner she had never met.

"What *can* we do?" protested the Connecticut couple.

"You can write to the governor of Ohio and demand that Sam be released."

"Can't you talk about anything except Sam Sheppard?" her husband interjected.

Ariane divorced Olaf Tebbenjohanns in 1957 after an unhappy six-year marriage. She insists that it had nothing to do with her belief in Sheppard's innocence. Their marriage was just on the rocks. Afterward, the wealthy Ariane spent considerably more time on the Riviera, but the indolent, carefree life there bored her.

Though she had written Sam Sheppard several times, she invariably tore up the letters lest she be considered a crank or an intruder. Finally, in March, 1959, she summoned the courage to compose a dignified, compassionate letter, which she mailed to brother Steve at the Sheppard Clinic. "Would it be possible to correspond with Sam directly?" she inquired.

Sheppard had received many letters via Steve from women all over the world who believed in his innocence. They wanted to correspond with and eventually meet him for romantic or other reasons. But Dr. Sam was bitter and had no interest in women during his nearly five years behind bars.

Something about this German woman's letter, though, tantalized Steve. It was meticulously handwritten on small crimson stationery with the simple word "Ariane" printed in white letters. On his next monthly prison visit he showed the letter to his brother.

"Write her and ask her to send her picture," said Sam.

Steve did. To lift his brother's spirits he enjoyed playing go-between. He wrote to Mrs. Tebbenjohanns, "Prison regulations forbid Dr. Sam to write to anyone other than his immediate family or lawyer, but he suggested that you write to me. I will bring your letters to him on my monthly visits. If he has any replies, I will send them to you."

That did it. Ariane Tebbenjohanns suddenly had a "cause" and some direction to her otherwise aimless life. "I wrote back more about myself and sent a picture of myself sitting on top of my Volkswagen and one later picture, skiing," she recalled.

Sam carried the cheerful, chatty letters of his mystery woman from across the ocean and read them at least a half dozen times daily. Steve scribbled Sam's reactions to her informative letters on backs of envelopes and airmailed them to her without comment. It was obvious to Steve that this woman was restoring his brother to the world of the living and enabling him to withstand his legal setbacks. When Dr. Sam was transferred to the Marion institution, in January, 1961, Ariane was allowed to write Sam directly for almost a year, even though the letters still had to go through Steve. In 1962 Ariane was placed on Sam's approved mailing list, and they corresponded directly.

Though they started as pen pals, the three-year correspondence developed into a courtship. The princess from across the sea and the imprisoned prince grew to know each other. "She was Sophia Loren, Marilyn Monroe, Doris Day, and Liz Taylor all wrapped up in one," Sam later explained.

On the Riviera in the summer of 1962, Ariane told an

American couple, "I've fallen in love with a convicted wife-killer in your country."

Still, the intelligent, sophisticated woman was prudent enough not to verbalize her loving feelings in her letters lest they unduly arouse a prisoner who did not know when, if ever, he would be released. Instead, she sent him books, a radio, and a lock of her hair, which he carried in a transparent cellophane sleeve. Without telling Sam she quietly sent a thousand marks ($253) to Bailey in Boston to help defray his client's legal costs. Immediately Bailey telephoned Steve, asking, "Did you ever hear of anybody named Ariane Tebbenjohanns?"

"Sure. She has been corresponding with Sam for three years and says she may be coming to America soon."

Ariane decided to do precisely that after receiving, at Christmastime, 1962, a small silver cross and chain from Sam. "You have made my life worth living," the grateful prisoner wrote her. Ariane's mother warned her that this transatlantic epistolary romance with a convict she had never met was "crazy."

"Are you doing this just because you want an excuse to go to America?" demanded her mother.

"No, I want to find out if my feelings toward Sam are just friendship or love."

On Sunday, January 20, 1963, Steve received a surprising person-to-person telephone call from New York City.

"Hello, Dr. Sheppard? This is Ariane. I am in New York. I am going to Marion to see Sam." She spoke a precise English, in a charming Continental accent.

Flabbergasted, Steve replied that he was glad to hear from her, but, well, what made her think she could possibly see Sam in prison?"

"I have a letter from the Marion superintendent, Mr. Lamoyne Green, saying that I can."

Steve swallowed hard; he finally found his voice.

"Well, bring the letter with you, and come here. It's easier to get to Marion if you come to Cleveland first. I'll pick you up at the airport."

"That won't be necessary, Dr. Sheppard. I don't want to trouble you. I can get a cab."

"Nonsense. We live not far from the airport."

"Very well, that is very kind of you. You can recognize me by my dark mink coat and silver blonde hair."

"My hair is probably more silver than yours. I'll be wearing a white sweater."

They recognized each other immediately. Steve suggested that she stay at a nearby motel, and that evening after dinner Steve and Betty Sheppard heard their visitor's bizarre life story.

Ariane was born in Germany in 1929 and grew up in Düsseldorf. Her father, Oskar Ritschel, developed a water purification process used throughout Germany. Ariane was the only child of her wealthy father's second wife. She had a half-sister named Magda, 20 years older, who was her father's daughter from his first marriage.

When Ariane was not quite a year old, Magda had married, over the strenuous objections of her anti-Nazi father, a man who was to assume an outstanding position in Nazi Germany: Dr. Paul Josef Goebbels. Magda's first husband had been a Jewish businessman. Three years before he became Chancellor of Germany, Adolph Hitler was the best man at Magda's 1930 marriage to Goebbels, who in 1933 was named Propaganda Minister of the Third Reich with complete control over press, radio, cinema, theater, and art. A warped and sadistic man, Goebbels was one of the most cynical, savage Nazis. In April, 1945, Goebbels and Magda killed themselves and their six children as Berlin was falling to the Soviet troops.

Ariane told the spellbound Sheppards that she hardly knew her half-sister because, after her marriage, Magda had lived in Berlin while she was growing up in Düsseldorf. She had never lived in the same house with Magda. Occasionally, Magda and Goebbels came to visit them. Ariane recalled that early in 1940, when she was ten years old, her father quarreled violently with Goebbels. "My father denounced the Nazis for their persecution of the Jews," she remembered. "And I heard Goebbels shout at him: 'If you weren't my father-in-law, I would have you thrown into a concentration camp.' "

When Ritschel died in 1941, the Nazis boycotted his funeral. Ariane and her mother continued to live in the city of Düsseldorf on the comfortable lifetime trust fund he had established for them.

As a teenager Ariane said that she had been a member of the Hitler Youth Organization but had not joined the Nazi party or been a sympathizer herself.

"Do you think my relationship with Magda would hurt Sam's case?" Ariane asked her host.

Steve Sheppard answered thoughtfully, "I don't see why. You were only a child then, and your parents weren't Nazis. You and Magda had the same father but not the same mother. You're probably interested in Sam's case because you hate all kinds of oppression."

Steve had planned to drive Ariane to the Marion prison the next day, but one of Ohio's blizzards prevented the trip. Ariane decided to go alone by train. The normally three-hour trip took eight hours. The train's heating system broke down in Fostoria, and Ariane and the other passengers shivered there in the blistering cold. She checked into a hotel after midnight but hardly slept. A taxi brought her to the prison before 9:00 A.M. on January 24, 1963.

"There's a blonde stunner out there in a mink coat to see you," a guard teased Prisoner 98860.

Ariane strolled jauntily into the unscreened conference room, wearing a fashionably tailored suit beneath her mink, and smiled at the prisoner. He found his first words to the woman, who now seemed more beautiful to him than any of her photographs. "How about giving me a big kiss?"

Since there were five curious guards peering at them, she discreetly kissed him on the cheek.

"It wasn't love at first sight," Sam later told me. "It was love *before* first sight."

"If I ever had any doubts about his innocence, they were eliminated during that visit," Ariane later remarked to me. "The beautiful Riviera and the crazy life I led there no longer seemed important to me."

They sat down at a secluded table in the large room. They held hands. They chattered about his life in prison, hers outside, his son, her daughter, their future plans if he was released. They vowed that their love was stronger than prison bars, hopefully agreeing, "Our day will come."

"Oh, I forgot to cut the bread," Ariane apologized.

Sam summoned a guard, who brought a 16-inch bread knife.

"You're sure trusting me," quipped Sam, whose honor status had permitted the extraordinary visit.

"She made a complete list of everything I needed so that she could send it to me," Sam later recollected. "It felt wonderful to know that somebody cared. She gave me real hope of becoming a member of society again with a home and happiness. Those who ridiculed us have never been in prison, or they might have understood."

Near the end of their four-and-a-half-hour visit, the prisoner stammered, "Ariane, I'm in no position to ask you . . ."

With a joyous laugh that indicated an extrasensory perception, she cut him short, saying, "Go ahead and ask, Sam, because the answer is yes!"

He handed her a dove on a silver chain with "Sam-Ariane" engraved on the back; he had made it in prison. He trembled as he placed it around her neck. From her own neck she removed an American Indian goldpiece which dangled on a golden chain. She encircled Sam's neck with it.

This jewelry exchange symbolized their engagement.

He felt like sweeping her into his arms, but the presence of guards restrained his feelings. When she left, he kissed her fervently, not knowing whether he would ever see her again.

"It was fifteen below zero, but it was the warmest day of my life," she later told me.

To Sam, the strange woman symbolized the words of Matthew (25, 36): "I was in prison and ye came unto me."

Blonde Bombshell

Five days after her bizarre betrothal, Ariane requested permission to attend Dr. Sam's commutation hearing in Columbus. Steve and Bailey agreed, but later they considered the decision a tactical error. Steve had announced the Sam-Ariane engagement the day before the hearing. When Ariane arrived at the hearing, she was greeted by a swarm of photographers and reporters who considered their genuine romance merely a Sheppard family publicity stunt. The German woman honestly believed that public opinion had put Sam in prison and that only public opinion would get him released. That evening the new celebrity was interviewed on many Columbus television and radio stations. She said some undiplomatic things about American justice, and pledged to carry the Sheppard case to President John F. Kennedy, Attorney General Robert F. Kennedy, and the German press.

The next day the American press sensationally revealed the controversial woman's relationship to Goebbels. Ariane was called a Nazi, a "Teutonic Marilyn Monroe," and a host of unprintable epithets. A neo-Nazi organization in the United States even tried to launch a campaign to protest the "persecution" of Dr. Sheppard. Immediately Ariane called the ex-Nazis "idiots" and angrily told the press, which scantily reported it: "*They*—not Dr. Sam—should be in prison."

As a result of this publicity flurry, the good will that Dr. Sam had created as a model prisoner for more than eight years vanished almost instantly. Hostility toward the Sheppards erupted anew.

Commissioner Koblentz swiftly struck Ariane Tebbenjohanns's name from the visiting and mailing list of Prisoner 98860. A letter that she had written to Sam in Marion was returned to her marked "Undeliverable." Enraged, the determined woman had her love letter published in the *Columbus Dispatch* so that Sam would see it. Koblentz then visited Sheppard in Marion and warned him, "You better send that blonde back to Europe," before ordering Dr. Sam himself carted back to the Ohio Penitentiary in chains.

Not only the Ohio authorities but Bailey and the Sheppard family now wanted to muzzle Ariane. When Richard returned from a holiday in Jamaica, he was furious at Steve for the way Steve had handled the Ariane affair; Richard had never even heard of her until he read about her in the Miami newspapers. "That was the nearest that Richard and I have ever come to a break in our friendship," Steve once said to me. On reflection, however,

Richard realized that Steve's motive was entirely to cheer and help their younger brother.

Frankly, some of Ariane's publicity techniques were puzzling. Still, she convinced this at first skeptical reporter of the sincerity of her love for Sam Sheppard. Though difficult to understand, Ariane was easy to like if one took the trouble to know her. There was far more beneath her flamboyant exterior than her seemingly zany antics suggested.

After she came to this country to battle for her future husband's release and vindication, I periodically discussed the case with her. Ariane was—and is—no ordinary person but a complex, sophisticated woman of Continental elegance and dramatic flair. Her few friends have come to know her as sensitive and warmhearted, despite her exhibitionist facade. She could talk a blue streak and make considerable sense. She could be charming and feminine or withering and scornful.

Because her visitor's visa was soon to expire, Ariane returned to Germany in March, 1963, to see her daughter and mother and to settle her business affairs. Ohio skeptics, who quickly dismissed her as a "phony" and a "publicity hound," predicted that the boisterous woman would never marry Sheppard but would remain in Germany now that the headlines had died down.

They were wrong.

Ariane, ever the woman of surprises, returned to Ohio quietly four months later, in July, after applying to become a permanent resident and eventually a United States citizen.

Ariane rented, under a two-year lease, a five-room brick row house in residential Rocky River. "When Sam and I get married after he gets out of prison," she explained to me, "I don't want him to have to live in a hotel or some uncomfortable rented place. This will be his home."

She furnished the house lavishly and tastefully with her prize possessions, shipped from her home in Germany. A royal purple color scheme dominated the eighteenth-century French living room. On the wall of the small upstairs bedroom—the room she had reserved for Sam's son Chip—she hung two photographs of Marilyn Sheppard. She purchased two cars, one for Sam and the other for herself.

After Ariane had settled in, despite the public hostility toward her she immediately resumed her crusade for the Sam Sheppard cause, which was again dormant. Although she had rarely worked in her life, she toiled around the clock on her strange mission. "If I had to talk about my own innocence to people, I couldn't do it," she explained. "Anything I do for myself, I'm no good at, but I have to do things for Sam because he isn't out here to do them for himself."

The dedicated Düsseldorfer talked about Sam Sheppard to anyone who would listen. "Nobody can outtalk me on that," she crowed. She never turned down an invitation to discuss the case. When we went into an Ohio drugstore to purchase an *Argosy* magazine containing a story about the Sheppard case, she scolded me, "Why didn't you tell the clerk *why* you were buying the magazine?" The emotion she invested in even the most minute details of her crusade was staggering.

The determined woman seized every opportunity to be interviewed by the press and to appear on radio and television to tell the Sam Sheppard story. Once when she was allotted 12 minutes for a radio interview, she protested to the producer, "Twelve minutes isn't enough time to tell Sam's story!" Another radio-TV official offered her a job, but she declined, saying, "No. My life belongs to Sam Sheppard." One morning I appeared with her as a guest on Long John Nebel's New York 12:00 A.M. to 5:00 A.M. radio program. By the time dawn arrived, I was wilted but not Ariane. She could have continued hours longer, looking as fresh as her highly styled hairdo.

All of her energy was poured into her crusade, and she was scrupulously faithful to her imprisoned fiancé. An attractive man-about-New York who had made an unsuccessful pass at her mused over a Scotch, "Imagine that kook turning *me* down for a con in the can!"

Forbidden to communicate with Sam, she arranged with prison visitors to smuggle letters in and out. In letters to his family and lawyers Dr. Sam ingeniously utilized codes to include messages for Ariane, such as making words in a letter spell out "I love you."

Released convicts brought gifts to her from Sam. One delivered a dozen long-stemmed roses on her birthday. Another purchased for her a black bra and panties, at Sam's request. Another brought her a ring made by Sam from a round lamb chop bone and polished like sparkling ivory.

Every month she drove to the Culver Military Academy in Indiana to pick up Sam, Jr., in her Volkswagen. She would drive him to the Columbus Penitentiary to visit his father and wait outside while Sheppard tried to sneak a glimpse of her in the parking area. Sam's son and she became great friends.

One afternoon while Sam was still in prison I walked with Ariane on the lakefront beach in back of the Bay Village house in which Marilyn had been murdered. We paced the scene of Sam's story. We checked the facts with the amazing psychic impressions of a Dutch sensitive, Gerard Croiset, in a unique experiment conducted at Holland's University of Utrecht Parapsychology Institute, which were later reported in my *Croiset the Clairvoyant* biography.

Suddenly Ariane blurted out, "Not only in my mind but in my heart I know that Sam couldn't possibly have killed Marilyn. There was no reason for him to do it. He was happy with her. If he were guilty, he couldn't have lived with himself all these years and be the man that he is today. Oh, I know a lot of people say, 'But he lied about having an affair with another woman.' Well, if all the men who had lied about affairs were accused of being murderers, there wouldn't be enough jails for them."

The worldly German woman added, "This type of thinking upsets me because I had to fight a *different* kind of prejudice. In my travels I have found that many people hate me just because I am German. Other people don't like me because I wear long earrings, eye makeup, and don't dress or live as they do. Therefore, they say: 'Oh, she must be no good.' That's one reason I didn't want my daughter to come here."

The Sheppard zealot deeply missed her nine-year-old daughter, who lived with Ariane's mother and stepfather outside Düsseldorf. The absent mother telephoned, wrote, or taped a weekly letter to her daughter in Germany.

"I hardly know my own child anymore," she told me tearfully in mid-December, 1963. "My heart is in the middle of the Atlantic between my Iris and my Sam. I'd like to fly there to spend this Christmas with her, but Sam doesn't want me to fly. He says if the plane crashed, his life would be over."

In fact, Ariane's dilemma became academic. At Christmas time she was in the Bay Village, Ohio, hospital suffering a "nervous breakdown" from overexhaustion. "I always thought I was made of rock," she wrote me from the hospital.

Ariane's dogged persistence began to give Ohio skeptics pause. "So what if she is playing Joan of Arc," conceded one. "She's doing a helluva job fanning the Sheppard fires." Despite her exhibitionism she was increasingly accepted as a public relations and financial bulwark in Sheppard's fight for freedom. Granted that her motives may have been complex in seeking fulfillment through her "cause," she was the first to admit, "Sam is the important one—not me. He's the one who should be free."

Soon the Sheppard freedom cry would again reverberate throughout Ohio's legal thickets.

7

THE RELEASE

FEDERAL JUDGE CARL A. WEINMAN, chief judge of the United States District Court in Southern Ohio, called Lee Bailey into his private chambers in Dayton on Friday morning, May 1, 1964.

The judge picked up from his desk an advance copy of *Parade* magazine containing my lead cover article titled "Will Sam Sheppard Go Free This Week?" This article was scheduled for publication the following Sunday in his local *Dayton Daily News* and 83 other Sunday newspapers.

The judge sternly inquired of the lawyer, "Mr. Bailey, are you trying my case in the pages of *Parade* magazine?"

"Oh, no, Your Honor. Sure, I knew about that story and that it *might* be published sometime. But I didn't know when, if ever. Jack Pollack called and talked to me, but he talked to everybody else on the case, too, I hear."

Judge Weinman shuffled some papers on his desk and said nothing. He had already scheduled a final pretrial conference on May 6, when he would decide whether it was necessary to hear oral arguments from the State of Ohio and Bailey. The judge had felt that they would not be needed because of mutual agreement on all points. But if he had any intention of freeing prisoner Sheppard that week, he most certainly would not do so now.

After he dismissed Bailey, Judge Weinman's mind perhaps drifted back to some of the other principals in the habeas proceedings, but he probably thought more about Bailey's exemplary conduct during the habeas proceedings and the Boston attorney's timely petition, which needed a ruling.

Despite Bailey's infectious optimism, Prisoner 98860 was pondering an alternative, if the habeas petition failed or was not acted upon. He was assessing a job proposal to submit to the parole board in October, when his minimum ten-year sentence would be officially ended. He considered living temporarily with his oldest brother Richard and trying to secure a sales job with a drug or surgical instrument company. Another thought was to work as a mechanic with a boat-building company in California through the intercession of his friends there. Still another idea was to obtain a construction position in Tennessee with the help of Marilyn's relative, Mary Brown, and her architect husband Bud.

Ariane, who wanted her Sam out immediately on any terms, urged him strongly to accept parole if he could get it. But Bailey's heart by now was deeply set on his habeas petition. "We had a hell of an argument," Bailey later admitted to me. "It ended by my telling her [Ariane] that I was going to Columbus to see Sam and that I would do everything in my power to undermine her advice because she didn't know what she was talking about."

Then the parole dilemma became academic.

Judge Weinman Rules

On the afternoon of July 15, 1964, in a historic decision in a case that had divided the judiciary and bar for nearly a decade, Judge Weinman released an 86-page ruling that Dr. Samuel Sheppard's 1954 conviction was a "mockery of justice" and that he should be released immediately on a $10,000 bond.

In a biting decision the federal judge in Dayton ruled that Sheppard's constitutional rights had been shockingly violated on five counts during his trial: (1) failure of trial Judge Blythin to grant a change of venue in view of the pretrial publicity; (2) failure of Blythin to disqualify himself despite uncertainty about his own impartiality; (3)

improper introduction of lie detector testimony; (4) the court's inability to maintain jurors' impartiality; and (5) unauthorized communications to the jury during their deliberations.

"Each of the aforementioned errors," Judge Weinman wrote, "is by itself sufficient to require a determination that petitioner was not afforded a fair trial as required by the due process clause of the Fourteenth Amendment. And when these errors are cumulated, the trial can only be viewed as mockery of justice."

In a stinging rebuke to the Cleveland press, Judge Weinman, who had studied six huge scrapbooks of clippings on the case from the Cleveland newspapers, concluded, "If ever there was a trial by newspaper, this was a perfect example. And the most insidious violator was the *Cleveland Press*. Freedom of the press cannot be permitted to overshadow the rights of an individual to a fair trial." The federal judge cited an opinion of U.S. Supreme Court Justice Frankfurter about freedom of the press not being an absolute. The decision was Earl Warren—Ohio style.

Judge Weinman was careful to point out that he was not ruling on Sheppard's innocence or guilt. That was not the issue before him. The judge ordered the state of Ohio or Cuyahoga County to retry Sheppard within sixty days or his freedom "shall be final and unconditional and the bond canceled."

This was Dr. Sam's first court victory in nearly ten years. He was now in the bizarre legal position of being an indicted man accused of a crime—as he was back on August 17, 1954—having been neither tried nor convicted for it.

My *Parade* article prediction suddenly aroused some post mortem interest, more than any Sunday supplement story deserved. After Judge Weinman's ruling *Parade* managing editor Edwin Kiester, Jr., asked Bailey to write a sequel article explaining the inside facts of the decision, but editor Jess Gorkin decided not to publish it. These are some extracts from Bailey's unpublished article:

> The announcement of Judge Weinman's decision was in keeping with the manner in which he conducted this case from the outset. During our first meeting,

he had laid down the ground rules. This was a complex and difficult case, he said, but with determination and professional conduct, it would be handled as thoroughly and swiftly as good legal procedure would permit. Counsel were expected to stipulate to every fact which was not reasonably in dispute; briefs would be filed on all serious questions of law. It was to be a dignified proceeding, handled in routine fashion with deference to the rights of all parties concerned. Judge Carl Weinman was an experienced, relaxed, no-nonsense jurist. I respected him from the outset, and still do; I think that any lawyer foolish enough to cross him would regret such recklessness immediately. He handled the Sheppard case, for as long as it was before him, with a gentle but rock-firm hand.

On July 15, 1964, the day Barry Goldwater was nominated, I was driving home in the early afternoon. Two days before, my associate and I had won the reversal of two murder cases in the Massachusetts Supreme Court. I intended to take the following day off to do some sailing. Suddenly the word came over my car two-way radio. My secretary was breathless. "Mr. Bailey—Sam Sheppard—he's getting out—the writ is granted—the phones are ringing—hurry back. . . ."

Judge Weinman's clerk had called all counsel to advise that an order had been entered freeing Sam Sheppard. The press would have the news shortly, he felt, and he wished counsel to know first. This was just another case, it seemed, being announced in routine fashion. Here was a judge who was above sensation, above drama, announcing a landmark decision on one of the few days in the year when it would have to be buried in the news of a bigger event.

What Jack Pollack smelled [in the *Parade* article], as he later explained, and what led him to his conclusion that Sam's release was imminent, was the one salient fact which so many others had missed: Sam was now in *federal court* for the first time. Rights guaranteed by the Constitution of the United States, which had been denied to Sam by the dozens, are protected by federal judges. Such was the case here. No new precedent has been set, for the law enunciated by Judge Weinman has been law for some time. It only remained for a completely impartial court to weigh the events of the Sheppard trial against what the Constitution guarantees every citizen, and a horrible imbalance became apparent.

Taking Sam Sheppard away from the custody of Ohio authorities was the greatest thrill I have ever had. I only regret that it was not done, as it should have been, ten years ago. They were wasted years, and Sam will never get them back.

My piddling *Parade* article did not make—but certainly reflected—legal history in Ohio.

Prison Gates

"Pack your shit, Sheppard. You're going home."

A guard in the penitentiary at Columbus barked these words at daybreak, July 16, 1964, into the cell of Prisoner 98860, who had spent nearly one quarter of his 40 years behind bars.

Samuel Holmes Sheppard had waited 3,639 days for this message and had expected it to be expressed in loftier, more lordly language.

He rolled off of his creaking bedsprings and accepted through the bars the pink slip that signified his release. He had counted these bars a thousand times, but somehow they looked strange. He still could not quite believe in the miracle pink slip—the symbol of discharge in industry. Suddenly he became conscious of the coughs of other rising convicts and the morning groans of the antiquated plumbing. Nervously he fumbled for his pipe.

Although usually a sound sleeper, he had hardly closed his eyes since he had heard, late on the previous afternoon, Judge Weinman's ruling. The word of his astounding release moved through the prison cells and corridors faster than a man on his way to the moon, but to Sam it was still a vague dream. He had heard the bitter comments of Ohio and Cuyahoga County officials before he tried to doze off, that they would rearrest him on another charge if he ever stepped outside the prison gates. Dr. Sam hoped for the best, but, as always, he expected the worst.

The night before he had skipped supper, preferring to stay glued to the radio. When the breakfast bell sounded, he wanted to pass up that meal, too, but he decided that he needed some coffee to wake him to what was euphemistically called the "real world."

In the mess hall the convicts cheered noisily as he strolled in clutching his pink slip. Some of the guards applauded, and others banged their sticks on the table, vainly attempting to restore decorum from the bedlam. The departing prisoner just smiled as he sipped his coffee with a few of the prisoners who had been closest to him. You don't say goodbye when leaving prison—not if you have any sensitivity. A man leaves prison alone.

In the clothing room he was given a prison-made suit; he was not permitted to don the new suit that Ariane had purchased for him, but he was allowed to wear the new white shirt and dark tie that she had delivered by Chip.

His personal belongings were returned to him, with the exception of his diary, legal papers, and some letters that the censor had never permitted to leave the penitentiary. Suddenly he felt bold and took a calculated risk because he had heard on the radio that Bailey would have federal marshals arrest anybody who impeded his release. "If you don't give me back everything that is mine," he blurted out to the frisker, "I'm going to call Lee Bailey right now, and he'll have you behind bars in a federal penitentiary yourself before sundown for an illegal search and seizure!"

"We do this with everybody, Doc," the guard weakly protested, as he permitted the ex-convict to get by with all of his possessions. The bluff had worked.

In the deputy warden's office he sweated out three of the longest hours of his life. There, he and others heard radio newscasts about how Attorney General Saxbe, who was in San Francisco attending the Republican National Convention, was conferring with state officials on methods to prevent his release, that if he was unable to achieve that, he would speedily appeal Judge Weinman's ruling.

The official order for Sam's release came shortly before noon. He was ushered into the prison accounts office to check his bank balance. The final stop was in the warden's office. Three persons were present: Warden Ernest Maxwell, Ohio Corrections Commissioner Maury Koblentz, and a representative of the Ohio Attorney General's office. Prisoner 98860 shook hands with the latter and with Warden Maxwell, but when Koblentz stretched out his heavy palm, Dr. Sam walked swiftly past him. This was the man who had ordered him thrown into the "hole" and who had banned all communication with Ariane.

As he strolled across the prison yard, prisoners craned their necks at the barred windows and cheered wildly, as did many of the guards. As the huge metal gates swung open, his heart pounded. The gates clanged behind him. There was no ritual about it: one minute you're in, the next minute you're out. It's almost like life itself.

Most released prisoners leave in total anonymity, but not Dr. Sam Sheppard. Outside, a throng of spectators, many of whom had been waiting for hours, applauded. One woman kneeled and prayed for the released prisoner. Another threw her rosary beads at him. Two truck drivers, approaching in opposite directions, stopped their huge vehicles in the middle of the street and shouted, "Hi, Doc!" and "Good luck, Sam!" A passing motorist, noticing the throng that was delaying traffic, said to his passenger, "Well, if it isn't President Lyndon Johnson, it's gotta be Sam Sheppard."

Warden Maxwell, a guard, and the released prisoner elbowed their way through the boisterous crowd into a waiting state of Ohio automobile, which took them to the federal building in downtown Columbus. There, another exhilarated mob greeted him. Onlookers observed that his face, which the world had come to know so well, was still boyish despite his thinning hair, now flecked with gray.

Lee Bailey was waiting. So was brother Richard, who was on hand to sign a $10,000 bond. It was the first time in ten years that Sam had entered a court unchained. He started to say to Richard, "I only wish Dad and Mom were here now," but somehow the words could not emerge.

Ariane remained in Rocky River, on the advice of Bailey, Steve, and Richard. They had figured that no added excitement was needed. Steve also decided to stay at home. Warden Maxwell gave Sam a check for $287, which terminated his prison account.

During the jam-packed news conference that Bailey held

shortly afterward in a large hearing room in the federal building, the cameras ground incessantly as the reporters fired a barrage of questions. Would Sam open that clinic in India now? Would he go to Vietnam, where doctors were needed? Would he join the Peace Corps? Was he going to marry Ariane?

He answered all the questions forthrightly—except two. When a representative of a hostile Cleveland newspaper addressed him as "*Mr.* Sheppard" and accented the word needlessly, he winced but remained silent. When another newsman asked, in good faith, "How come you're so tanned?" he snapped bitterly, "I'm told Dreyfus looked that way when he left Devil's Island."

Sam, Bailey, and Bailey's then wife Froma (nicknamed Wickie) drove to the Arlington Arms motel outside Columbus where Ariane, who was driving in from Cleveland, would later join them. I was in the party and checked into the room adjoining Bailey's. During the drive to the motel rumors flew over the car radio that Judge Weinman had been reversed by a higher federal court and that Sheppard would be rearrested momentarily by a federal marshal. It was a psychological war of nerves.

At the motel Bailey heard on the radio that Federal Judge Lester Cecil of the United States Sixth Circuit Court of Appeals had stayed Judge Weinman's order, that Sheppard's $10,000 bail had been revoked, and that he was to be rearrested. "If only for my family's sake," Sam philosophized, "I don't want to go back. But if I have to, I will."

Bailey promptly telephoned Judge Cecil, who said yes, he had issued a temporary stay pending a hearing, which meant that Judge Weinman's decision would be reviewed. But he had not ordered Dr. Sam back to prison, nor had he revoked the bond.

When Sam heard this news he shouted with happiness and jumped into the motel pool for a swim.

Before doing so, he gave me a two-dollar bill, writing on it: "For Jack. This represents a half month's pay during my incarceration." (He had earned four dollars a month during his ten-year imprisonment.) From the pool, he cried: "I'm free! Godammit, I'm free!"

Days of Freedom

What is freedom? Chains can manacle the heart and mind in or out of prison walls.

When he was first released, America's most celebrated ex-prisoner was not sure whether the world or he had changed in ten years. Whatever the case, he treasured every moment of his freedom.

As Sam and I were sharing some of the aromatic tobacco I had sent him while he was in prison, he remarked casually, "It's funny. I now probably have a deeper appreciation of the little things in life that people outside prison take for granted. I enjoy the companionship of my family and friends more than ever before. I love being able to drink fresh orange juice again and to smell a chicken roasting in the oven. I get a bang out of being able to take a shower alone. I get stir-crazy looking at flowers in the green fields and the blue sky in the sunshine; I love to walk by the water and hear children laugh. The simple things in life can be so damn beautiful!"

Even window-shopping excited him. It was immaterial what was displayed; everything exhilarated him. He could stare for hours if he had the time. It was worlds apart from that of armed guards patrolling a prison turret.

The released prisoner nurtured a passion for freedom. Whenever he entered a room, he flung off his shirt and his shoes and socks, so that he could touch the carpet with his bare feet.

He had an almost adolescent anticipation about getting his driver's license back. He had not been behind a wheel in ten years. "Cars are so different now," he observed.

His entire attitude was affirmative. He was pleased when I quoted him the famous line of Harold Russell, the World War II veteran who had four artificial limbs, which he already knew: "It's not what you've lost but what you have left and how you use it that counts." Another quotation, translated from Sanskrit, delighted him even more:

> Look to this one day. For it and it alone is life. In the brief course of this one day lie all the verities, all the realities of your existence—the joy of living, the

splendor of beauty, the glory of action. Yesterday is but a dream. Tomorrow is only a vision. But today, well lived, will make every yesterday a dream of happiness and each tomorrow a vision of hope. Look well, therefore, to this one day, for it and it alone is life.

Suddenly he felt tortured with family obligations. First and foremost was young Sam. There were many fish that he had to catch with his 16-year-old son, who that fall would be a senior at the Culver Military Academy, in Indiana.

Yet Sam was still in legal limbo. His court battles were far from over. On July 17, the day after his release, it was announced that a three-judge tribunal of the United States Court of Appeals would review Judge Weinman's decision on July 22.

With at least five more days of freedom assured, free man Sam Sheppard decided to take another plunge.

8

THE REMARRIAGE

THE SHEPPARD FAMILY and Bailey did not want Sam to marry Ariane immediately. They thought that they needed time to get to know each other under more normal circumstances.

Yet they also knew that Sam was a healthy male who had been celibate for a decade. He could not risk a fornication charge by Ohio authorities, who would have rearrested Sheppard for sneezing in public if they could. "If Sam stopped at my apartment for a cup of coffee and stayed half an hour," Ariane pointed out, "some narrow-minded people who remember that he committed adultery ten years ago might say, 'Look, he's at it again.' "

Since the marriage seemed inevitable, even if Sam had to return to prison, everyone agreed that it should take place outside Ohio. Why risk having the groom rearrested as he and his bride were exchanging vows?

Wacky Wedding

Paul Holmes suggested that the couple marry in Chicago under the auspices, financial and otherwise, of his newspaper, the *Chicago Tribune*, which would naturally have an old-fashioned scoop. Illinois had no waiting period between the marriage application and the granting of a license, unlike many other states, including Ohio. All that was required ahead of time was a blood test for both parties. It seemed a sensible idea and was a justifiable pay-off to Holmes, who swiftly made all the arrangements for the blood tests, license, marrying judge and bridal suite.

Dr. Sam wanted his son to be best man at the wedding, but Steve protested vehemently that it would be improper, would throw the boy into the publicity spotlight. Steve himself decided not to attend the wedding, partly because his relations with Ariane and Sam were somewhat strained. When asked by the press why he was not going to the wedding, Steve explained that he was "busy in surgery." Brother Richard, likewise, decided not to attend. Bailey was chosen as best man and his wife Froma, as matron of honor.

With Ariane behind the wheel and Sam beside her in her shiny Lincoln Continental, and with Bailey, Holmes, and Froma as passengers, the "elopement" began on the afternoon of July 17, 1964, the day after Sam's release. It wasn't exactly the type of elopement either the bride or groom had dreamed about. Six cars jammed with reporters and photographers started to tail them from Columbus.

The locale of the wedding was kept secret. An eager young *Life* magazine staffer had a hot tip that the wedding would take place in Washington, D.C., and was preparing to fly there from Columbus to scoop the reportorial caravan. However, when he checked the site with me, I didn't have the heart to lie to him. "If I were you, I wouldn't fly to Washington but to Chicago, if only for refueling," I said. *Life* saved on traveling expenses.

When Ariane drove past the Ohio penitentiary, her husband-to-be protested, "Did you have to go *this* way?"

She volunteered, "Honey, I'll take another route."

But Sam quipped, "No, the prison looks fine from the outside."

Noticing a low-flying helicopter from the Ohio Highway Patrol circling above them checking their speed and direction, Bailey cautioned, "Ariane, drive ten miles under the posted speed limit until we get the hell out of Ohio into Indiana!"

The elopement continued in the shadow of fear. The

news reports persisted that Sam would be momentarily arrested and returned to prison. Ariane stared fearfully at every passing police car, worrying that her prospective husband would be hauled back to prison. Once, seeing an officer at a red light strolling toward them, Ariane, in an agitated voice, warned, "Don't get out of the car, dear. That policeman is looking at us." Taking her right hand temporarily from the wheel, she touched him tenderly and said, "Darling, don't worry, you'll never have to go back to prison. If you ever do, I'm going to ask them to give me a room with you."

Though technically free, the groom had his small duffel bag all packed in case he had to return to the penitentiary. To ease the tension the eloping party sang songs endlessly, including "The Prisoner's Song" and "I'm Only a Bird in a Gilded Cage."

They arrived in Chicago at midnight in a blinding rainstorm after a wild drive over some dark back roads in order to lose their tailing cars. The elopers managed to shake off all except one pursuing press car, which, when it arrived at the *Chicago Tribune* parking lot, was ordered off the premises by uniformed armed guards.

The eloping couple was hustled upstairs to meet the editorial brass by Holmes. But how were Sam and Ariane going to get out of the newspaper building and into their bridal suite in the Conrad Hilton hotel? They were to be married in the hotel the following afternoon by Magistrate Nicholas J. Kure. In the old Ben Hecht *Front Page* tradition, they sneaked out in the back of a dark *Tribune* delivery truck.

It again rained on Saturday, their wedding day. "But it was the brightest rainy day of my life," the ecstatic groom later told me. Before the ceremony, 49 hours after his release, Sam gave his bride a handwritten note: "Ariane, my dearest, our day is finally here. We both love you more each day. Your two Sams." The second signature was Chip's.

That evening the bridal party was the guests of *Chicago Sun-Times* columnist Irv Kupcinet at the Pump Room. After Ariane hesitantly accepted her husband's invitation to dance, he wisecracked, "I'll bet you thought I'd forgotten how—that I only danced with men!"

On Monday morning the Sam Sheppards flew to New York for a two-day honeymoon at the Hotel Pierre, where a superb series of pictures was taken of them by *Parade* photographer Ben Ross. Of course, *Parade* gave the photos to the couple. In amusing contrast, Sam and Ariane both later complained to me that the sponsors of their wedding, the *Chicago Tribune*—"the world's greatest [and one of the richest] newspaper"—refused to pick up their $150 hotel tab!

On Wednesday morning, July 22, Dr. Sam and the second Mrs. Sheppard were back in court in Akron, Ohio.

Lakefront Lovebirds

At Akron, Ohio, on Wednesday afternoon, July 22, 1964, a three-judge panel of the United States Sixth Circuit Court of Appeals heard the state of Ohio's plea to reverse Judge Weinman's ruling and put Sam Sheppard back in prison. Cuyahoga County Prosecutor John T. Corrigan (no relative of Sheppard's original lawyer) and Gertrude Bauer Mahon argued that Judge Weinman was wrong because 20 judges had previously upheld Sheppard's conviction.

Federal Judge Lester L. Cecil, of Dayton, asked Bailey, "Does your client plan to settle down now and not make a public spectacle of himself?"

Bailey's beefy cheeks reddened. "A spectacle was made of this case by others long before now," he snapped.

Judge Cecil, Judge Paul C. Weick, of Akron, and Judge Clifford O'Sullivan, of Port Huron, Michigan, debated their knotty decision privately for more than two hours while Dr. Sam, Ariane, and the lawyers sweltered in the courtroom. Finally the judges decided to pass the legal buck to its regular session, which would meet in the fall. Meanwhile, they stayed Judge Weinman's decision but ruled that Dr. Sam could remain free until then by posting a new $10,000 bond in Columbus.

The Sheppards eagerly returned to their Rocky River house and tried to live a quiet suburban life as a normal couple. Compared to their spectacular prison romance and wedding, it *was* quiet.

Still, they remained public pigeons. People stared and whispered whenever the couple appeared in public. "We practically have to disguise ourselves so that people won't recognize us," Sam complained, more in sorrow than in anger. "If only they would leave us alone."

They installed an unlisted telephone, but curiosity seekers somehow managed to secure the number.

Late one evening their home phone rang. Ariane answered and spoke to an agitated woman whom they didn't know, calling from California. "Is your husband going to kill you too?" the caller demanded. "One moment, please, I'll ask him," Ariane replied. Putting her hand over the receiver, she relayed the message to her equally amused husband who was puttering around the house in slacks, sipping a soft drink. Ariane returned to the telephone and whispered, "Yes, he's coming at me now with a 21-inch knife!" She hung up.

Their lack of privacy drew Sam and Ariane even closer together. Though they enjoyed good relations with their neighbors, they did not socialize with them or even with Sam's brothers. They shopped together and went nearly everywhere together. Sam even accompanied his wife to the beauty parlor twice a week. They grew so devoted that they rarely left each other alone except when Sam did his daily reading of the latest medical textbooks in neurosurgery and she wrote or taped letters to her daughter Iris. They shared everything except the housework. They could afford but would not trust any maid or cleaning help. When I asked Sam who did the housecleaning, he said, "Me! Who else?"

Their love seemingly now had more solidity than when they had first met in the Marion prison. "Ariane and I are more in love than ever," Sam mused. "She has suffered as much as I have during the past few years. And she's a wonderful, rare person who has made me feel alive again. Every time I look at her, hear her voice, feel her touch, it makes me forget my bad years."

Ariane became less ostentatious. While she was the same friendly, impulsive Continental charmer who laughed easily, even at herself, she had become more relaxed. Instead of being considered a publicity hound, she was now respected as a woman who knew what she wanted and got it.

When Ariane became pregnant, she and Sam were ecstatic. However, she had a three-month miscarriage on

Christmas morning, 1964, Sam's first Christmas outside prison bars in ten years. The loss depressed both of them. Sam blamed the miscarriage upon the legal cloud that hovered over them and her constant worry over his possible rearrest.

"Ariane in some ways means the return of Marilyn," Sam told me shortly afterward. "She gives me a new appreciation of Marilyn and family life. A man without a loving wife is only half alive." He proudly showed me photographs of Marilyn and Ariane when both were ten years old. "Isn't the resemblance amazing?" he asked. "They could almost be taken for sisters. Marilyn's aunt thinks so too."

I never heard Ariane utter a harsh word about Marilyn. She and Sam talked naturally about his first wife. When I visited them in May, 1965, Ariane sat in the living room flipping through some folders and then remarked casually, "Sam, you never told me about this love letter you once wrote to Marilyn."

No less casually, Sam replied, "It never occurred to me."

Because they wanted more privacy, they decided to purchase a secluded lakefront $40,000 house in Bay Village, about a mile from the house where Marilyn had been murdered. The down payment, they agreed, was to be made with Ariane's funds and with a book publisher's advance for Sam's autobiography and a motion picture option on his life story.

The Sheppards rarely went to the movies or watched television. When asked why, Sam explained, "Well, for one thing those television programs and movies about doctors are junk."

"Including the one called 'The Fugitive,' which is supposed to be based on your case?"

"Yes, including that one. It doesn't catch me at all. It would be ridiculous of me to say that I am a better man for what happened. Yet I think my experience has left me not only older but wiser. I have learned many things—patience, forbearance, discipline, the importance of family and friends, the joy of freedom, the value of laughter, the need for hope.

"I also learned that injustice can strike anyone, anywhere, and that it is vicious in its relentlessness. My family reared me in an atmosphere of love and loyalty. At the time of the trial, I was totally unprepared for the accusations that confronted me."

On May 5, 1965, as they were looking forward to moving into their idyllic lakefront retreat, they received a devastating blow.

The United States Sixth Circuit Court of Appeals, acting upon the October 8, 1964, hearing in Cincinnati, in a two-to-one decision, overruled Judge Weinman and ordered Sam Sheppard to return to the penitentiary within 20 days to continue his life sentence. The majority decision was written by Judge O'Sullivan, who had sat at the Akron hearing ten months earlier, and was concurred in by Judge Harry Phillips, of Nashville, Tennessee. A vigorous dissent was written by Judge George Edwards, Jr., of Detroit. Bailey advised Dr. Sam to go into hiding lest bloodthirsty Cuyahoga County officials try to rearrest him.

Employing every legal maneuver, Lee Bailey received permission for his client to remain out of prison on bail, despite Cuyahoga County protests, while he appealed the case to the United States Supreme Court. But Sheppard's ordinarily confident attorney was deeply worried. Were the issues important enough for the high court to review the lower courts? Bailey prepared a monumental appeal—probably the epic brief of his career.

Six months later, on November 15, 1965, the Supreme Court announced that yes, it would finally hear the Sheppard case—more than a decade after the complex case began. It granted *certiorari*.

Nine years and one day after denying *certiorari* the nation's highest court reversed itself—and caught up with the Dutch Uncle counsel of its late Justice Felix Frankfurter.

9

THE SUPREME COURT

A FUNNY THING HAPPENED on the way to the Supreme Court.

It was a casual but amazing remark by columnist Dorothy Kilgallen, reported by thousands of newspapers, magazines, and radio and television stations around the world.

Time magazine termed the Kilgallen remark, "The most damaging charge against Judge Blythin." The *Saturday Evening Post* assessed it for Sheppard in these words: "Like manna from heaven it fell."

In his autobiography Bailey described the remark as "lucky" for the Sheppard defense and admitted that it was a "central issue" before the Supreme Court. Dr. Sam himself, in his so-called autobiography, devoted more than two pages to discussing the remark, with generous credit to my intermediary role. He later told me, "Jack, if Dorothy Kilgallen hadn't said that, my case before the Supreme Court would have been much tougher." The *Saturday Review* editors, on January 7, 1967, stated: "Mr. Pollack was instrumental in getting evidence before the United States Supreme Court showing the unfairness of Dr. Sam's trial."

Bailey rushed the remark at the eleventh hour to fair-minded Judge Weinman, who was deeply shocked by it. In his Akron appeal, the Sheppard attorney cited the comment as "new evidence." When the remark finally reached the Supreme Court, it became a bone of contention between opposing lawyers and astounded justices. Nearly half of the entire hearing time on the Sheppard case was devoted to it. Clearly, it influenced the court's ruling.

Kilgallen Assist

This is the brief background of the remark, originally published in the *Overseas Press Club Bulletin* as the lead cover article in its April 16, 1966, issue, nearly two months after the Supreme Court hearing on the Sheppard case but a month and a half before its decision:

> On March 17, 1964, an OPC Book Night arranged by Anita Diamant Berke was held on *The Minister and the Choir Singer*, a study of the Hall-Mills murder case. The panel included the book's author, lawyer William M. Kunstler, columnist Dorothy Kilgallen, NBC newsman Gabriel Pressman, and Irene Corbally Kuhn (who covered the Hall-Mills case). During the discussion, Miss Kilgallen casually mentioned that when she was covering the Sheppard case in Cleveland back in 1954, shortly *before* the trial, the late Judge Edward A. Blythin called her into his private chambers. As he was donning his black robe preparing to ascend the bench, the Judge said, "Miss Kilgallen, it's nice to see you. But why should a company like Hearst send a journalist of your stature to a small town like ours to cover what appears to be an open and shut case. Sheppard's guilty as hell! There's no doubt about it!"
>
> Immediately an articulate writer in the audience, M. D. Morris, scolded Miss Kilgallen for being derelict in her duty for now belatedly disclosing Judge Blythin's ten-year-old bias. "If you had reported Judge Blythin's prejudice at the time instead of keeping silent," Morris insisted, "it might have changed the venue and entire complexion of the case."
>
> Obviously hurt by this criticism, Dorothy Kilgallen quietly replied, "Things said to a journalist in confidence should be kept in confidence."

As an old Washington peacemaker, I tried to ease the tension by rising and saying, "I happen to have as my guest tonight the brilliant young attorney on the Sheppard case—Mr. F. Lee Bailey of Boston. Perhaps the chair can prevail upon Lee to say a few words."

Lee did—with his customary eloquence. And I felt sorry for Bill Kunstler that the rest of the evening was devoted to the Sheppard—not the Hall-Mills—murder case.

After the meeting, in my battered old station wagon, I drove Bailey back to his hotel and Kunstler and his wife Lotti and Morris home. All that we talked about was Dorothy Kilgallen's amazing statement. Lee Bailey, who, then a venerable 31, had the earmarks of a Clarence Darrow, cryptically chirped, "I may be able to use Dorothy's remark."

The next afternoon in Boston, Bailey telephoned the Ohio attorney general's office and requested that Dorothy Kilgallen's statement about Judge Blythin be made part of the permanent record. Sheppard was still in the Ohio penitentiary, and his case would soon be ruled on by U.S. District Judge Carl A. Weinman.

A month later, Bailey and Assistant Ohio Attorney General David Kessler flew to New York (Bailey in his private plane) to convene with Dorothy Kilgallen in her East Side apartment. There, in a deposition, Dorothy repeated what Judge Blythin had said to her in her pretrial interview.

In her apartment, Dorothy Kilgallen repeated her astounding recollection of Judge Blythin's bias to both of them on May 9, 1964. Bailey immediately requested that this Kilgallen statement be made part of the permanent record in his habeas corpus petition before Judge Weinman, and it was so agreed by stipulation rather than formal deposition.

The Kilgallen statement to Bailey and Kessler read in part:

He was very affable. He shook hands with me and said, "I am very glad to see you, Miss Kilgallen. I watch you on television very frequently and enjoy the program." And he said, "But what brings you to Cleveland?"

And I said, "Well, Your Honor, this trial."

And he said, "But why come all the way from New York to Cleveland to cover this trial?"

And I said, "Well, it has all the ingredients of what in newspaper business we call a good murder. It has a very attractive victim, who was pregnant, and the accused is a very important member of the community, respectable, very attractive. Then added to that, you have the fact that it is a mystery as to who did it."

And Judge Blythin said, "Mystery? It's an open and shut case."

And I said, "What do you mean, Judge Blythin?" I was a little taken aback because I have talked to many judges in their chambers, but usually they don't give me an opinion on a case before it's over.

And so he said, "Well, he is guilty as hell. There's no question about it."

. . . . And the judge seemed genuinely surprised that there was so much interest in this particular case, which to him seemed to be a mere formality.

It developed that Dorothy Kilgallen was not the only person to whom Judge Blythin had verbalized his belief in Sheppard's guilt before the trial started. Edward T. Murray, a clerk in the Cuyahoga County Common Pleas Court, now also revealed that in July, 1954, before the trial began, Judge Blythin had casually remarked to him, while picking up his mail in the presence of three or four other persons: "Sam Sheppard is as guilty as I (the judge) am innocent."

Ironically, Dorothy Kilgallen, who turned out to be the Mystery Guest in the Sheppard "What's My Line" show, never lived to see the effect of her belated assistance to Dr. Sam. Unfortunately she missed what would undoubtedly have been one of the great thrills of her life. On December 8, 1965, she died.

The Supreme Court Hears

Sam Sheppard climbed the steps of a massive white marble building in Washington, D.C., on the morning of February

28, 1966, at 9:45 A.M. He walked up with his wife, son, lawyer, and lawyer's wife. Atop the building he saw four engraved words: "Equal Justice Under Law."

This was the end of the legal appeal road for him. There were 89 United States District Courts similar to Judge Weinman's and 11 United States Circuit Courts of Appeals like those that had heard his case in Akron and Cincinnati. But this was the nation's highest tribunal. Each year the Supreme Court rules on more than 2,000 cases, many of them momentous, and it is considered the bulwark of the American way of life, more powerful than any judicial body on earth.

It was the first time that citizen Samuel Holmes Sheppard had entered this breathtaking building. He gulped as he passed the 16 stately columns at the Parthenon-like entrance leading to the courtroom, with its 24 gleaming columns of Sienna marble.

Nervously, he took a seat in the first public row. He had been warned that it was difficult to hear in the courtroom, and he did not want to miss a single word. The hearing had been delayed four days, which was fortunate because he was down with the flu the day it had been originally scheduled.

As he waited for court to open on this day—over 19 months after his release from prison—his thoughts drifted back to the suspenseful life he had been living for nearly 12 years. It was as if he had been on the edge of a precipice; such a precarious balance had become his way of life. Could he ever look forward to the blessed day when the legal and prison shadows would disappear; could he live a "normal" life again?

Ariane sat on Sam's right. She was a far cry from the shrill woman who, when she had first arrived in this country, had screamed about "American injustice." This was the day that she had dreamed about when she first set foot in the United States.

On Sam's left quietly sat his namesake—his 18-year-old son Sam. The boy had flown home from India a few days earlier, cutting short his around-the-world cruise to attend his father's historic hearing.

As one of the 18 privileged reporters in the small press box a dozen feet away from them, I saw them flash a confident smile toward me. They did not wave. Inwardly I saluted them for their restraint and quiet courage.

Promptly at 10:00 A.M. the nine justices marched dramatically from behind the draperies into the hushed courtroom and took their seats.

"Oyez! Oyez! Oyez!" the court crier intoned. "The Honorable, the Chief Justice and Associate Justices of the Supreme Court of the United States. . . . All persons having business before the Honorable, the Supreme Court of the United States, are admonished to draw near and give their attention, for the Court is now sitting. God save the United States and this Honorable Court."

The central figure of the hearing intently studied the faces of the nine justices. He stared longest at Chief Justice Earl Warren, former Governor of California, who had been appointed to his lifetime post by President Dwight Eisenhower in 1953, a year before Marilyn Sheppard had been murdered. Sam appraised the eight associate justices, who flanked the Chief Justice in order of their seniority: Hugo L. Black, William O. Douglas, Tom C. Clark, John Marshall Harlan, William J. Brennan, Jr., Potter Stewart, Abe Fortas and Byron R. White.

Lee Bailey, arguing his first case before the Supreme Court, opened the argument as the appellant (or petitioner) and had the right to close it in his brief allotted hour. Since the justices have already read the briefs, this is generally enough time. Bailey allotted some of his valuable hour to Bernard Berkman, lawyer-chairman of the Greater Cleveland Civil Liberties Union, who, as an *amicus curiae* (friend of the court), cited the prejudicial newspaper publicity during the trial.

Bailey spoke swiftly and succinctly, firing his appeal points almost as if he were target-bombing. Anchoring his thumbs in the pockets of his vest, he quickly read excerpts from *Cleveland Press* editor Seltzer's autobiography, and mentioned the inflammatory Walter Winchell and Robert Considine broadcasts. Displaying an unusual interest in the case, seven of the nine justices peppered Bailey with lively questions.

Bailey was asked what new evidence he had which had not been available when the court declined to grant *certiorari* and hear the case back in 1956. He mentioned the

Dorothy Kilgallen deposition about Judge Blythin's prejudice. This statement, by a deceased columnist about a deceased judge, became, surprisingly, the highlight of the hearing. "One of the difficulties of this case," Bailey pointed out, "is that most of the persons originally involved in it are deceased."

Several hours earlier I had chatted outside with Mrs. Gertrude Bauer Mahon, the Assistant Prosecutor of Cuyahoga County, who exclaimed to me, "Nearly everybody from the original trial except me is dead. All these new people in the case don't know what it's all about! Only I do—and I know that Sam Sheppard is guilty!"

Ohio Attorney General William B. Saxbe considered the case important enough to argue it personally. In his rebuttal to Bailey he attempted to dismiss the Kilgallen statement on a technicality, saying that it had "come out accidentally at a cocktail party ten years ago."

Saxbe also argued that the Kilgallen statement had not been taken under oath. Later, in his closing remarks, Bailey seized upon this charge with the fury of an aroused tiger. He admitted that the Kilgallen statement had indeed not been sworn to but that it was solely because the notary public who had been summoned did not appear on schedule at the Kilgallen apartment. Assistant Ohio Attorney General David Kessler and Bailey had then agreed to waive the oath and take the Kilgallen statement regardless. Saxbe whispered to Kessler and then admitted to the court, "I'm afraid that's true."

In his drawling voice, which masked a diligent zeal, Saxbe, now U.S. Ambassador to India, then made a far more serious undiplomatic mistake. During his formal remarks he compared the Sheppard case to the notorious Sacco-Vanzetti case. The execution of Sacco and Vanzetti, in August, 1927, resulted in worldwide sympathy for them and set off thousands of demonstrations in many countries on their behalf.

"Sacco and Vanzetti were guilty, and so is Sheppard, regardless of everything the 'bleeding hearts' like Felix Frankfurter said," thundered Ohio Attorney General Saxbe.

The faces of the shocked justices bristled with anger. In calling the late Felix Frankfurter a "bleeding heart," Saxbe was slurring a member of their select group for 23 years, from 1939 to 1962. He had died only 9 months earlier, in April, 1965.

Justice Hugo Black, a judicial intimate of Frankfurter during those years, caustically told Saxbe, "I hope you don't want us to reexamine the evidence in Sacco and Vanzetti. The Sheppard case is difficult enough!"

Saxbe offered another argument: there was no evidence to prove that the jury had been prejudiced by the adverse publicity. "I believe the judge in the case ran a good trial and got a good jury," he said. "And we don't have to throw out the first amendment (freedom of the press) to preserve the sixth amendment (right to a fair trial)."

Sam Sheppard sat through the proceedings impassively with considerable self-control, his chin high and arms folded. His face reddened only once, and he tugged at his tie when Saxbe called him a "liar." His wife comforted him sympathetically.

The other spokesman against Sheppard was John T. Corrigan, the Cuyahoga County prosecutor, who echoed Saxbe when he said, "We have on trial the jury system of the United States."

The court's red light flashed, indicating that the hour for the prosecution was up. The entire hearing consumed only 2 hours and 20 minutes, with an hour recess for lunch.

After the hearing ended, a crowd gathered around Sam Sheppard on the court building steps. He said stoically, "All I want to do is to get the hell out of here and drive home."

Bailey rushed up and briskly said to me, "Get two cabs and we'll make a run for it to the Sheraton-Park for a breather." He had reserved a suite in that hotel.

In the pouring rain I managed to commandeer two cabs, and we dashed past the angry reporters and photographers. Sam, Ariane, young Sam, Bailey, and his wife Froma climbed into the first cab, and I followed in the other with Dennis Brock, a *Stern* magazine photographer.

At the hotel we sauntered down to the cocktail lounge where we relaxed in a secluded corner. But it was difficult to feel at ease. Dr. Sam voiced the concern of all of us when he said: "I wonder what the Supreme Court is going to do."

The Supreme Court Speaks

Back in Ohio, the state of Sam's birth and of his sorrow, Sam Sheppard awaited the Supreme Court decision. Whenever the telephone rang, his heart raced with anxiety. Would it be a message saying that he had to return to prison?

I assured Sam that he must have faith in the Warren Court. This hunch was based upon my studies of Earl Warren, of whom I had planned to write a biography.

Sleeping was not easy. Very often he would awake streaming with perspiration while Ariane slumbered, not certain whether he was in his bedroom with his wife or back in his prison cell. He would drift into the kitchen, open the refrigerator door, looking for a soft drink, angrily close the white contraption and meander into the living room to snap open the liquor cabinet and swiftly down a shot of straight Scotch instead. Sunday nights were the worst because Monday is the day on which decisions are handed down by the Supreme Court, though the date of a ruling is never divulged in advance.

On Monday decisions are the first order of business of the Supreme Court after new admissions to the bar are made. These decisions have been printed by a small staff from the Government Printing Office in the basement of the Supreme Court building since 1946. The rulings are highly guarded because any advance "leak" of a forthcoming Supreme Court opinion—which might, for example, affect the entire economy—could enable a speculator or some other character to profit mightily.

March passed. Then April and May. The court generally recessed for the summer in early June.

Dr. Sam wondered and worried.

At 11:40 A.M. on Monday morning, June 6, 1966, the telephone rang in the Sheppard apartment. Sam and Ariane had decided to delay purchasing their proposed lakefront home until the Supreme Court had ruled.

A reporter from New York was on the telephone. He told Ariane, "I haven't got all the dope yet, but it just came over the ticker that Sam was freed by the Supreme Court. Have you anything to say about this?"

"No, not now, but thank you very much for calling and telling us," replied Mrs. Sheppard ecstatically.

Meanwhile, Sam, Jr., had answered the front doorbell. A horde of Cleveland reporters was outside pressing for a statement.

The object of all this attention was upstairs snoozing because he had scarcely slept a wink the night before. Swiftly awakened, he learned the facts over the radio.

In a landmark eight-to-one decision favoring him, the United States Supreme Court had ruled that convicted Samuel H. Sheppard had received an unfair trial in 1954. It decreed that he was entitled to a new trial "within a reasonable time" or to be set free by the state of Ohio. The Supreme Court had upheld Judge Weinman's District Court ruling and had reversed the Sixth Circuit Court of Appeals.

The lucid, 29-page, 9,000-word decision was written by Justice Thomas Campbell Clark, a 66-year-old Texan who had been Attorney General of the United States for four years before being appointed to the Supreme Court in 1949 by President Harry S Truman. Clark was a modest man, fond of saying, "I didn't do anything; it was somebody else who got that done."

Justice Clark did not rule on Sheppard's innocence or guilt, and he did not attempt to muzzle the press. However, he strongly criticized the "carnival atmosphere" and "editorial artillery" of Sheppard's trial, writing that Dr. Sam was deprived of the "judicial serenity and calm to which he was entitled. . . ." He charged further that the "massive, pervasive, and prejudicial publicity that attended his prosecution" proved that Sheppard did not receive a fair trial consistent with the due process clause of the fourteenth amendment. . . ."

In speaking for the nation's top tribunal, Justice Clark implied that Judge Blythin, when conducting the 1954 trial, did not know how to run a court. "The erection of a press table for reporters inside the bar is unprecedented," scolded Justice Clark. Judge Blythin should have limited the number of newsmen, shielded witnesses from interviews, and instructed prosecutors and police not to talk outside the courtroom.

Justice Clark added: "... bedlam reigned at the courthouse during the trial, and newsmen practically took over the entire courtroom, hounding most of the participants in the trial, especially Sheppard. ... Trial courts must take strong measures to ensure that the balance is never weighed against the accused." Judge Blythin did not "fulfill his duty" to protect the jury from this press onslaught.

The Clark decision concluded with these words: "The case is remanded to the District Court with instructions to issue the writ [of habeas corpus] and order that Sheppard be released from custody unless the State puts him to its charges again within a reasonable time. It is so ordered."

The sole "no" vote on the Supreme Court was that of Justice Hugo Black, to whom freedom of speech was virtually a religion. Black refrained from writing a dissenting opinion, however. "I wasn't surprised by—and even expected—Justice Black's dissent," admitted Bailey.

A half hour after her husband's Supreme Court victory, Ariane Sheppard amazed the reporters and photographers swarming outside their home. Gone was the woman's familiar platinum-blonde upsweep hairdo. What the press now saw was her sudden new look: a dark auburn downsweep hairdo with bangs.

"Did you dye your hair?" she was asked.

"Oh no," Ariane explained. "I'm just wearing a wig now because everything looks so different to me."

In other quarters the effect of the decision was more solemn. The ruling was felt immediately by nearly every criminal court, district attorney, and prosecutor in the nation. It gave many court officials the power to do what they have always wanted to do with the press except when they were running for reelection. Some crime reporters wondered whether free-booting "circus trials" were doomed to go the way of vaudeville and tent circuses.

The decision inspired many sober thoughts and introspective doubts by responsible newspapers. The *New York Times* editorialized: "The Sheppard case has long been one of the scandals of American jurisprudence and journalism ... The Supreme Court has rectified that injustice by ordering the trial verdict set aside." The *Washington Post* termed Dr. Sam's 1954 trial "a reproach to American justice. . . . The conviction, therefore, had to be set aside." The *Louisville Courier-Journal* admitted, "To put it mildly, the U.S. press did not distinguish itself by fairness or moderation during the months preceding and during the trial."

The chastened *Cleveland Press,* throwing an olive branch, was more guarded, probably out of concern for Bailey's threatened lawsuit against the Scripps-Howard newspaper chain. It editorialized about "the fantastic public interest this case generated, not only here but throughout the world. The *Press*'s news coverage reflected this interest. . . . And its editorials were critical of police work which seemed, for a time, to be confused and inert. If there were excesses, as the court contends, they should be viewed against the circumstances of the case, which, as the *Press* once said editorially, became 'too much a part of all our lives.' "

Yet in a page-one news story the day after the ruling the *Press* gleefully cited a minor error in Justice Clark's opinion about the sequestering of juries in Ohio.*

Editor Louis Seltzer, recently retired, refused "under any circumstances to make any comment on any aspect of the Sheppard case—period. I'm going to be a stuck record and say nothing. I'm now the Sphinx."

The *Cleveland Plain Dealer* was more defiant, editorializing, ". . . the U.S. Supreme Court has narrowed the field open to the press. These justices accepted some unfortunately weak evidence and agreed with the defense's version . . . but the public has an important stake here too. No rule should allow judges to control or gag the only voice of criticism the public can count on to lay open perversions of justice."

A similar protest was voiced by Robert C. Notson, President of the American Society of Newspaper Editors. Notson warned that the decision might lead courts to "hide from public knowledge virtually all of the facts of law enforcement and the administration of justice. American

* This error was corrected in the published version of the decision distributed to law libraries and the legal profession.

newspapers have become increasingly circumspect in the handling of news of criminal matters. . . ."

On the Monday night of the Supreme Court decision Bailey flew to Cleveland for a strategy session with the Sheppard family about a possible retrial and suit against those responsible for Dr. Sam's ten-year imprisonment.

Though overjoyed by the decision, the first man in American history to have his murder conviction overthrown by the Supreme Court on the grounds that "prejudicial publicity" had deprived him of a fair trial still faced the question: would he have to go through a retrial? And though the United States Supreme Court had spoken, the next decision was not an easy one for the state of Ohio.

10

THE VINDICATION

JOHN T. CORRIGAN, prosecutor of Cuyahoga County, Ohio, faced the dilemma of whether or not Sam Sheppard should be retried. He probably did not relish a retrial any more than Dr. Sam or even Bailey did because of its myriad problems.

John Corrigan was no relative of Sheppard's defense attorney William J. Corrigan, although many headline-gleaning Ohioans still thought so, including some Clevelanders who had voted for him. Corrigan had been elected county prosecutor after being trounced when running for mayor of Cleveland in 1962 against incumbent Mayor Ralph S. Locher. The son of a retired policeman, John Corrigan was reared to respect law and order. During the Battle of the Bulge in Germany an enemy mortar shell deprived him of the sight of his right eye, and he suffered other facial injuries. He won three battle stars. Upon returning to civilian life to complete his college education and secure his law degree, the enterprising young man toiled as a laborer, plasterer, mailman, football coach, and door-to-door salesman. Now, as county prosecutor, his task was to defend the commonwealth. "We call him the Vindicator," said one lawyer, "because Corrigan really believes that he was elected to vindicate the rights of society."

Corrigan's Crusade

To Corrigan the Supreme Court decision was "absolutely unexpected." He realized the problems of a retrial. Some figures who played prominent parts in the first trial were dead. Witnesses had scattered, and he wondered just how much they could remember after 12 years. In any case, Sheppard's defense was now far stronger, thanks to the Supreme Court decision. Moreover, Dr. Paul Leland Kirk, whose posttrial findings were not available during the first trial, probably would agree to testify for the defense. Finally, Sheppard could be retried only on a second-degree murder charge because the jury had acquitted him of first-degree murder; the United States Supreme Court had ruled in 1957 against double jeopardy in murder cases.

Dr. Sam was not overenthusiastic about a retrial either, as my talk with him shortly after the Supreme Court decision convinced me. Still, in response to press queries, he crowed, "I'm all for a new trial because I am anxious to attain complete vindication. I know I can prove my innocence." Actually he was deeply worried about any jury. After all, a jury had convicted him in 1954. He was reluctant, too, to put himself and his family through the ordeal of a trial again. He and Ariane were working at making a go of their marriage; young Sam was entering Boston University in the fall; Steve and Richard were busier than ever at the hospital.

Even Bailey had mixed feelings about retrial. It would certainly involve a considerable personal and pecuniary burden on him. Still, the attorney's chemistry demanded constant challenge. Wasn't that why he had tried to run up a down escalator when he was a boy? With so many odds against the state of Ohio, Bailey believed it would not risk a retrial.

On June 10, 1966—four days after the Supreme Court decision—Corrigan put to rest all the speculation. In a televised press conference with 40 newsmen, who packed his steaming office, the Cuyahoga County prosecutor announced:

> In arriving at this decision, I am mindful that this is a government of law, not a government of men. In

keeping with this principle, I have made a determination that society was the victim of a most heinous crime, and society demands redress. However, society also affords to an individual a fair, impartial, and objective trial before a jury of his peers, and so we will present the case to them for their consideration.

Answering a barrage of questions, Prosecutor Corrigan added that Sheppard could remain free on his $10,000 bond until he appeared before the presiding judge in the Cuyahoga County Criminal Courts building; that he, Corrigan, would personally handle the prosecution in the trial, which would begin in "early fall"; that there would be no comment from himself or any member of his staff; that courtroom seats "would be available to the press and public on a first-come, first-served basis."

Dr. Sam, Ariane, and young Sam watched the Corrigan press conference on their living room television set. After switching the set off, Sam strolled into the kitchen to get a soft drink.

The bell rang at the front door. An impatient group of newsmen stood outside, awaiting an impromptu press conference. The man who would soon stand retrial sauntered out to the front steps, sipping his soft drink. Ariane presently joined him, sporting her familiar platinum blonde hair wrapped in a turban. Young Sam remained inside the house.

"This is wonderful," exclaimed Dr. Sam. "I'm ready to go to trial—tonight if necessary. This is the day I've been waiting for."

"Will your testimony be needed?"

"Maybe the case will be thrown out of court for lack of evidence before the defense side is even presented," he snapped.

"Will you take the stand?"

"You're damn right, I will!"

Associated Press photographer Julian C. Wilson pleaded, "Sam, how about a smile?"

Turning to Ariane he said, "The only time I can smile is when I look at you."

A reporter asked, "What do you and Mrs. Sheppard plan to do in the immediate future?"

Dr. Sam smiled even more enthusiastically. As he closed the door on the press, he quipped, "We plan to go in and have some lunch!"

Lee Bailey opined to newsmen in his Boston office: "It is doubtful that a fair trial can be held in Cleveland. We will have to do some careful looking. Neither Corrigan nor I want the trial prejudged." Bailey added that during the trial he would "hold back no punches," including the possible disclosure of Marilyn's real murderer. Cryptically, he said that the killer still lived in the Cleveland area.

Return Match in Cleveland

Rare is the adult Ohioan who did not then—or does not even now—have a fixed opinion about the guilt or innocence of Dr. Samuel H. Sheppard.

Now the state of Ohio was scheduled to clarify this uncertainty in the very same courtroom, barring a decision for change of venue, in which the original trial had been held 12 years earlier.

On September 8, 1966, defendant Sheppard appeared before Judge Roy F. McMahon, presiding jurist in the criminal division of the Cuyahoga County Common Pleas Court. Had he so wished, Judge McMahon could have named himself to hear the case. However, he agreed with the request of both the prosecution and defense to have a trial judge who was not seeking election in November and who had no connection with the 1954 trial. Three weeks later, at the end of September, John McMahon announced that the case would be assigned to Judge Francis J. Talty.

Judge Talty was an ex-trial lawyer, who, following 18 years of law practice, had been on the bench for 3 years. He was fast earning a reputation as a tough but fair judge.

Judge Talty's first written order curtailed the press coverage drastically, even more narrowly than the Supreme Court had indicated. All photographers were ordered to stay outside the Cuyahoga County Courthouse. The reporters who were privileged to cover the trial officially were barred from securing information other than what they could gather in the small courtroom. Interviews of the principals were banned, and the press was forbidden to go behind the bar railings. No telephones or teletype machines were permitted to be installed, no recording machines were allowed in the courtroom, and no sketches of the trial were to be made in the courthouse during the proceedings, recesses, or adjournments.

The press was assigned 14 seats. Twelve were given by Judge Talty to representatives of the Cleveland newspapers and radio and television stations. Only two seats were reserved for out-of-town news representatives: the Associated Press Arthur Everett and United Press International H. D. Quigg. Both reporters had covered the 1954 trial for their wire services. Among those refused press seats and who had, of course, requested them, were representatives of the *New York Times*, the *New York Daily News*, the *Chicago Tribune*, *Life*, *Time*, and *Newsweek*—among the most widely distributed and most influential publications in America. A *New York Times* reporter stood in line at daybreak to secure one of the 26 coveted public seats. He slipped a man up front a $20 bill to secure a more advanced position in the line, but he was bounced at the door. He protested to Judge Talty, who was unsympathetic to his plea. One of the most harsh press bans was against the *Chicago Tribune*'s veteran Paul Holmes, who, if only because of his long and conscientious concern with the case and his 1961 book about it, merited admittance to the press box. Bailey tried to rectify this by inviting Holmes, a member in good standing of the Wisconsin Bar Association, to join him as co-counsel at the trial table. Judge Talty swiftly denied this privilege in chambers. Holmes, however, did manage to attend the trial without accreditation, as did other ingenious reporters.

Two weeks before her husband's second murder retrial began, on October 24, 1966, Ariane Sheppard flew back to Germany, presumably to visit her sick stepfather. The rumors flew. Had she left Sheppard? Had he dumped her? Was their marriage breaking up? Would she really *not* talk to the press about her husband, herself, or the retrial, as Bailey had ordered? Would she return for the retrial?

I had a drink with Ariane at the Plaza Hotel in New York City the night before she left and learned the answers to some of these questions. Yes, she planned to come back for the retrial, as she later did, during the time when the jury was being selected, three weeks later. Among other reasons, she was going to Germany to bring back the $25,-000 that was needed for legal fees. She tearfully mumbled something about having just signed, or was considering signing, a separation agreement with her husband but that she still loved him deeply. The woman whose romantic love drama had astonished the world added, "I hardly know my own child anymore. I sometimes wonder if I made the right decision."

She was leaving, I gathered, at least partly because she had quarreled with Bailey, who had ordered her not to talk to the press.

This strictness didn't appeal to Mrs. Sheppard. "Nobody can stop me from talking to the press if I want to," she said. "Not even the great Lee Bailey. Sure, I admire Lee because of his brilliant mind, but he uses Sam and me. Every time he comes to Cleveland, he has the press meet him at the airport before he ever sees us. But what I can't forgive Lee for is the way he makes fun of us behind our backs, and he even makes jokes about how Sam walks."

Bailey's first move in court was to request a change of venue. Motion denied, snapped Judge Talty. How dare anyone think that he could not conduct a fair trial in Cleveland?

Picking a jury of seven men and five women—the same ratio as in the first trial—consumed more than a week. Bailey strove to get young, intelligent persons on the jury, especially new Cleveland residents who had no preconceived opinions on the case. Corrigan wanted older, more mature Clevelanders on the jury. Bailey was assisted in the jury selection by Dr. William J. Bryan, Jr., of Los Angeles, a physician-attorney whose seminar on hypnosis, memory recall, and the "art of persuasion" the Boston lawyer had attended in 1961, before accepting the Sheppard case. Bailey rejected a potential male juror who admitted being a regular reader of the *Cleveland Press*. On the other hand, Corrigan rejected a woman prospect who said that she had once played bridge with Steve Sheppard's wife Betty.

Bailey was happy that the foreman of the jury turned out to be Ralph Vichell, an engineer of 33—Bailey's age. The other male jurors were Russell D. Jefferson, a mailman; Carl D. Lindbloom, an Internal Revenue agent; William Nicholson, an advertising man; Michael A. Spinelli, a repair shop manager; Charles W. Stephens, another mailman; and Arthur Wykoff, a Federal Reserve Bank supervisor.

The women jurors were Yolanda Cowan, manager of the hosiery department in a retail store; Frances J. Grodjinski, a great-grandmother; Norma Koch and Sara K. March, housewives; and Betty Peters, a bookkeeper. The alternate jurors were two women: Cecile Horneski and Marion Pipoly.

After the jurors were chosen, Judge Talty decided to sequester them in hotel rooms except when in the courtroom or jury room, for the *entire* trial. Although Ohio law requires that jurors be sequestered in capital trials after they begin deliberations, it is subject to the discretion of a trial judge whether to do so during a trial. The jurors in Sheppard's first trial were sequestered only for their 5 days of deliberations, after a 65-day trial. Mindful of the Supreme Court's decision, Judge Talty earlier had cautioned the 46 veniremen who took the witness stand before the jury was chosen not to read or listen to any reports about the case. "If you are listening to the radio or watching television," he admonished, "you will do one of two things if you hear anything about the case: walk away or turn off your set." Judge Talty instructed the jurors that they could make telephone calls to their families in their hotel rooms *before* deliberations began. However, all of these calls would be monitored by court officers. Jurors, the judge said, absolutely must not discuss any aspect of the case.

The jury was escorted to the nearby Statler Hilton Hotel, where Bailey and his aides happened to be staying. Immediately upon hearing of this, the Bailey party checked out and settled in the Hollenden House.

As in the first trial, at the very start the jury was brought to the Lake Road murder house. This was the first time that Bailey had visited the house with Sam, and he peppered him with questions about the controversial areas. To the man who had harbored so many happy memories—and one tragic remembrance—of this house, it was a painfully poignant experience.

Apart from the visit to the scene of the crime, the two

trials were diametrically different. The 1954 trial was a cacophonous circus. The less flamboyant second trial was a streamlined model of decorum, with strict rules for press and public conduct imposed. The first trial had dragged on for 9 weary weeks. The second took only 18 courtroom days. The first trial heard 70 witnesses; the second, a mere 33. Susan Hayes, the star prosecution witness at the first trial, was conspicuously absent at the second, not being called as a witness. The adultery question was barely introduced as a murder motive by the state.

Even the state's 1954 trial witnesses testified with considerable restraint and brevity. Witness after witness tried—but failed—to offer precisely the same testimony as in 1954.

J. Spencer Houk, the former Bay Village mayor-butcher, divorced from his wife Esther, remarried and an automobile salesman, was again a prosecution witness. When cross-examining Houk, Bailey briskly asked: Why had he not immediately telephoned the police after Sheppard had called him and exclaimed, "Spen, get over here quick! I think they've killed Marilyn!" Why did Houk not bring a gun with him since "they" might still be in the house and armed? Why did he risk bringing his wife along? Had he ever been in Marilyn's bedroom before seeing her corpse? Did he have a key to the Sheppard house?

Houk denied that Marilyn gave him a house key; he also said that he had not been with her when a delivery man came to the Sheppard home.

Esther Houk was asked by Bailey: how did she know that Marilyn lay upstairs slain on her bed? Sam did not mention this when she and her husband arrived. Why did she start a fire in her fireplace the night of the murder?

The Houks' answers, according to many court observers, were vague or noncommittal and generally indicated that they had never thought about it at the time.

When Coroner Samuel Gerber took the stand, it was a confrontation for which Bailey had waited five long years. The Boston attorney saved his lengthiest and most penetrating cross-examination for the coroner. Gerber testified that the bloodstains on Marilyn's pillow had resulted from some "object." In his direct examination Corrigan carefully sidestepped calling it a "surgical instrument" and had probably cautioned Gerber, Bailey suspected, not to use this term. But Bailey, taking a calculated risk, tried to draw out the articulate coroner and get these two words onto the record. Finally, under persistent questioning, Gerber exclaimed, "Well, it looked like a surgical instrument to me."

Bailey heaved a sigh of relief and confidently proceeded at his brilliant best to coast downhill to his goal.

"Well, now, Dr. Gerber," said Bailey, "just what kind of surgical instrument do you see here?"

"I'm not sure."

"Would it perchance be an instrument that you yourself have handled?"

"I don't know if I have handled one or not."

"Of course, you have been a surgeon, have you not, Doctor?"

Gerber shook his head reluctantly. Bailey pursued his prey with merciless irony.

"Do you have such an instrument back at your office?"

"No."

"Have you ever seen such an instrument in any hospital or medical supply catalog or anywhere else, Dr. Gerber?"

"No, not that I can remember."

"Tell the jury, Doctor, where you have searched for this instrument during the past 12 years?"

"Oh, I have looked all over the United States," admitted Gerber—golden words to the defense.

"My goodness," said Bailey in mock surprise. "Then, please, by all means tell us what you found."

"I didn't find one," Gerber conceded.

Corrigan and Leo M. Spellacy, his able assistant, looked as if they wanted to throw Marilyn's pillow at their prize witness. Even Judge Talty, a former trial lawyer, appeared amused by the Boston attorney's scathing cross-examination.

"Now, Doctor," Bailey continued, "you know that Sam Sheppard was and is a surgeon, don't you?" Gerber nodded. "Now you didn't describe this phantom impression as a surgical instrument just to hurt Sam Sheppard's case, did you, Doctor? You wouldn't do that, would you?"

"Oh, no. Oh, no."

Doubtless the jury quickly got the idea that Bailey wanted it to have: the murder weapon could have been a simple pair of household pliers, a flashlight, or some equally commonplace implement.

Bailey had several other questions that he wanted to get on the record. "Did you, Coroner, tell a young intern at the Bay Village Hospital about a month before Marilyn was murdered that you intended some day to 'get' the Sheppards?"

"No! Whoever says that is a liar!" roared Gerber.

"Did you not tell a reporter a week after the crime that you thought the murderer was a woman?"

Gerber heatedly denied this.

After the coroner left the stand, Bailey summoned witnesses who contradicted the coroner on his denials.

Corrigan placed greater faith in the testimony of his final witness: Mary Cowan, the laboratory technician in Coroner Gerber's office. However, her competent, calm testimony about the blood spatters on Marilyn's and Sam's watches confused the jurors, just as the blood evidence had during the first trial. Corrigan countered with a sharp left hook when, discussing the blood spots on Sheppard's wristwatch, he said: "This watch tells more than the time. It tells us who the murderer of Marilyn Sheppard is."

Bailey bluntly asked Mary Cowan, "Does it not appear, Miss Cowan, that this weapon was swung in a left-handed arc?"

"It would seem so," she said, much to the delight of the defense counsel.

Steve Sheppard testified briefly about the seriousness of his brother's injuries on the murder morning. This was again corroborated by Dr. Charles Elkins, the neurologist, who testified that the defendant had suffered a fractured second cervical vertebra and a spinal cord injury—which Sheppard could well have sustained by jumping out of a second-floor window. But Corrigan argued that Sheppard's injuries resulted from Marilyn's waving arms and kicking legs. "Sam got clipped good," he insisted.

Bailey's heavyweight witness was Dr. Paul Leland Kirk, who came from his University of California criminology laboratory in Berkeley to testify for almost an entire day, putting on the record the meat of his 1955 posttrial affidavit. Among other things, Kirk claimed that the bloodstains on the murder bedroom wall clearly showed that (1)

Marilyn was definitely slain by a person whose O-type blood was different from her husband's A-type blood; (2) the killer was left-handed, while Dr. Sam was right-handed, and (3) the blood on Sam's wristwatch, which Mary Cowan had testified came from "flying blood," actually reached the watch by direct contact. Corrigan cross-examined Kirk briefly with merely a handful of questions, perhaps because a skilled cross-examiner knows when *not* to cross-examine a witness in detail.

In an attempt to refute Kirk, Corrigan called as a rebuttal witness Dr. Rogers W. Masters, a Cleveland blood expert. Under Bailey's cross-examination Dr. Masters admitted that he was experienced in studying whole blood but not dried blood. Bailey shrewdly pulled out of his pocket one of Dr. Masters's scientific papers, in which the chemist admitted that fingerprint powder does not contaminate dried bood. The paper confirmed a point that Bailey was trying to prove.

Throughout the entire testimony defendant Sheppard sat at the defense table listening to every word, sometimes looking a little bleary-eyed. During the first trial he had been on the witness stand for three and a half days, but Bailey decided that his client was in no condition to testify. The reason that he gave Sam was: "You have already told your story many times, and telling it again would only make you vulnerable to the prosecution's pot shots."

However, a far more important reason to Bailey was that Sam Sheppard had begun drinking heavily—straight vodka instead of soft drinks—and was mixing alcohol with a variety of pills. Bailey never let the prosecution know his master plan of not having his client testify. On the contrary, Bailey leaked it all around the court corridors, "Of course, I'll have to put Sam on the stand later."

Corrigan seemingly bought this fabrication and was awaiting Sheppard's testimony. The prosecutor, it was rumored, planned to bring in to testify an Ohio penitentiary convict known as "Frenchy." "In return for clemency," Bailey wrote in his autobiography, *The Defense Never Rests,* "according to my information, Frenchy would claim that Sam had conspired with him to kill Spencer Houk after forcing Houk to write a suicide note in which he would exonerate Sam and implicate himself in Marilyn's death."

Whether or not this real or imaginary Frenchy would have told the truth was immaterial. His testimony might have provided the excitement for an otherwise dull trial, as Bailey trials go. Many prisons harbor shabby characters who will "confess" to anything in open court or judicial chambers in an attempt to reduce their sentences or save their own skins.

As it happened, neither Sheppard nor Frenchy testified, much to Corrigan's surprise. Had Frenchy taken the stand and knifed Sheppard, it is doubtful whether he would have escaped slaughter himself back in the Ohio penitentiary. Prisoners have their own code of conduct.

In his hour summary to the jury Bailey excoriated the prosecution's case as "ten pounds of hogwash in a five-pound bag." He likened the state's case to that of a woman searching around a gutter under a high street light. When asked why, she explained, "I'm looking for a dollar bill that I dropped 50 feet away."

"Then why aren't you looking over there?"

"Because the light is better here," she answered.

Judge Talty's 23-page charge to the jury gave it a choice of three possible verdicts: (1) guilty of second-degree murder carrying a life sentence with parole possible after 10 years; (2) guilty of first-degree manslaughter with a maximum sentence of 20 years with parole permissible after 11 months; and (3) not guilty.

At 10:45 A.M. on November 16, 1966, the jury climbed the staircase to its third-floor room. The Cleveland bookies gave six-to-five odds for Sheppard's acquittal. In Las Vegas they were twenty-to-one for acquittal. The differential in these percentages troubled Bailey, the legal gambler. Though confident, he said, "Anything can happen in Cleveland."

Instead of going to a restaurant at noon, the jury ordered box lunches sent in. All afternoon they deliberated while the Sheppard party waited in their hotel rooms. The jurors were brought back into the courtroom before going out to dinner. At 7:30 P.M. they were deliberating again. By this time Dr. Sam was trembling with the waiting. "If it goes the wrong way, Sam, I'll do everything I can to keep you from going back to prison," Bailey comforted him.

Judge Talty telephoned Bailey that he was sending the jurors back to their hotel for the night and to hurry over with the defendant, who had to be in court when the jury was sent to retire. When Bailey arrived back at the courthouse, Judge Talty astonished him by saying that he had a verdict. At 10:15 P.M. the jurors sauntered in. The jury had deliberated less than a day, as compared to five days in 1954. All the jurors solemnly avoided the defendant's eyes, but Bailey and Russell Sherman, his associate defense counsel, detected what they thought was a wink from one of the male jurors. Dr. Sam held his breath.

The judge quickly unfolded the sheet and read: "We find the defendant not guilty."

Sam Sheppard's heavy right arm dropped like a sledgehammer on the table as he cried, "It's about time!"

Indicating displeasure with a reproving stare, Judge Talty was sternly silent as Bailey chided his jubilant client, "Take it easy, Sam. We're still in an open court."

When promised that no additional commotion would disrupt the court, Judge Talty thanked the jurors and discharged them. They were ushered out, and court was adjourned.

"I want my wife," cried the exonerated man. Ariane had already edged her way forward to her husband and fell into his arms. They both sobbed with joyful relief.

Back at the Hollenden House there was no formal victory celebration. However, Bailey turned to the throng of pro- and anti-Sheppard newsmen and quipped, "You friendly people wearing white hats are invited to join me for liquid refreshments. The rest of you wearing black hats can go to hell."

Newsmen learned that five ballots had been required. On the first ballot seven jurors voted for acquittal, four for guilty, one undecided. The older jurors at first voted guilty. Foreman Ralph Vichell revealed, "At no time did we consider a first-degree manslaughter verdict as an alternative to the second-degree murder charge. It was a question of guilty or not guilty of murder." Then he added, "I don't think the case has been solved." Several days later another juror admitted that many fellow Clevelanders had telephoned irritably, saying, "How could you ever have acquitted him when everybody knows he's guilty?"

The acquitted defendant, who had gone for broke after ten years of prison and a little more than two years of jittery freedom, who had spurned the questionable freedom of an almost certain parole, was now legally free. With deep bitterness he said to me, "It's not the kind of education I'd recommend to anybody. Twelve years is a helluva price to pay."

A Lawyer Writes a Letter

Dr. Sam's court victory in Cleveland sweetened his cup of bitterness as no change of venue could ever have done. Still, although legally a free man, he continued to feel, in some ways, like a prisoner in the United States of America. The mark of Cain was still on him in countless persons' minds and would be on him forever, he feared, unless he was *really* cleared. The parallel with Cain was not the same in *his* mind as it was in the minds of many individuals who still thought him guilty despite his acquittal.

A jury of his peers in a court of law had decided that husband Samuel Sheppard had not killed his wife. Who had? A bushy-haired intruder? A dope-crazed burglar searching for narcotics in a doctor's home? A neighbor? A woman? Who?

Shortly after he was first convicted, prisoner Sheppard had confidently predicted, "Some day the person or persons who murdered my wife will be found out."

In July, 1961, William J. Corrigan, Sheppard's first defense lawyer, was standing in his private office in downtown Cleveland with his back to Steve Sheppard. The attorney was gazing out of the window at the pigeons flying in the square below and ruminating about how free they were compared to his imprisoned client. When he had first accepted the case, Bill Corrigan had assumed that his client was guilty. But as the trial progressed and time wore on, he grew convinced that his client was truly innocent.

Suddenly he turned and said, "The person who killed Marilyn is living with a terrible guilt, Steve. This person wants to forget the crime but never can. Probably not even confession would fully relieve this guilt. After all, this person hastened the deaths of both your mother and your father. Imagine how this person must feel whenever he reads your brother's name in the newspaper or hears it on the radio or television. Some day this person will be coerced, by some means, into telling the truth." Then he added, "I wish that I could be around when that happens, but I'm afraid that will not be so."

Three weeks later Bill Corrigan was dead.

Now Sheppard's second lawyer, flush from his courtroom triumph, concentrated on the question, "Who killed Marilyn?"

In his closing arguments to the jury during the retrial, which were not reported, Lee Bailey had claimed: (1) A woman had killed Marilyn Sheppard; (2) A man had made the two attacks on his client. In short, *two* persons were involved in the crime. Dr. Sam had said, in his dazed, shocked condition, "*they*'ve killed Marilyn. "Some one was angry, angry enough to kill," insisted Bailey.

Shortly after his client's acquittal Lee Bailey sat down in his private office in Boston, closed the door, and told his secretary that he would receive no telephone calls and no visitors. He had decided to write a letter.

Lee Bailey had a lot to say. Lawyers' letters are generally terse, cold communications. However, Bailey, who once had yearned to become a writer, began writing a long, highly emotional, uninhibited letter revealing his deep indignation on crucial aspects of what was the most exhausting case of his entire career.

Because of the coming of age of the telephone and telegraph, letter writing is believed to be a dying art. Yet no form of communication or branch of literature can be more intimate or revealing than a letter setting forth what the writer deems to be the truth.

Lee Bailey addressed his letter to Police Chief Fred Drenkhan, of Bay Village, Ohio. Drenkhan was the first police officer to step inside the Sheppard house on July 4, 1954, when he was a lowly patrolman. Drenkhan and Sam Sheppard had often shared rides on accident calls and chow at police functions in Bay Village. During Sheppard's first trial Drenkhan had testified for the state for almost two days and was one of the officers who had first arrested his former friend, on July 30, 1954. At the retrial Drenkhan, who had since become Bay Village's chief of police, again testified for the state, repeating more concisely his earlier testimony, including the facts that neither the murder weapon nor the defendant's T-shirt had been found.

Bailey's *j'accuse* letter to Drenkhan was 15 single-spaced typewritten pages. Though its contents were never made public, it is known that the letter named names, implicated others, set forth extensive, hitherto unknown information, and charged that *two* persons who were now at large had murdered Marilyn Sheppard.

The letter almost burned Police Chief Drenkhan's hands when he read it. It was obviously not something that he could just file and forget; it required official action. As a result of this letter, a Cuyahoga County Grand Jury issued subpoenas. Key persons were summoned to appear before it, behind closed doors, and to furnish testimony that had not emerged at either of the two Sheppard trials. The individuals were Bailey, Dr. Sam, Drenkhan, former Bay Village Police Sergeant Jay Hubach, former Cleveland Detective Patrick Gareau, a practicing attorney, J. Spencer Houk, and his former wife Esther.

After an alleged two-week investigation the Cuyahoga County Grand Jury, on December 15, 1966, concluded that there was "no basis for the charges. . . . They were merely the opinion of an attorney representing a client and are wholly unsubstantiated and without merit."

In Freehold, New Jersey, where he was defending Dr. Carl Coppolino, Bailey snapped back: "Ridiculous! A damn whitewash! Exactly what I expected. Cleveland is trying to protect itself from ten years of sin against Dr. Sheppard."

The grand jury investigation was dropped.

It is doubtful whether Lee Bailey's epistle will ever be included in any forthcoming "Treasury of the World's Great Letters." Nevertheless, it raised the blood pressure of some Ohioans, who were not accustomed to reading such letters from lawyers—not even from this brash barrister.

Medical License

Meanwhile, Sam Sheppard, who had recently moved with his wife into their posh new lakefront home at 27204 Lake

Road, in Bay Village, Ohio, was doing battle on the medical front.

The exonerated ex-convict, now 43-years-old, yearned desperately to get his medical license restored immediately. "I'm a doctor, and I want to help people," he remarked. "I owe that to my father. I can't forget the past, but I hope somehow to enjoy the future and practice medicine. I'm trying not to let yesterday spoil today and tomorrow."

Sheppard's medical license had been taken from him after his 1954 conviction, and it was suspended indefinitely on April 2, 1957. Now he formally applied for its return. But the Ohio Medical Board seemed to be stalling; it took no official action.

"You call this rehabilitation?" he mused bitterly. Why, he wondered, must his medical colleagues make it so difficult for him to return to respectable society? In prison he had tried to keep up with the latest developments in medicine. After being released he had diligently brushed up by reading the latest medical textbooks and discussing new techniques, especially with his brother Richard. And Richard and Steve wanted him to return to their hospital. Unfortunately, the question was academic to Sam because his license had not been restored.

"My husband has received many offers from doctors and hospital groups all over the country," Ariane told me. "He has an offer to practice in California, and he likes it out there. Perhaps that might be a good place for him to start all over again. But the decision is entirely his. I'll follow him to the end of the world if necessary."

Since Ohio was seemingly reluctant to return his license, he decided to apply in California, where he had graduated from medical school in 1948.

On May 25, 1967, he appeared for 45 minutes before the California Board of Osteopathic Examiners. He stressed that during 7 of his 10 years in prison he had performed hundreds of operations under the supervision of prison physicians. At the hearing Dr. Arthur Miller, senior attending physician at Los Angeles General Hospital, testified that he would trust Sam—once his medical school roommate—to operate on him or any member of his family.

Nevertheless, Wallace Thompson, administrative officer of the board, ruled eleven days later that Sheppard had to pass written examinations within six months in obstetrics and gynecology, general medicine and therapeutics, surgery, public health and pediatrics, as well as oral examinations in the field in which he intended to specialize. All of this indicated to Sam that the board was giving him a hard time.

Enraged, he wrote to Robert K. Steinberg, his Beverly Hills, California, attorney: "The provisions of the board are not only surprising but insulting. They preclude any fair testing since not one of the board members could stand simple examination himself. We must appeal to a higher court. I have been tried, retried, and tested too often. Give them hell!"

However, some people close to Sam felt that if he did not take quite such an unyielding, even hostile, attitude toward the licensing authorities, Ohio—and even California—might act in his favor. Sheppard told me flatly, "I'm a doctor, and I want to stay one. But it seems to me that a lot of my colleagues here in the states don't want to let me."

Dr. Sam's dedication to his profession was evidenced during his retrial when an elderly man collapsed in the court hall. Instantly, defendant Sheppard rushed over, took his pulse, and tried to examine him, but he was ordered away by an attendant.

Another matter that irritated Sam was the public confusion of his case with that of Dr. Carl Coppolino—possibly because both were defended by the same attorney. Although Coppolino was acquitted in New Jersey earlier, he was sentenced to life imprisonment in Naples, Florida, on April 28, 1967, for the murder of his wife Carmela. A week after the defeat, Lee Bailey contended on the Johnny Carson show, "The Coppolino case is becoming another Sheppard case."

Sam Sheppard took strong exception to this. He insisted that not only the verdicts but the evidence in the two cases were diametrically opposite. Joseph Frank, a perceptive New York attorney who made a special study of both cases, stated, "The circumstantial evidence in these two trials was totally different, even though Bailey played the same tune about a hostile press distorting the truth. But Bailey plays the tune he thinks can help him."

Disheartened by the disappointing anticlimax of his legal victory, especially what he considered bureaucratic pussyfooting in restoring his medical license, Sam Sheppard angrily said, "Screw you! I'll go to Europe and practice there. I'm a doctor. I'll go anywhere that people are sick. I probably won't make as much money as in the United States, but I learned in prison that peace of mind is more rewarding."

At Ariane's urging, the couple left on what was Sam's first trip to Europe, visiting the Riviera, Germany, and England. "I'll enjoy showing him the places I know so well," she said.

On December 14, 1967, when Sheppard was staying at the home of Ariane's mother in Duisburg, West Germany, the Ohio Medical Board suddenly reinstated Sam's license to practice osteopathic medicine and surgery.

Unfortunately, just as love, wealth, wisdom and life's other treasures sometimes arrive belatedly for many persons, so did Dr. Sam Sheppard's medical license renewal come too late for him.

Expatriate Pitch

During his refreshing European trip in the summer of 1967 Dr. Sam Sheppard, a physician without a license, suddenly returned to the land of his birth feeling like a man without a country.

In late September, 1967, Sam visited New York with his son and confided to me privately that he had decided to forsake the United States and begin life anew as a doctor on the French Riviera. "This is the only way I can make the most of the years left to me," he said.

With his cooperation I speedily wrote a superficial but exclusive and widely publicized article entitled "Why Dr. Sheppard is Quitting the United States," which was published as the lead cover story in the Sunday, November 12, 1967, issue of *Parade*.

The following are some extracts from the complete article:

Fearing that he may never find peace of mind or resume medical practice in his native land, he is quitting the United States to start a new life on the French Riviera. . . . The embittered, 43-year-old Sheppard complained:

"I'm sick of being continually on trial in this country. Too many people make me feel like an outcast—the staring, the finger-pointing, and the hard time they give me. I found out recently when I spent some time in France that nobody paid any attention to me. That's the way it should be."

But Sam Sheppard still lives a life of torment in the U.S. He hasn't been able to get his medical license restored. He's still a victim of whispers, rubbernecking, hate mail, and crank calls. And, worst of all, Doctor Sam believes that authorities here know who really killed his wife but for some reason are dragging their feet.

Another reason for Sheppard's planning to live abroad is his determination to preserve his three-year marriage with his glamorous, Continentally elegant Ariane, who never felt comfortable in the United States. Her preference is the Riviera, and Sam now agrees. . . .

The ballyhooed Sheppard marriage underwent far more than normal stress. Rumors of public quarrels, separations, and possible divorce were continually spread. "Those rumors began as soon as we were married," Sam recalls. "Many people wanted to see our marriage bust up. I'm sure it would have made them very happy. But Ariane and I have overcome our difficulties and are now more in love than ever."

"Can't you see?" Sam told me. "I have to try to forget all these things. I have to start all over again somewhere else."

During recent months abroad with Ariane he determined on the Riviera as his "somewhere else." He has taken an option on a secluded house in Cap d'Ail with a swimming pool and terrace. And here in Bay Village, a for-sale sign has gone up on his six-room brick Colonial lakefront home, about a mile from where Marilyn was slain in her bedroom. . . .

"We're trying to get $50,000 for it, if we can," Sam admits. . . . One of the first things real estate broker Harry Whitmer did was to discard the entrance doormat with its lettering: "Stay Away."

Probably the only thing that could get Sam Sheppard to change his mind would be if Ohio or California were suddenly to give him his license back —and he could persuade his wife to settle in the U.S.

Today, though Dr. Samuel Sheppard is not a man without a country, he plans to try another one tomorrow only because he feels his own didn't give him the freedom he had earned after ten years in prison.

As a result of the article the Sheppard home was deluged with a horde of invaders, who tramped over the lawn and shaggy white rugs and plumped down on the furniture. An art-minded group from the Bay Village Women's Club canceled a discussion about antiques to tour this lakefront Valhalla.

Art-loving and God-fearing, Ohio is also a press-fearing state. The *Parade* supplement was avid Sunday morning breakfast reading in key newspapers in four Ohio cities. By far the greatest influence of the article, according to my information, was that it helped to spark the Ohio Medical Board into action. Shortly after the article's publication and the consequent pro-Sheppard mail, the board suddenly restored Dr. Sam's medical license.

Expatriate Sheppard, who had returned to Europe shortly before the publication of the *Parade* article, was so delighted that several weeks later, on January 8, 1958, he returned to the United States. Looking relaxed and smiling easily on a below-zero day, he warmly announced to the Cleveland press that he planned to practice medicine in Bay Village and that he was applying to five Ohio hospitals for reinstatement.

My reportorial face was red. *Parade* editor Jess Gorkin demanded, "Where in the hell is Sheppard going to practice—in Ohio or on the Riviera? What are the facts?"

I put the question to Sam himself.

"Yes, I changed my mind," admitted Dr. Sam. "I found out it would be slow and difficult to bring my French or German up to the standard needed to practice over there.

Also, the money situation is a lot different in Europe than here. Most important, I want to stick around Ohio to pursue the question of the tragedy as far as is legally possible. I've got to lick this thing on home base first if I ever want to live with myself. Steve told me that when I got out of prison, and he's right. It took me three and a half years to understand this. If I can't make it here, I might be able to join the Peace Corps. They still have an application of mine that they haven't processed. But it's great to be back here where I belong."

Movie Exploitation

Sam Sheppard decided to return to Ohio for another reason: he had unfinished business to conduct.

Paramount Pictures announced that it would soon start shooting a documentary film about Sam Sheppard, and he was likely to be called in for consultation.

The brain behind this proposed Sheppard movie was producer Brad Dexter, a former actor who reportedly had catapulted in the Hollywood hierarchy shortly after saving Frank Sinatra from drowning. He became associated with Sinatra Enterprises and produced *The Naked Runner*, starring Frank Sinatra. An ecstatic Paramount Pictures press release stated, "Brad Dexter is a producer who knows what he wants and then gets it accomplished."

Apparently Sam Sheppard did not like what was being accomplished. He asked me to check out the matter for him. The film was originally announced as *The Sam Sheppard Story*. Then it was changed to *The Sheppard Murder Case*, to be based on the transcripts of the two trials and material from Dr. Sam's "autobiography," *Endure and Conquer*, which was rushed out one week after his acquittal.

Hollywood has a whimsical logic all its own. The studio's plan to dramatize the actual Sheppard case was suddenly abandoned. Instead, studio officials decided to make a movie about an ambitious, tough criminal lawyer defending a case similar to Sheppard's. For some reason the emphasis was switched from Sheppard to Bailey. In fact, the title of the film—as late as May, 1969, after two weeks of location scenes were shot in Colorado Springs—was *Petrocelli: Lawyer.*

Brad Dexter even wanted Lee Bailey to play the leading role, deciding that no professional actor could possibly possess the lawyer's "dynamic intensity." After all, Joseph Welch, the Boston attorney in the Senator Joseph R. McCarthy hearings, played himself in *Anatomy of a Murder.*

Conceding that he had some "ham" in him, Bailey remarked, "The only time I have ever really acted was in front of juries." This impromptu wisecrack raised so many eyebrows at the American and Boston Bar Associations that Bailey later denied in Boston that he ever said it (even though many newsmen in New York heard it at a Paramount press conference).

In his autobiography Bailey discussed his later censure by the Boston Bar Association. He wrote that one of the five "matters of concern" to the grievance committee was: "A report that I intended to play myself in a movie about the Sheppard case. . . . I had indeed been asked to play myself in a documentary about the Sheppard case. I had replied that I would have to see the script and that I could only make such a decision after conferring with bar association officials. (I never did play in the film.)"

The lead role was brilliantly acted by Barry Newman, a comparatively unknown Broadway actor who had never appeared in a film before. According to most critics he was the movie's one redeeming feature.

Shortly before the film was released in February, 1970, the title was changed from *Petrocelli: Lawyer* to *The Lawyer.* The Paramount promotion literature now crowed that the film was "suggested by the Sam Sheppard Murder Case" and that the lead character, Tony Petrocelli, was "inspired by attorney F. Lee Bailey, of Boston, Massachusetts." The second most important character in the film—the doctor accused of murdering his wife—was named Dr. Jack Harrison. (Somebody's joke or attempted defamation of me?) The lawyer in the movie doesn't give a damn about his client's innocence or guilt—only his acquittal.

Dr. Samuel Sheppard, whose life had "suggested" this picture, saw it for the first time in Columbus, Ohio, a month before another great tragedy. His verdict of *The*

Lawyer: guilty of being the most dreadful movie that he had ever seen. He sentenced himself to consuming a bottle of vodka. To the inebriated, disintegrating man his alcoholism was merely a misdemeanor compared to the colossal crime that Hollywood had committed against his life story.

For all that, the life story itself, *Endure and Conquer*, upon which the movie was based, was no masterpiece. When reviewing Sheppard's book in *Saturday Review*, I wrote:

> Dr. Sam Sheppard's personal account is . . . illuminating and disappointing. . . . Because Sam's tragedy has been spoken of as an American Dreyfus case, his could have been an epic book. Regrettably the autobiography misses widely owing to its patchwork composition and ghostwritten flavor. The inevitable suspicion persists that *Endure and Conquer* was tailored for a prearranged motion-picture sale. Had Sam Sheppard—free man and ex-convict—written it entirely in his own words, from his own heart, the resulting book might have been less facile but far more touching. . . .
>
> Nevertheless, Sam's innermost feelings don't penetrate the bulk of his book. . . .
>
> Sam's relentless recitation of familiar facts tends to numb the mind and emotions. What the reader—painfully conscious of the man's agony—wants to know of Sam Sheppard's personal story is not told. Whether as a result of natural reticence, an emotional block, legal caution, or publication pressure, the book's tone is too often flat, corny, even self-righteous. . . .

My opinion was not very different from that of many other reviewers.

11

THE TRAUMA

LEE BAILEY accepted the dormant Sheppard case in November, 1961, without any fee, retainer, or guarantee that he would ever earn a nickel. No one can deny that his Herculean labors in springing his client from prison in July, 1964, triumphing before the Supreme Court in June, 1966, and exonerating Sheppard in a retrial merited a highly justified legal fee. What Lee Bailey did for Sam Sheppard in five years can never be measured in mere money.

Worthless Net Worth

Ever since the young Boston lawyer took the case, he had vowed to sue those who he claimed were responsible for his client's wrongful 1954 conviction and subsequent ten-year imprisonment for their "net worth."

In its June 20, 1966, issue *Newsweek* reported that Sheppard was threatening "to sue the paper (the *Cleveland Press*) for $151 million." Bailey, no amateur with figures, mentioned punitive and compensatory damages of at least $200 million when deploring how the press "play God. . . . They make judgments and ruin people by writing stories. . . . When you have that much power, you have that much responsibility . . . let the press, for its abuses, pay the bill!"

A month after Sheppard was released from prison, the triumphant attorney wrote a letter to editor Seltzer, a copy of which was secured by and published in the *Sun Press*, a suburban Cleveland newspaper. The letter read in part:

> This is to advise that claim is hereby made against you by my client, Dr. Samuel H. Sheppard, for damages suffered by him as a result of your misconduct and that of the *Press*. The damages were occasioned by gross defamation, and by the deprivation of his civil rights to a fair trial which arose directly from your interference with legal processes in the case of State *v.* Sheppard, Cuyahoga County Common Pleas, 1954. A further claim for malicious prosecution will ripen when this case is finally resolved in Dr. Sheppard's favor through the failure of the County to try him again, and will be presented at that time.
>
> By your callow and ruthless acts, you robbed Dr. Sheppard and his entire family of each ounce of human dignity you could slice away. You took a man who was immersed in the greatest personal grief, and smothered him in your own brand of muck. You caused, brutally, the death of both of his parents. You stole from him his right to a fair trial in a fair court, and did each thing in your power to cause his conviction, despite his obvious innocence, for the most heinous of crimes, with his life nearly as the prize. You sought, and nearly took, all that this man had. The fair measure of malice of this kind is reciprocal. I now seek as compensation all that you have—and I refer to yourself, the *Press*, and Scripps-Howard. Our *ad damnum*, if suit need be filed, will reflect the net asset value of these three defendants.
>
> You may have your attorneys contact me if you desire. However, to avoid wasting attorneys' valuable time, let me be clear in stating that no offers will be entertained which do not tender both substantial sums—very substantial—and some arrangements for the total vindication of Dr. Sheppard. If this cannot

be done through negotiation, we will trust an unpressured jury to see that justice is done.

Seltzer did not reply to the letter, and what he said privately is not known. What is known is that three years later, on November 13, 1967—almost a year after his retrial acquittal—Dr. Samuel Sheppard filed through Bailey two damage suits in the United States District Court at Cleveland. The first suit accused the E. W. Scripps Company, publisher of the *Cleveland Press,* and Louis B. Seltzer, its recently retired editor, of conspiring with Dr. Samuel R. Gerber, Cuyahoga County Coroner, to secure the conviction of Dr. Sheppard for the murder of his wife Marilyn in 1954. The second Sheppard suit, a malicious prosecution action, charged that Seltzer and the Scripps Company had carried on an editorial attack that had caused public officials to accuse Sheppard of murder. As a result, claimed Sheppard in his suits, he was imprisoned for approximately 10 years, lost 13 years of income as a physician, was saddled with attorneys' fees, and lost his reputation and the respect of his community. These suits asked for damages, including punitive damages.

However, nearly eight months later, on July 3, 1968, Federal Judge James C. Connell, sitting in the U. S. District Court at Cleveland, dismissed the two damage suits. His decision was appealed. A year and a half later, on January 22, 1970, the United States Sixth Circuit Court of Appeals in Cincinnati upheld the lower court's dismissal of these suits. In dismissing them, the Federal Appeals Court blamed what it termed the "deplorable" atmosphere of the first trial predominantly on Judge Edward Blythin.

If these judicial setbacks disheartened Bailey, he did not show it. Instead, he devised another method to collect his legal fee from his client.

Bailey's legal fee in the Sheppard case was solved in part by having the bulk of Dr. Sam's earnings from the movie rights and his autobiography assigned to Bailey in part payment until it was paid. The Boston attorney set a nominal $150,000 fee, which was far from exorbitant in view of his major accomplishments.

After accepting other seemingly hopeless cases without fees, Bailey ingeniously attempted to collect fees by controlling the rights to some of his clients' life stories through the sale of or royalties from books and movies and magazine articles stemming from his clients' notoriety. "Lee has to get paid some way," one of his friends explained.

In an article on February 23, 1967, by Richard Reeves, the *New York Times* headlined: *Trial Books Help Pay Bailey Fees.*

> F. Lee Bailey has received hundreds of thousands of dollars in book and movie rights as his payment for representing celebrated defendants in nationally publicized trials during the past year. The 33-year-old criminal lawyer controlled the sale of book and movie rights to the stories of Dr. Samuel H. Sheppard and Dr. Carl Coppolino. . . .
>
> "Sheppard assigned book rights to me until his fees are paid," said the lawyer, who refused to disclose the amount of any fee. A source in the publishing industry said Mr. Bailey received $100,000 to $150,000 for representing Dr. Sheppard from August, 1965, until the Cleveland osteopath ... was acquitted last November. . . .

Three years later, on September 20, 1970, a *New York Times* Sunday magazine article by Paul Wilkes reported: "In Sheppard's case, Bailey went in with no assurance of a fee and came out with $100,000 earned from the sale of a book and movie."

However, while in Philadelphia promoting *The Lawyer,* Bailey was quoted in *The Jewish Exponent* on February 13, 1970, by Leon E. Brown: " 'I represented Sheppard for five years and received about $60,000'. . . . Bailey said he only held these rights until the legal fee was paid by Sheppard. He said that it was paid and that he no longer owns any rights to the book or film."

On the other hand, William V. Levy, who helped to ghost-write Dr. Sam's autobiography, was quoted in the *Akron Beacon-Journal* on April 7, 1970, in these words: ". . . Sheppard received between $60,000 and $70,000 in royalties for the book, while Paramount Pictures purchased movie rights for $125,000. Most of the money was given to Sheppard's attorney, F. Lee Bailey, for legal fees. . . ."

It so happened that shortly after my *Saturday Review* review appeared I happened to be in the Cambridge, Massachusetts, courthouse covering the trial of Albert De Salvo, the alleged Boston Strangler. Everybody was anxious to glimpse De Salvo in his first public appearance. Lee Bailey marched out with his notorious client, who was handcuffed to a court bailiff.

Bailey, who seemingly has eyes in the back of his head, spotted me in the crowded corridor and leaped over toward me, momentarily forgetting his client, who stood transfixed amid the throng of curious onlookers. Bailey plumped a firm hand upon my shoulder and said, "You killed the sale of Sam's book with your review in the *Saturday Review*. Don't you know I own the book?"

"What was wrong with the review?" I weakly protested. "Sam, Ariane, and Steve seemed to like it."

"Nothing was wrong with it. Everything you said was true. Sure, it was a lousy book. But why did you have to say it? I'm sure you could have written a better one."

"Lee, no book review—not even in the *New York Times*—kills a book if there's public interest in it. Lots of best sellers are never even reviewed."

Meanwhile, during this lofty literary discussion, Albert De Salvo, who confessed to having killed 13 women, impatiently glared at his attorney and me. He looked as if he would have been happy to have added both of us to his list.

Malpractice Muddle

At this time the former prisoner was trying to rehabilitate himself in society *without* his lawyer.

Before Sam Sheppard's medical license was restored by Ohio, he attempted to earn a living by selling automobiles in Rocky River—and he even sold me his own 1964 Lincoln Continental convertible (one of the worst purchases I ever made!).

Dr. Sam left the used car business after his medical license was restored, and because he was determined to remain in Ohio, he decided to try to join the Youngstown Osteopathic Hospital, where he had treated a case in March, 1968. In May he was accepted as a member of the hospital staff. In June the Ohio Academy of Osteopathic Medicine approved his transfer there.

The Sheppards were living in their Bay Village home, which they had decided not to sell. Now they quietly rented a one-bedroom apartment in a modern building in Youngstown, where they spent a happy summer. One neighbor recalls seeing them often laughing and splashing in the building swimming pool when Sam was not on hospital duty. Another remembers, "Dr. Sam was always a gentleman, helping us with our groceries, dogs, or luggage or holding the elevator or helping us in the parking lot." No neighbor recollects ever hearing the Sheppards quarrel. Life for them was seemingly serene.

But all that soon changed. Dr. Sam suddenly found himself a defendant again in other looming courtroom battles involving other deaths.

On September 7, 1968, a Youngstown widow, Marcia Lopez, sued him and the hospital for $530,000, charging negligence in the death of her husband Samuel. The lawsuit on behalf of the widow Lopez and her three minor children contended that Dr. Sheppard had been negligent in lacerating an artery while performing a spinal operation on Samuel Lopez on August 6. This alleged negligence resulted in hemorrhaging, which caused the patient's death, the suit charged. It claimed that the hospital had been neglectful in selecting Dr. Sheppard for its staff and permitting him to perform an operation when he had not practiced for ten years.

However, Dr. Sam's defenders, citing hospital records, claimed that the patient's death had been accidental. Although the artery had been cut and internal bleeding had occurred, it had not occurred until after the operation.

A similar $685,000 lawsuit was filed by the same attorneys, Norman Goldberg and Nathaniel R. Jones, on September 17, against Dr. Sheppard and the Youngstown Osteopathic Hospital. This second suit was on behalf of Martin L. Duffy, fire chief of Liberty Township, about the death the previous May of his wife, Mary A. Duffy, after an operation for the removal of a disc. Like the first suit, it claimed wrongful death but asked for additional money for pain and suffering on the part of Mr. Duffy. This second suit differed also in that it charged that Dr. Sheppard was guilty not only of negligence in the operation but also of failing to provide Mrs. Duffy with proper postoperative care. She had died 16 hours after Sheppard had operated on her. The suit claimed that Dr. Sam was negligent in that he had lacerated a blood vessel, which ultimately caused the patient's death.

The total amount of damages claimed against Dr. Sam and the hospital in these two suits was $1,215,000.

Pressure was put upon the hospital to fire Dr. Sam, but officials did not request his resignation. However, when Sheppard heard that the hospital's insurance companies would not issue it any further malpractice insurance unless he resigned, he did so, on December 3, 1968. Without malpractice insurance coverage it is virtually impossible for any hospital or doctor to function. One major malpractice suit can ruin any hospital or doctor.

"I didn't want to get the hospital into any trouble because of me," he explained. He then shrugged and added, "I kind of expected this would happen. There are people in this state who are still out to get me."

A month later, on October 29, 1968, the insurance company that had written the policy presumably protecting Dr. Sam against malpractice damages asked a federal court in Cleveland to relieve it of responsibility in the two suits. The Fidelity General Insurance Company of Chicago claimed that the policy it had issued to Dr. Sheppard on February 15, 1968, specifically excluded major surgery and that his application had stated that his practice would be 90 percent general practice and 10 percent treatment of mental illness. The insurance suit quoted Sheppard as saying beforehand that he "performed no major surgery and did not require coverage for major surgery."

However, on October 10, 1970, nearly two years later, the insurance company lost this motion. United States District Court Judge Ben C. Green, in Cleveland, ruled that Sheppard's 1968 application for malpractice insurance clearly indicated that he intended to conduct neurosurgery in addition to the practice of general medicine.

Nearly a year after Dr. Sam had resigned from his relatively brief stay at the Youngstown hospital he was slapped with a third malpractice suit for $750,000, by a father on behalf of his son. The suit was against Sheppard, the

Youngstown Osteopathic hospital, and Dr. William J. Lurie, a doctor of osteopathy. On October 15, 1959, the *Youngstown Vindicator* reported:

> The suit, filed by the law firm of Pfau, Comstock & Springer, is aimed largely at Dr. Sheppard. Plaintiff is James Evans, now 11, . . . through his father, Robert J. Evans.
>
> The petition states that young James fell June 15, 1968, and broke his right arm. He was taken to Dr. Lurie, who sent him to the hospital. He was put in care of Dr. Sheppard, who operated on the boy and set his arm.
>
> The petition says Dr. Sheppard told the parents that it was "the best job of bone setting" he had seen and the treatment was "going to be 100 percent."
>
> Since then, the plaintiff says, he has gone through painful operations and corrective treatments, the arm developed swelling and loss of circulation, and that young James never will have proper use of his injured arm.

The Sheppard malpractice suits made headlines from Maine to California. Ironically, one out of five of America's nearly three hundred thousand M.D.s then had at least one malpractice suit, according to American Medical Association surveys. But these routine malpractice suits are rarely reported in the general press because few, if any, of the sued physicians have the notoriety of Dr. Sam Sheppard. Today such suits are Big legal Business.

Dr. Sam's malpractice suits, though, were only the *beginning* of his renewed anguish. The day after he resigned from the Youngstown hospital he received another devastating blow.

Düsseldorf Damsel Divorces

The cover story of the November 27, 1966, issue of the *National Enquirer*, a weekly tabloid whose masthead modestly described itself as "The World's Liveliest Paper," was entitled, "Why Sam Sheppard's Strange Marriage Is Working."

The article was based upon an interview with the late Dr. Frederic Wertham, a prominent psychiatrist who directed the first psychiatric clinic in a major American court. Dr. Wertham concluded by saying that there was every chance that the marriage would succeed.

Two years later psychiatrist Wertham's prediction proved to be somewhat less than accurate.

While he was still reeling from the malpractice mayhem, Dr. Sam Sheppard's marital world suddenly collapsed—for the second time in 14 years. His first marriage had been ended by death. His second marriage appeared to be ending by divorce.

On December 3, 1968, Ariane Sheppard sued her husband for divorce in the Cuyahoga County Common Pleas Court—the same Cleveland tribunal in which Dr. Sam had undergone his two previous trials. She demanded that her husband be restrained from seeing her lest he "perpetrate on her acts of violence, do her irreparable damage and great bodily harm." The divorce petition charged gross neglect and extreme cruelty and requested the court to enjoin Dr. Sheppard from "touching the person of the plaintiff . . . for her protection." Ariane told the court that she feared for her safety, having been threatened by her husband on several occasions. She asked for temporary and permanent alimony, payment of her legal fees, and the exclusive use of their home in Bay Village, which was in her name. Mrs. Sheppard was immediately granted an injunction that restrained her husband from attempting any contact with her or molesting her in any way.

The Sheppards' Youngstown neighbors were stunned by her charges. They remembered them as a model couple and Dr. Sam as a paragon of exemplary conduct. He had never, to their knowledge, quarreled with his wife. Both had always appeared attentively solicitous of each other's welfare.

The press had its expected field day. For example, the *New York Daily News* used the front page of its first edition on December 4, with photographs of both Sheppards, to blare: *Fearful Wife Sues Dr. Sam.*

More news was made on the following day when Ariane

held a Cleveland press conference. She wore no wedding ring, and she dabbed her tearful eyes with a violet handkerchief. To protect her life, she said, she had moved out of their Youngstown apartment and the Bay Village Lake Road home to a secret address. She complained that her husband had another woman (a former babysitter now living somewhere in the East, where she thought he was hiding); that he had stolen her money, car, jewelry, clothing, and "personal things"; that he habitually carried a pistol, knives, and a hatchet, although she admitted that he had never struck her; that he used vile language and threw empty bottles at her. He had also thrown her out of the car in the rain in Boston, and she had had to walk to town because she had no money, she said. Furthermore, she claimed that on November 13 her husband had come into the bedroom of their Bay Village home when she was asleep and had threatened her life with a pistol. She had hidden in the closet and later had gone to the police for protection before moving out. She referred to her husband as "irrational" and "that maniac."

"I was very willing to make a go of my marriage," she told the reporters. "When I married him, I knew that he was under great strain. I tried to understand; I thought it would work itself out. I went to Europe for ten days before the retrial. I had to put some distance between us. I also had to get $25,000 to pay Lee Bailey, who had asked for that much money to defend my husband. While I was abroad, Sam put five thousand miles on my Thunderbird and sold our second car. After he was acquitted, things grew steadily worse. He said to me, 'I don't need you any more—I'm free of you.' I never knew from one moment to the next how he would act. He became despondent and lost touch with reality. He went on the Johnny Carson television show and told that story about having a gun with him the night the verdict was returned. But I know that wasn't true. For years I have been paying his bills. I even sold my major interest in a company in Germany. I put about $200,000 into the marriage. He couldn't afford to hire an office girl, so I performed secretarial duties for him in Youngstown. I felt that I was the one person who could help him, and I tried as long as I could. But when he woke me in the middle of the night, pointed a gun at my head, and called me a thief—that was the end. I had to call the police. You can't call the police on your husband and continue to live with him. Some people can, but I can't. I can't help him any more. He needs medical help."

Deputy sheriffs were unable to locate Dr. Sam to serve him the temporary restraining order. Rumors flew that he was in Cleveland, in Youngstown, and in Boston visiting his son. The estranged husband was finally located in Columbus on December 10. He denied his wife's charges but said little else. It was not that the embroiled husband was exercising restraint or wisdom; it was just that he did not have much to say about the charges of the woman whom he had once professed to love more than life itself. To him divorce was another serious defeat.

Had Dr. Sam contested his wife's divorce action, it could have dragged on for several years. But he decided not to contest it. In early October, 1968, several days before Sam and Ariane met, in court, for the next to the last time, Sam tried to effect a reconciliation, according to his wife. "But I had gone through too much and couldn't go through any more," Ariane said. When the decree was finalized, in October, 1969, the judge ordered Sam to pay his wife $300 a month in alimony. Thus the lovebirds, who had met for the first time in prison and had spent only four and a half hours together before deciding to marry, now, after four and a half years of sweet-stormy wedlock, ended their romance.

Obviously, one asks: Why? At the start of their marriage both of them had said, "The important thing is that we have found each other." But marital tension was inevitable for the Sheppards from the very beginning. It was aggravated by the continual hounding by the press, by the pointing of people, the whispering, the vicious hate mail, the crank phone calls, and their own propensity to exhibitionism.

At first, all this drew them together. While at the beginning of their marriage Sam's emotional, psychological, and economic dependence upon his strong-willed wife deepened, as a basically independent male he rebelled inwardly at this feminine dominance.

"Ariane sometimes looks after him almost too well," insisted one insider. "I know that she loves him—as much as it is possible for her to love anyone. But I wonder if she doesn't box him in too much with her affection and attention. He doesn't have any male friends any more and doesn't seem to want or need any. Sam's whole life has become Ariane. I wish he would go bowling, sailing, or golfing with the boys like he used to. But he's not interested. He just wants to be near Ariane and defers to her judgment too much."

Ariane's protective attitude toward her husband included considerable financial assistance. To help defray his increasingly heavy legal expenses, she drew upon the income from her late father's estate. When she considered dipping into the principal, her husband rejected the offer, he said, and cashed in the balance of his $100,000 insurance policy. Sam felt justified in doing so because his son had already been provided for with a $50,000 inheritance from Marilyn's father.

During a visit with the Sheppards in July, 1966, *Parade* photographer Ben Ross took me aside and remarked perceptively, "Sam's getting stronger now, and Ariane's getting weaker. He's asserting himself more." After Ben left for New York with the pictures he had shot, Sam and Ariane dined with me at the Valley View Motel restaurant, where I was staying. They kept me up all night with their private complaints about each other as the three of us lounged on reclining chairs facing the motel's swimming pool. I was in the middle chair, so first one and then the other would claim my attention as they unburdened themselves about their real and imaginary grievances toward each other and members of their families.

Some of my unpublished notes reveal the following comments from Sam:

"She bugs me and crowds me too much."

"She pushed me out of bed with her feet like Marilyn used to do."

"When I called her Marilyn once by mistake, she said 'Thank you' in a cool way and was mad at me."

"Did you notice how she was hopping up and down on my Honda motorcycle? I think she *wanted* me to crash."

"She picks on young Sam. I don't expect her to feel as close to him as I do, no more than I feel as close to Iris as she does."

"She got out of the car last night because she said I was driving too fast. She said I threw her out, but I really didn't."

"She's talking about a divorce a lot lately."

"I'd like to get away from everybody and out of this state."

Ariane, of course, voiced many complaints about Sam.

At eight o'clock in the morning, when the motel restaurant had opened again, we hobbled in to breakfast after a sleepless night. I was exhausted. I felt that I had just witnessed another performance of the ugly marital fury that I had seen in *Who's Afraid of Virginia Woolf?* on Broadway. I must have looked like the wrath of the devil, but both Sheppards looked punchy until we had swallowed our welcome black coffee. Since they knew that I was genuinely fond of both of them, they sensed that I was deeply troubled about their dangerously rocky marriage and about whether I would mention it in *Parade*.

In a wild stab at heavy-handed levity, Sam quipped, "Hey, Pollack, lay off my wife when I'm not around. She's my girl."

Ariane, who can be extremely sensitive, quickly interposed, "Sam, we kept Jack from sleeping, and we're now bothering him with all our silly troubles." She lit a cigarette and then threw this haymaker: "Why talk about it? We're not getting divorced yet."

Her husband's face suddenly froze. "Who said anything about divorce?" he demanded of her.

Ariane ignored his remark. Like a playful kitten, she turned to me and said, "If you write anything not nice about me, Jack, I'll sue you. And Lee Bailey won't represent me. I know *other* lawyers."

On the evening that Ariane Tebbenjohanns Sheppard filed for divorce, the first telecaster to report her version was a close friend, Cleveland commentator Dorothy Fuldheim, who said that she could not understand how Ariane could have married Sam Sheppard. In Dorothy Fuldheim's words, "Ariane is a woman of impeccable taste. She has a good sense of humor, is good looking, has breeding, is educated, and has wealth. That's the great enigma. *Why* did she do it? She probably thought it was the greatest love story of the century. She's a romanticist. If Sam had been like-minded, it might have worked out." Fuldheim also reported that she had asked Ariane, before the July, 1964, Chicago wedding, "What if you don't like him in bed?" The bride replied, according to telecaster Fuldheim, "I can always leave him."

Every man, woman, and child who has ever experienced a bitter divorce feels the deep hurt and realizes that it takes time—and care—for emotional scar tissue to heal. A stormy divorce is a traumatic experience. No principal ever emerges from it completely unscathed.

In the case of Samuel and Ariane Tebbenjohanns Sheppard the hidden hurt never really healed.

New Life, New Wife

After his divorce Dr. Sam Sheppard, harried by domestic and professional headaches, moved to Gahanna, a suburb of Columbus in central Ohio.

There he rented an apartment and opened a small office in a building across from a fire station. Although he had wanted to move to California to practice in that state, it was necessary to have a doctor of medicine (M.D.) degree, which he did not have.

In Gahanna Dr. Sam confined himself to general practice, deciding to do so alone. "I don't want to subject anyone else to my bad fortune," he remarked. Furthermore, he felt he should establish his practice before attempting to become affiliated with any local hospital.

"I'll take care of sick people," he promised, "but refer my surgical patients. I'll refer those who need surgery or obstetrics to a good M.D. I never felt any animosity toward medical doctors."

The estranged husband felt no animosity toward his ex-wife either, saying, "When the chips were down, Ariane came through like a champ. She's still a champ. I wish her love. It is just that I have a son and had a wife. It was difficult to separate the two. She wouldn't let my son in the house."

When asked about Cuyahoga County's latest crime sensation—the January 9 murder of Marlene Steele, wife of Municipal Judge Robert L. Steele—he said, "I haven't followed the case. But I hope that the accused person gets a fairer shake than I did."

Soon afterward Sam encountered George Strickland, a professional wrestler, who opened up a new world to him. Sheppard, a physical fitness bug, had always enjoyed all forms of athletics, especially wrestling. One of the thorns between him and Steve, who had reared his son, was that his brother had encouraged the youth to pursue scholastics rather than athletics—which father Sam would have preferred.

Now with the encouragement of Strickland, who suggested becoming his trainer and manager, Dr. Sam decided to become a part-time professional wrestler for charity. "Wrestling is a good way to show that men over 40 can stay in good physical condition," he exulted. "And why not? I've wrestled ever since I was a sophomore in high school. My father pushed me into medicine. Wrestling and other athletics are more enjoyable when you don't have to depend on them for a living. I'm going into it for the sport."

Psychiatrists might suggest that an explanation for Sam Sheppard's wrestling mania was that he wanted to touch somebody, get close to somebody. He was searching for love, warmth, and bodily contact, just as other affection-seeking adults cuddle children and others pamper animals. Sam Sheppard was more "secure" in wrestling than in medicine or marriage, psychiatrists might explain. The rejected husband desperately wanted to be loved, even by strangers. I once accompanied him into a grocery store where, after purchasing a six-pack of beer, he left a 15-cent tip on the counter to the clerk's astonishment.

When it was announced that Dr. Sam Sheppard was grappling with a new career, on July 30, 1969, many editors reading the dispatch from Columbus on the news ticker cried, "Somebody must be kidding." Once more the ex-convict became a press pigeon. Professional wrestling is generally considered a crooked sport, suitable for shabby late-show television entertainment. Even the most inexperienced public relations pundit would have agreed instantly that wrestling was bad for Sheppard's "image."

Still, Dr. Sam made it clear that he was not trading his

stethoscope for a pair of wrestling trunks. "I'm a doctor, and my practice will always come first," he insisted.

Far more important, he said, "This is my way of contributing something. I'll probably get the same bang out of this as when I volunteered to be injected with live cancer cells during the prison research project. My share of the gate receipts will go to the Sloan-Kettering Cancer Research Foundation, excluding expenses." Then he wisecracked, "But my expenses come high."

When Sheppard the wrestler was played up as a public clown, he angrily told newsmen, with more candor than wisdom, "Maybe I'll make more money as a wrestler than as a doctor. I'll be the cleanest, meanest, damnedest wrestler you ever saw."

His first match, on August 9, was held before jam-packed stands at Waverly High School, for the benefit of the Pike County Cancer Society. His opponent was "Wild Bill" Scholl, a behemoth weighing in at nearly 300 pounds.

In the locker room Wild Bill snarled at him, "Amateurs shouldn't wrestle us professionals."

"I'll show you what kind of amateur I am," snapped Sam.

The antagonists marched out to enter the ring for their star match. Although outweighed by nearly 100 pounds, Sheppard hurled Wild Bill over his shoulder to the mat several times. The fat man whined in pantomimed pain on each occasion. The last time Wild Bill rose, shaken. Utilizing his medical knowledge, Dr. Sam poked two fingers into his opponent's mouth and pressed on the sensitive madibular nerve underneath the tongue. Wild Bill shrieked in agony and toppled to the floor. The referee raised Sam's hand in victory. The crowd cheered Sheppard thunderously. The match had lasted not quite seven minutes.

Nursing his disappointment in the dressing room, Wild Bill protested, "I coulda beat the hell out of you, Sheppard."

"Wanna fight again right here?" retorted his elated foe.

Wild Bill declined.

Wrestler Sheppard also teamed up with manager George Strickland in some tag team matches. One of their most spectacular victories was achieved in the Akron Armory against Porky Pig and Jack Murphy on September 27.

On October 21—two months after his first match—during a West Coast wrestling tour, Dr. Sam again stunned critics and defenders. He slipped away to Chihuahua, Mexico, to marry. His third bride was pretty 19-year-old Colleen Strickland, the daughter of his wrestling manager.

It didn't seem to bother either of them that Colleen was half his age. "I've never been happier," he said. "He's so kind, thoughtful, and wonderful in every way," she said.

The marriage took place 14 days after Dr. Sam's divorce had become final.

When Ariane heard the news, she was reported to have said, "People thought I would be upset, but I'm not. I didn't have to divorce him. It was a good idea, his marrying a 19-year-old girl. When men get older, they start looking at younger girls. I'd like to marry again myself, but I don't have anyone at the moment."

Shortly after the newlyweds returned from Mexico, Dr. Sam closed his Gahanna office. With his bride he moved into the three-bedroom ranch home of the bride's parents, George and Betty Strickland. Out of their comfortable living room Dr. Sam continued his medical practice on a more limited scale.

Dr. Sam's new sanctuary with the Stricklands was the nearest thing to a "home" that he had known since his family had collapsed on that July 4 morning in Bay Village in 1954. Sam saw his son occasionally, but either he was abandoned by his brothers or made no overtures himself to reestablish relationships with them. The Stricklands were warm, affectionate, outgoing people.

"But Sheppard at times appeared to be the loneliest man in the world," Lacy McCrary observed in the *Akron Beacon-Journal.*

Although Sam would never admit it, he deeply missed Steve, from whom he had become estranged ever since his release from prison. His devoted brother had done more for him than anyone in the world during his ten years behind bars. Though there was never a public breach between them, they rarely saw each other socially after Sam was free. Part of the reason was probably because Steve and

Ariane both had possessive, strong-willed personalities. Each worried constantly about Sam's welfare.

Typical of his inner yearning for Steve was the way he signed his letters to me: "Fraternally yours." Once he even said to me, "I feel closer to you than to either of my brothers." I assured him that his feeling was extravagant nonsense because both Steve and Richard were fine brothers. Late one evening in 1967, when Sam was drunk, he drove me to the Bay Village Hospital and exclaimed in the driveway, "God, how they've ruined this hospital since my father ran it! Steve resents the fact that I'm a better surgeon than he is. He *wanted* me to stay in jail because it gave him status."

I answered as calmly as I could, "Sam, you don't really believe that crap, and neither do I. This is what Menninger calls your love-hate pattern toward Steve."

Sam Sheppard said nothing, but his silence indicated agreement.

Steve left Ohio in the spring of 1968 to become an M.D. psychiatrist in California. The following year he received a National Institute of Mental Health grant to study prisons and mental hospitals in Europe. Meanwhile, his younger brother was wrestling back in Ohio, and he seemed to need some mental treatment himself.

Because of his growing notoriety as a wrestler, Dr. Sam received tantalizing offers to wrestle in Europe, Japan, and Australia. However, he declined all of them because he did not want to relinquish his medical practice. Ariane had hoped to see Sam and his new wife at brother Richard's home during the 1969 Christmas holidays, but Dr. Sam never got there.

"He was too busy with his wrestling tours," Ariane said.

Was he happy wrestling? Or was his new top billing merely an escape for him? Did he think that he was on the way up—or down?

Whatever his sober thoughts, Dr. Sam began to spend more time wrestling. But he was now grappling with himself. Though he may have evidenced a strong outer wrestling grip, the more important grip on his own life was weakening.

On April 3, 1970, he took ill.

Fallen Figure

Dr. Sam Sheppard said that he was down with the flu.

For three days he refused to see a doctor. On Sunday evening, April 5, 1970, his temperature rose to 104 degrees. He felt weak, but he still refused to see a doctor and forbade anybody to call one. When his young bride of six months and his mother-in-law tried to sneak into the kitchen to telephone for a doctor, he overheard them and yelled at them to stop.

He tried to get up from his bed but found it difficult to walk without falling. His womenfolk made up a bed for him on the living room couch, where he lay, half awake and half asleep. He was spitting blood.

At 3:00 A.M. he got up from the couch, stumbled, and tried to walk into the kitchen, 20 feet away. His mother-in-law heard him and rushed to help him. He asked to be left alone. But he banged his head on the kitchen wall and fell. He then insisted that they leave him lying on the floor.

His wife and mother-in-law quickly put down pillows and blankets on the floor near where he had fallen. With great effort, the two women pulled him over to this makeshift bed.

He complained about being thirsty. He was brought a glass of water. He ordered his mother-in-law to bring him an injection of Librium, a tranquilizer. Reluctantly she did so. He moaned in pain and started to shake violently. He was incoherent and seemed only half conscious.

Delirious, he mumbled scattered, confused words, trying to voice the jumbled, irrational thoughts that were racing through his disorganized mind. First he said something about the malpractice lawsuits pending against him, then went on, please, somebody, help him to get out of prison, and don't let anybody ever take him back. He wanted to move to California with his wife, where he could practice his specialty. Why did his mother let his father down? His father had cancer, but he didn't let any of the three boys know it. Damn right, he goofed off in San Francisco on his book tour. He was pissed off at those TV jerks ordering him to be here at 3:31 and there at 8:21 and somewhere else at 11:29. No, he never carried any concealed gun into court in his jockstrap like he had said on television. He only said this to get sympathy. Sure, he knew who killed Marilyn, and he could prove it.

His delirium indicated a man who had been brainwashed, who had a terrible sense of doom—but not of guilt—hanging over him. He had lost his will to live.

At 7:00 A.M., when his condition seemed to worsen, his mother-in-law desperately opened his medical kit looking for something. She tried mouth-to-mouth resuscitation. There was a smell of blood and internal bleeding. He coughed out a huge gush of blood. His wife called the operator, asking for an ambulance. A police emergency squad car arrived swiftly. Somebody put a stethoscope on his chest, but it was too late. Sam Sheppard was dead.

Compared to the dramatic life that he had lived, it was an undramatic death on the morning of Monday, April 6, 1970. Had Samuel Holmes Sheppard, osteopath, ex-convict, wrestler, been given a choice, it was not the way he would have preferred to leave this earth. He won the freedom to die on the floor, outside prison walls, twisting in agony.

In his wallet was a photograph of his first wife Marilyn, for whom he had never ceased to grieve. On a nearby bookshelf lay legal documents of his two trials, including the affidavit of Dr. Paul Leland Kirk, the California criminologist, exonerating him of Marilyn's murder.

As I write this, I am watching a fly, caught on flypaper, but still alive. The trapped fly's legs are kicking; it is still struggling for freedom. In some ways this helpless fly reminds me of Sam Sheppard, who walked on legal, medical, and marital flypaper for 16 years. Finally he stopped moving—after fighting a losing battle.

Investigators from the coroner's office and detectives examined the body and took photographs of it for over an hour before removing it to the Franklin County Morgue. Later it was transferred to the Ohio State University Hospital for a more extensive autopsy. But no autopsy could ever uncover Sam Sheppard's deep emotional wounds.

The cause of Sam Sheppard's death was as confusing in the news media as the reporting of the murder had been. One news faction swiftly reported that the controversial man had died of cancer, which he had probably contracted during a volunteer prison experiment when he had been injected with live cancer cells. This was aided by comments from his widow, mother-in-law, and attorney, all of whom said or indicated that the deceased man had told them that he was dying of cancer, about which he appeared to have a phobia. Bailey informed newsmen that his client had cancer, according to what Sam had revealed to him several months earlier, and that he "took a lot of medication to relieve the pain."

Fearing a possible posthumous lawsuit, this cancer flurry prompted considerable reaction. On April 7, 1970, the *Cleveland Press* coyly reported: "Ohio Penitentiary officials produced records to refute any suggestion that Dr. Sheppard carried cancer in his body out of the pen when he was released in July, 1964. . . ."

Franklin County Coroner Robert A. Evans was quoted the same day as saying that an autopsy had turned up no signs of cancer but that the official report would come later. In an addendum, the coroner said that it was ". . . obvious that Sheppard drank a great deal, but I found no evidence to indicate that he had consumed liquor recently." This reassurance must have relieved America's liquor industry.

This booze story was played up by a second segment of the press. Even the normally cautious *New York Times*, despite shifting the assessment to Coroner Evans, reported on April 7 that "the osteopath had been drinking up to two fifths of vodka a day. . . ."

A third news group bought the liquor-pill theory. Alcohol, when consumed heavily together with tranquilizers or barbiturates, is considered highly dangerous. This combination was responsible for the death of Dr. Sam's surprise ally, Columnist Dorothy Kilgallen. Ariane Tebbenjohanns Sheppard strengthened this theory by saying that she had tried to persuade her husband to reduce his drinking and drug consumption. "If he hadn't been on drugs, he would not have been such a mean person—which he was not, basically," she said.

The statement by Betty Strickland, his mother-in-law, that she had given Dr. Sam an injection of Librium four hours before his death seemingly precipitated some concern by its manufacturers. The drug is advertised in medical journals as being effective "for severe anxiety"—although it is doubtful whether Librium or any other drug could have relieved Sam Sheppard's inner anxieties. Possibly inspired by some backstage public relations pundit, an anonymous "pharmaceutical expert" was speedily quoted in the Ohio press as saying that it would have taken "huge amounts of alcohol and Librium"—which is only a "mild sedative"—to have killed Dr. Sam Sheppard or anyone else.

The Franklin County Coroner's Office was so deluged with inquiries about Sheppard's death that on April 8 a spokesman stated: "We are not taking any more calls on the Sam Sheppard case and will have nothing to report until next week."

A week later, on April 14, the official autopsy report was released. Coroner Evans announced his ruling after extensive pathological tests: Sam Sheppard had died of "natural causes" brought on by "liver failure." There was no evidence that he had cancer or had received any "massive single dose" of any drug before his death. Moreover, there was no trace of heavy drinking found in the body.

This liver failure was caused by a "pathological transformation . . . a fatty metamorphosis of the liver." This fatty buildup, Coroner Evans explained, was a prelude to cirrhosis. Cirrhosis causes serious hardening and contraction of the liver and shuts off vital bodily functions. The huge amount of blood that Dr. Sam had vomited shortly before dying was a symptom of liver failure, which could have been brought on by faulty diet or by drinking. "This was not something that happened all of a sudden," the coroner added. The liver failure had begun to show up in skin discoloration.

Coroner Evans would not amplify the cause of the liver failure. "That would be purely speculative and might also be an invasion of privacy," he stated.

Either Lee Bailey entertains a contrary view of his client's death or he erred in reporting the official findings. Rejecting his preliminary cancer theory, in his book published in December, 1971, he wrote, "But the cause of death was found to be an overdose of pills."

I have my own view of the reason for Sam Sheppard's death. I think he committed suicide—not technically but virtually. He wanted to die. He had what Sigmund Freud called the "unconscious death wish." He was a physician who could not heal himself. He could periodically save other people's lives but never his own. His repeated verbalization about being doomed with cancer was another childish cry for pity as a reject of society. He overanesthetized himself with alcohol and drugs to ease his inner torture. His private prison confined him by stronger chains than any iron bars or stone walls could. Dr. Sam could no longer stand the inner pain. The man who had espoused athletics and pampered himself with vitamins and proteins in an attempt to stave off death at last welcomed it. Only in death could the man who had been out of prison less than six years finally feel free.

Ariane Tebbenjohanns Sheppard flew up from Hollywood, Florida, where she had been visiting friends.

"I really have been expecting this," she told the press in a voice filled with emotion. "I have had a very strange feeling the past two months that something would happen to Sam. I can't explain it. He was doomed for a long time. He never realized that he needed help. Even though I divorced him, I stayed in the United States because I thought he might need a friend. I guess I can go home now. I had no hard feelings for him. I would have stuck by him if he had let me . . . he couldn't help himself."

As for regrets, Ariane unhesitatingly said, "Yes, I regretted that I didn't accomplish with him what I wanted. He became so strange, I couldn't reach him. He was a very tragic figure. At our divorce he hardly knew where he was. He was the victim of a lot of circumstances during the past 16 years . . . whether he was guilty or not."

When asked if there were any happy times in her four-and-a-half-year marriage, she answered simply: no.

Then, in a resigned tone, she concluded, "I never carried any hatred. I believe that is all I want to say now."

The second Mrs. Sheppard conferred with Colleen Strickland Sheppard and her family about the funeral arrangements, which all agreed should be strictly private. Ariane suggested Sam should be buried in Bay Village near his parents.

"He would be all by himself in Columbus, where he doesn't belong," she insisted. "He has been a little lost dog. I think a child like that should go back to his parents."

She doubted that Marilyn's remaining family would want him beside the slain woman's ashes in the family crypt. Some members of Marilyn's family had apparently never accepted his exoneration.

His widow reportedly had said that there was no room for him in the Sheppard family plot in Cleveland, but Dr. Richard Sheppard was quoted in the *Cleveland Plain Dealer* on April 7, 1970, as saying that there was a plot available in Sunset Memorial Park, in nearby Olmsted Falls, "next to our parents."

Regardless of their difference of opinion over the burial site, Ariane and Betty Strickland embraced and exchanged kisses when they met at the funeral chapel on the beautiful spring morning of April 8, 1970. Looking lean and drawn, Ariane accompanied Dr. Richard Sheppard, his wife Dorothy, and their two children.

Dr. Richard Sheppard and his wife had just returned from a month's vacation in Hawaii and had found a "Happy Easter" telegram from Sam at their home. "When we last talked," reported Richard, "Sam never mentioned that he was sick. He seemed in fine spirits."

Conspicuous by their absence were the deceased man's namesake, his 23-year-old son who was in Spain, and Stephen Sheppard, who was in Broadstairs, England. Each sent a telegram of condolence. Were they unable to get back in time between Monday and Thursday or would returning for the funeral have been too painful?

The scheduled 11:00 A.M. services were delayed ten minutes until Lee Bailey, visibly shaken, arrived. Before leaving for Ohio he told an interviewer, "Sam was getting more and more religious. He gave me an ancient Bible last Christmas. He told me that he wouldn't live six months."

The 20-minute service was conducted by the Reverend Dr. Alan Davis, of Bay Village, who had known the deceased man for more than 40 years. Reverend Davis had served at several Methodist churches in the Cleveland area.

Before beginning his service in the main chapel Reverend Davis ousted an NBC network camera crew, despite their protests that they had made prior arrangements with the widow to film the eulogy. Their television cameras were removed. They waited outside with other cameramen and at least a dozen reporters. Although the services were presumably private, some newsmen managed to slip in with the crowd of mourners.

"In many ways Sam Sheppard's life was an open book," said Reverend Davis. "But much remains a mystery, as it should be, known only to God. The life of Sam Sheppard was not self-made but was God's creation." Only recently, confided the minister, Sam had told him that he believed "both at home and in prison and back home again, God is with me."

Sam Sheppard lay in his casket wearing sunglasses, a blue suit, white shirt, and dark tie. According to his wishes, some of his medical instruments were placed beside him. In the coffin with the deceased man was a wristwatch placed there before the service by a man who said, "Sam was always so good to me." A woman outside the chapel, who said that she had followed Sam's travails closely, remarked, "Maybe in this world we live in we're too quick to judge."

The interment took place at the monumentless Forest Lawn Cemetery. The pallbearers included Dr. Richard Sheppard, Lee Bailey, Richard Nolan (Sam's prison friend), young Billy Strickland, and his father, George Strickland. At the cemetery Strickland said to a friend, according to *Columbus Dispatch* reporter Ned Stout, "Meet you out at the party house."

Colleen Strickland Sheppard, the 20-year-old widow, was composed until she kissed the bronze metal coffin before it was lowered into the grave. Colleen broke into tears and ran to the family car.

When their son-in-law had moved in with them, the Strickland family had listed the telephone in his name. Even after his death they still received threatening calls. One telephoner, according to Mrs. Betty Strickland, had said, "You murdered Sam Sheppard. Beware!" The Strickland family was placed under police protection.

Another call the Stricklands received at that time was from the *Dayton Daily News*, requesting an in-depth interview with Colleen Sheppard on her "Last Days with Sam." The young widow said fine but that she had to talk to her father first. According to staff writer Jo Ann Knout, Strickland pleaded in a choked voice, "I'm not trying to be mercenary. But while things are warm, we want to do the best by him. There's nothing deader than yesterday's news. We don't want the money for ourselves. We just want to pay off his bills. Make out the $500 check to Schuman and Jones medical supply house to help pay his bill of about $3,000 for equipment. The women will both be available Tuesday, but I'll be on tour. I'm sure they can give you all the information you need."

When the reporter asked if such an arrangement had been made with other newspapers, Strickland said no, not since Sam's death. However, when he was alive, a London newspaper had paid $1,500 for a picture layout while they were on a wrestling tour in Tennessee.

"The day he died we were completely unorganized," Strickland reportedly added. "Those were just news reports anyway. No one has really interviewed Colleen in depth. There are many things that she could tell of their last days together, such as the song they called 'Our Song.' We'll co-operate with you in any way. I'll even come down to $400. All I want is to do right by Sam and pay his bills."

Strickland was right about Sam's indebtedness.

On April 16, 1970, a week later, the Internal Revenue Service filed a lien against Samuel Sheppard's estate for $11,425.80 in unpaid 1968 federal income taxes. But his mother-in-law explained that Sam had left no money in the bank and had no assets. "Let them come—there's nothing here," she said. Dr. Sam had one insurance policy, she pointed out, which named his son as the sole beneficiary. Sam had been trying to pay off his debts incurred from his long legal struggle and was gradually reducing them, she added.

Nearly two weeks later, on April 28, the Franklin County Probate Court revealed that Dr. Samuel Holmes Sheppard had left an estate of only $5,000, mostly in accounts receivable from his medical practice. The estate estimate listed no real estate. His mother-in-law was named the administrator of the estate by Probate Judge Richard Metcalf.

On August 19, four months later, Betty Strickland was named as one of the defendants in a $300,000 lawsuit because of the alleged faulty operation that Dr. Sam had performed on James Evans in June, 1968.

Thus, even in death, Sam Sheppard was being attacked in the news.

Shortly after his death, apart from the story for which George Strickland had requested $500, Colleen Sheppard was quoted in other Ohio newspapers: "He was an excellent husband in every way. Just three weeks ago, for no reason at all, except his love for me, he bought me a little ocelot. Every time he got any money, he gave it to me. I will marry again when the time is right. If I ever marry a man that old, he would have to be just like Sam."

One of the most illuminating observations about Sam Sheppard's tragedy came from Coroner Samuel Gerber: "I feel sorry for the family. Had Sam straightened out, he would have been a fine doctor. He was very intelligent. This was the biggest case of the century in Cuyahoga County, and it will still be discussed 50 years from now."

Sam Sheppard was dead at age 46, but his case—especially the persisting mystery about the murder of his first wife—is still very much alive.

12

THE GUILTY

SAM SHEPPARD made no "death-bed confession." If he had any private knowledge or evidence about his own—or about any one else's—guilt in Marilyn's tragic murder, the central figure of the case took it with him to the grave.

At first the 1954 jury said Sam had killed his wife. Then the 1966 jury said he had not. Is the question now academic, even historical, as is that of "Who killed McKinley?"—the twenty-fifth President of the United States—as a reminder for those who know Sam Sheppard's name better. History has recorded who killed McKinley but not Marilyn Sheppard.

Who Murdered Marilyn?

Yet countless men and women apparently still care, and they are not all Ohioans. Furthermore, most are even now sharply divided in their opinions. In many minds, the murder question remains unsettled, as is evidenced by the questions posed to me by all manner of persons. "Did Sam do it?" is the perennial query. Though people are no longer highly excited about the subject, widespread curiosity persists over Dr. Sam's innocence or guilt. Those believing him guilty often ask about his missing T-shirt, his bloody watch, and other evidence that they deem incriminating.

On the other hand, Sheppard defenders frequently ask, "Why wasn't the murder weapon ever found?"

America may have forgotten the McKinley assassination but certainly not the Sheppard murder. The clouds still hang over Cleveland, and the haze lingers over other parts of the state of Ohio.

Sheppard's zealous lawyer Lee Bailey never wavered publicly or privately in asserting his complete confidence in his client's innocence. Moreover, in his book, Bailey even argued that the question of Sam's innocence was irrelevant in his trials just as in the trials of many of his other clients.

Ariane Sheppard, two years after her former husband's death, on May 7, 1972, said on the Long John radio program when I appeared with her: "Yes, I definitely say Sam was innocent. The facts prove it. He was the most brilliant and at the same time, the most stupid man about life that I have ever known."

Criminologist Kirk concluded in his classic affidavit that Marilyn was murdered by a left-handed person. Theoretically this should make attorney F. Lee Bailey a possible suspect, since he happens to be left-handed! My remark is obviously absurd. I make it only to draw attention to the spurious "accusations" and even "confessions" of hallucinating or self-seeking individuals behind bars and elsewhere who sought the limelight in the Sheppard murder case.

For example, back in September, 1954, before the first trial had even begun, Steve Sheppard made a wild goose chase trip to Trenton, New Jersey, to interview a prisoner who had "confessed" to his jailer that he had murdered Marilyn. Sam's brother swiftly appraised the "confessor" as a disturbed personality.

Another obviously disturbed Cleveland woman, who signed herself "Jane Doe," wrote to her minister in February, 1955, a long, detailed letter, saying, in part: "Sam Sheppard did not kill his wife. I did not kill her. But I was an unwilling witness to the act. It was my husband who did it . . . he said he was going for a walk to get a paper, but he did not return until after midnight . . . I went out to look for him. . . . My husband recently had a brain tumor and died. . . . I cannot allow an innocent person to be punished for this terrible crime. . . . I have been unable to eat or sleep since I witnessed it.... I pray that God and the Sheppard family will forgive my husband, who was not responsible for what he did...."

During the 1966 retrial, Bailey made a stab at ferreting out Marilyn's murderer. His surprise first witness was a bakery delivery man. As Gene Lowall reported the episode in the February 1967 *Argosy:*

> The witness, John Krakan, said he had been a bakery-goods deliveryman in 1954 and had frequently delivered bread and other supplies to the Sheppard house. Krakan said that, on several occasions, he saw a man sitting with Marilyn in the kitchen having coffee. On one occasion, Krakan testified, he saw Marilyn give a house key to the man, whom he assumed to be Dr. Sam. Krakan said he was surprised to overhear Marilyn say, as she handed over the key, "Don't let Sam see this.'" Another time, he said, he saw the man "caressing" Marilyn.
>
> Long after Sam's conviction Krakan was shown a picture of a man by a Lorain, Ohio, newspaperwoman, who asked if it was the man he had seen in the Sheppard house. Krakan said it was and then told the identity of the man in the picture. Bailey asked the witness to divulge that name, but Krakan was interrupted by an objection by Corrigan. A bench consultation with both attorneys was then called, and after that a recess. Krakan did not resume the stand, but apparently a telling point had been made with the jury.

The name of J. Spencer Houk, the former mayor of Bay Village, has likewise been bruited about as Marilyn's possible murderer. The suggestion emerged during the 1966 retrial. In the November 3, 1966, *Columbus Dispatch,* Mary McGarey wrote:

> J. Spencer Houk told a Criminal Court jury Wednesday how he and Sam Sheppard, once close friends, each suggested the other as the killer of Sam's wife, Marilyn.
>
> Seated a few feet apart, Sheppard, the defendant in

a retrial for the murder, and Houk, the state's third witness, rarely met each other's eyes as the former Bay Village mayor-and-meat-merchant testified. . . .

He told of the conversation with Sam and Dr. Stephen Sheppard several weeks later, during which they told him of a Cleveland psychiatrist's theory "they thought I should know about"—that a schizophrenic personality had committed the crime.

They described the schizophrenic type to him, Houk said, as a "loner" or somebody secretly in love with a woman, who if that woman became pregnant, would have an urge to kill. Marilyn was pregnant when she was murdered.

Later questioned by defense attorney F. Lee Bailey on this incident and asked if he felt Sam or his brothers were pointing suspicion his way, Houk said, "I had a feeling they were trying to tell me something."

It was his own turn, the day before the inquest, Houk indicated, when he suggested to Sam that, if Sam had murdered Marilyn, "You should tell the truth. . . . Your friends will stand behind you."

Sam replied that he hadn't, "couldn't have, and that Marilyn wouldn't have wanted him punished," Houk recalled. And Sam did say, he added, that Dr. Alan Moritz, Cleveland psychiatrist and medical criminologist, "had expressed a keen interest in me."

Bailey questioned Houk closely about his "frequent" visits to the Sheppard home in the six months preceding Marilyn's death during the hours Sam wasn't home.

Houk replied that, as often as two or three times a week, "It was not unusual for her to call," and ask him to drop something off from a store for her or to cash a check for her. . . .

Bailey also made much of the Houks' response to Sam's first summons on the day of the murder—why they drove the short distance, why Houk failed to take his shotgun or other defensive weapon to a murder scene "where someone with the disposition to kill might be awaiting you," why Houk as both mayor and safety director didn't call police immediately from his own home.

Houk answered repeatedly, "I just didn't consider it."

Asked if he had made any effort to circulate or broadcast Sheppard's description of the man he had seen on the murder morning, Houk said he had told police officers about it but could not remember exactly which ones.

Bailey questioned Houk closely on why Mrs. Houk, on their arrival at the Sheppards, had gone directly to Marilyn's bedroom without Sam's telling them where the body was, and why Houk later had gone directly to that room.

Houk said he had been on the second floor of the Sheppard home only once before, as he recalled. He said he had taken lunch to Marilyn one day when she was ill but that she then occupied another bedroom.

When Bailey questioned the former mayor about Marilyn's clothing, her position on the bed, anything he noticed about bloodstains or other features of the room, Houk responded at one point: "I don't remember. I just stayed a minute. It was a hell of a thing to have to see. . . ."

In a further half hour's questioning by Bailey Thursday, Houk admitted he had been in the bedroom in which Marilyn was killed. He said when he arrived at the house one morning in April of 1954, he went directly to the room, found her sleeping, and left.

On redirect examination Corrigan drew from Houk another conversation with Sam during which Sheppard expressed regret about the trouble the murder was causing the Houk family.

Houk said he questioned Sam about a police officer's statement that Sam had "spoken to me" about his attentions to Marilyn. He said Sheppard replied, "Spen, it's a damn lie."

Following Houk to the stand was his former wife, Esther, the first person known to have entered the bedroom after Sam said he found his wife murdered. . . .

Toward the end of his questioning Bailey asked Mrs. Houk about the reason for Houk being hospitalized in 1954 about the time of the trial.

She replied quickly that it was because of "severe strain from intense pressure and he was crushed his best friend . . . would intimate he had anything to do with this."

There were slight discrepancies between the stories of Houk and his former wife.

Granted, Sam Sheppard did not murder Marilyn. But *somebody* must have.

A bushy-haired man? A burglar? A drug-seeking prowler? A neighbor? A woman? Two killers? Somebody who knew and resented Sam or Marilyn—or both—whose fury exploded into murder?

In his book about the Marilyn Sheppard murder case, published in 1961, Paul Holmes, in what he called "pure hypothesis," cautiously speculated: "Nevertheless, I think it was more likely that the murderer was a person who had at least some slight acquaintance with either Sam or Marilyn, or both, and to borrow a thought which Sam himself gave me after the trial, I suggest the possibility that this murderer may have been a woman."

In a skeptical news story published in the *Cleveland Press* on August 7, 1961, headlined *Book Offers Theory on Sheppard Slaying*, Al Ostrow wrote, in part:

> Theories that Mrs. Marilyn Sheppard was killed by a woman and that a flashlight was the murder weapon are advanced in a new book, *The Sheppard Murder Case*. It was written by Paul Holmes, a Chicago newspaperman.
>
> The woman killer, according to the Holmes hypothesis, discovered her own husband in Mrs. Sheppard's bedroom.
>
> Both husband and wife, the author theorizes, may have entered the Sheppard home in Bay Village separately and gone upstairs without noticing Dr. Sam Sheppard sleeping on a downstairs divan.
>
> The intruding husband, the book continues, may have been the "bushy-haired man" Dr. Sheppard says knocked him unconscious when he awakened and ran upstairs to see why his wife was screaming.
>
> After this, Holmes writes, the woman killer and her

husband may have cleaned up the place, planting various false clues to mislead investigators, and then fled the scene, "safe from the law at the price of living with themselves and each other, welded together by their terrible secret, held in eternal thralldom to a crime they can never talk about, never forget and never expiate."

Holmes concedes that his theory cannot be proven, but insists it "might have happened" and is as plausible as the prosecution contentions accepted by the jury that found Dr. Sheppard guilty of second-degree murder. . . .

Two years later I chanced to examine some little known research on the controversial case, which indicated that a woman and a "bushy-haired man" might have been involved in Marilyn Sheppard's murder: the unpublished raw material of Harold Bretnall, a New York private detective who had recently died.

Bretnall had been employed secretly for six years (1955-1961) by the two Sheppard brothers to search for proof of imprisoned Sam's innocence. The detective was writing an admittedly partisan pro-Sheppard book entitled *The Big Frame*—which he had planned to dedicate to Steve when he died suddenly in November, 1963, at age 65.

Bretnall, whose specialty was corporate investigations, concentrated on discovering evidence that he claimed the Ohio authorities had suppressed or ignored—an unidentified tooth chip found in the murder bedroom; a triangular fragment of leather; and unexplained scrapings from under Marilyn's fingernails. Among other things Bretnall contended that he had in his possession a pair of Marilyn's bedroom slippers, whose soles revealed, according to him, that she had made a post-midnight trip out of the house prior to 3:00 A.M., before she was attacked.

Bretnall insisted that his *new* evidence and his unearthing of the 1954 trial's *forgotten* evidence added up to the firm fact that somebody other than Sam Sheppard had killed Marilyn. His conclusion was based in part upon Dr. Sam's early words over the telephone after discovering his wife's murder: ". . . I think they've killed Marilyn." Sam's *"they've"* beat on Bretnall's brain until he reconstructed the crime after piecing together his unique findings. "The answer to the Sheppard case riddle," he wrote, "lies in Bay Village. Sam is innocent."

Bretnall had reputedly done confidential investigations for dozens of America's top corporations, including General Motors, Standard Oil, RCA, Bendix Aviation, American Canners Association, American Bank Note, and Pabst Brewing. He had also been a central figure in the New York City wire-tapping scandal and an investigator for the late Tennessee Senator Estes Kefauver's much publicized Crime Committee.

Typical of his probing for business clients was the time that he saved a company $10,000 in a personal injury suit. A woman suing claimed that she had developed a rash after eating ketchup from a bottle which had contained a dead mouse. Investigator Bretnall produced signed affidavits that this woman had had the same rash fifteen years earlier, and her doctor had diagnosed it as an allergy to fish. A favorite Bretnall ploy was to gain entrance into homes, offices, and hotel rooms by saying, "I'm a private detective who's checking on some suspected jewel thieves across the street." For some strange reason people cooperated.

During his Sheppard investigation Bretnall was warned that it would be impossible for him to interview a sick patient in a Cleveland hospital who had some evidence. One day he jauntily strolled past the hospital receptionist carrying his attaché case and went directly to the patient's room as the nurses respectfully greeted him, "Good morning, doctor."

Bretnall's sleuthing methods—which he claimed to have used effectively in his Sheppard case investigation—included collecting and studying home and office trash by renting a pickup dump truck, bribing janitors and junkmen, and even renting an office in a building in order to switch his own burlap trash bag left outside his door for the bag he wanted. "Give me the trash from any office for a week and I'll tell you the company's secrets," he insisted. "Stenographers often make mistakes near the ends of their letters and then throw them in the wastebasket."

Private eyes frequently "bleed" their clients by telling them what they *want* to hear. But Bretnall's primary motive in the complex Sheppard case, he contended, was professional curiosity. "You could put in your eye what I got paid by the Sheppards," he snapped. When he first talked to Sam's brothers in August, 1955, he said, "I'll take the case only if I can give it to you straight, even if you don't like what I find."

"Okay with us," they agreed.

The deeper Bretnall probed, the more convinced he became that the wrong person was behind bars for Marilyn's murder. He never transmitted all of his findings to the Sheppard brothers because he never got around to organizing all of them. In his files I saw a typical early Bretnall memoranda entitled: "One Hundred Questions I've Asked Myself One Hundred Times." They included such queries as: "Whose blood was spilled in Marilyn's room? It wasn't hers or Dr. Sam's. Whose tooth [chip] was found in Marilyn's room? What really happened to the murder weapon? Who got to the scene of the crime first? *Where* and *when* was Sam's green bag really first found? Whose hair was found under Marilyn's nails? It wasn't Sam's. Who knew the Sheppard house so well they knew the easiest way out when Sam gave chase?"

Bretnall had planned to disclose in his book his explosive new findings, which had not been made public during the 1954 trial. He considered but rejected turning over his material to Ohio authorities because he feared they would only scorn it. "Many officials would rather let an innocent man rot in jail than ever admit that they had been wrong," he said to Steve Sheppard one day. Bretnall's investigation convinced him that Cleveland authorities had concealed and even altered key evidence during the trial, which, if produced, would have indicated Sheppard's innocence: (1) police photographs of the house's interior; (2) 3 x 5 inch index card containing the results of a test on a speck of blood found on Marilyn's wristwatch; (3) evidence that a dark colored car was parked near the Sheppard house on the murder morning; (4) scaring off of some pro-Sheppard witnesses; (5) wiping off of fingerprints in the murder house by the police themselves.

Bretnall explained why Dr. Sam did and did not do certain things that have long puzzled students of the baffling case: Why did he not turn on the lights? Why did he not pick up a poker from the fireplace when chasing the bushy-haired man? Why did he not telephone for help immediately after his beach encounter?

When the Cleveland Police Department attempted to collect the $10,000 reward posted by the Sheppard family for the arrest and conviction of Marilyn's murderer, Bretnall scathingly wired the reward arbitrators on July 10, 1959:

> For almost four years I have directed an investigation into the murder of Marilyn Sheppard on July 4, 1954. I am informed that efforts are being made on behalf of certain members of the Cleveland Police Department to claim the reward of ten thousand dollars for the arrest and conviction of the murderer of Marilyn Sheppard based on the theory that the murder was committed by her husband, Dr. Sam Sheppard.
>
> Since the final solution of this crime is imminent solely through my efforts, the payment of such reward to members of the Cleveland Police Department or anyone else except me would be wholly unwarranted and legally subject to return if paid in error. I respectfully submit the following facts:
>
> There are now, or recently were, in the possession of the Cuyahoga County Prosecutor's office numerous tangible pieces of evidence which establish the complete innocence of Dr. Sam Sheppard.
>
> Among these many items are the following:
>
> 1. A tooth fragment measuring 5/32 x 1/8 inches which came from the mouth of the murderer;
>
> 2. A leather fragment approximately triangular in shape and measuring 1/4 x 1/4 x 3/8 inches on the sides, torn from the glove worn by the murderer;
>
> 3. An original record from the office of the Coroner of Cuyahoga County indicating tests from blood on the deceased's watch worn when murdered, showing both A and B cells. Neither Dr. Sam Sheppard's blood nor the blood of his murdered wife contained any B cells. Thus the presence of a bleeding third party in the murder bedroom is proved.

I have in my possession photographs taken at my direction of all of the items enumerated above while the items were either in the custody of the Ohio Supreme Court or the custody of the Cuyahoga County Prosecutor's office.

The writer of an anonymous letter which describes in detail the events at the scene of the murder was located by me after a three-year search. This person, a Cleveland property owner, confirmed personally the facts set forth in the letter. The original of this document is in my possession.

A prowler seen at the time of the murder in front of Dr. Sam Sheppard's residence by a number of reliable witnesses has been positively identified by his former brother-in-law, who saw him there at the time.

The only metropolitan Cleveland Police who may be entitled to any interest in this reward are those who have cooperated with me in establishing the complete innocence of Dr. Sam Sheppard.

Three months later the arbiters dropped this hot potato and ordered the reward money returned to the Sheppard family.

Bretnall died a year and a half before Dr. Sam was released from prison. They never met, though both had looked forward to their meeting. Shortly before he died, Bretnall wrote: "Marilyn Sheppard was murdered by someone who was a frequent visitor to the Sheppard home. A gigantic fraud has been perpetrated by Ohio officials. In my book, I plan to take them apart one by one. I only hope they stay alive long enough to read it." After carefully ruling out all other possibilities Bretnall concluded that Marilyn's killers were a woman and a bushy-haired man living in bondage with their dreadful secret.

Though not as scientific as Kirk's classic affidavit on Dr. Sam's innocence, Bretnall's findings went beyond it in some ways. True, much of his evidence was circumstantial—but so was most of that which originally convicted Sheppard.

Bretnall's evidence was not used during Dr. Sam's retrial in 1966 largely because his attorney believed that he had so many *easier* ways to get his client acquitted. Bailey knew about the Bretnall material to which I had access and said that he would request it if he needed it.

In any case, Kirk, Bretnall, and the retrial exonerated Sam. He did *not* murder his wife. Who did? The finger of suspicion, according not only to Bailey but to more impartial observers, still points most stubbornly to a couple—a woman and a man.

Could it be that the man was having an affair with Marilyn, that his wife found out about it and tried to kill her, only to be interrupted by her husband, who, out of guilt, rushed to her aid and "finished the job"?

This theory may have much to recommend it, not least the gossip of Bay Village. And it may not be coincidental that a tooth chip belonging to neither Marilyn nor Sam was found in the bedroom after the murder and that the teeth of one Bay Village resident were reportedly extracted immediately after the crime.

EPILOGUE

THERE WERE *two* victims in one of the century's most sensational murders: Marilyn *and* Sam Sheppard. One was brutally slain. The other was pilloried in an astonishing travesty of justice.

If Sam Sheppard could speak from the grave, would he say anything now that he did not or could not say during his comparatively brief lifetime? Could he have added anything that might have stripped the case of some of its mystery?

Sixteen years of hell—twelve of them in legal limbo—do something to any human being, especially if a man has spent a decade behind bars for a crime that he did not commit. This may explain at least part of Dr. Sam's odd behavior after he gained his so-called freedom. Was he his own assassin?

Or were the roots there earlier for the fall, the rise, and the fall again of Sam Sheppard? Was there anything in his genes that may have influenced his actions?

Whatever the reason, why did this tormented soul, whose life touched hundreds of other lives for good or ill, remain entrapped in controversy and encircled by notoriety? Was it because he was tortured with some inner demon that he felt was trying to destroy him?

America does not know how to deal compassionately

with its temporary press pariahs. One man who was accused of treason and spy-related charges after released from prison, became a stationery salesman. Another man, who was involved in a television quiz scandal, was last reported as doing encyclopedia research.

"If somehow Oswald and, to a lesser extent, Ruby were necessary sacrifices to the public interest, Dr. Sam Sheppard should not have been," wrote Donald M. Gillmor, University of Minnesota School of Journalism Director, in the July, 1971, *Current History*. "Here there were no overriding social rights at stake."

Unlike Senator Edward Kennedy, who has managed to come back considerably in public esteem since the Chappaquiddick tragedy, Sam Sheppard could never organize his life constructively after regaining his freedom. "Why did we spend all those years fighting for him?" reflected one insider. "Look at what Sam did with his life afterward." His attorney, in his book, wrote: "He won his freedom, and he won exoneration. But he couldn't win back his life." Bailey sadly added this cryptic sentence about his client in a radio interview on December 7, 1971: "I'm not sure we won anything for Sam in the long run."

Perhaps this pathetic figure was overly tormented—or was too emotionally ill—to enjoy the free years left to him outside prison walls. His post-prison life need not have been an epic one. A useful one would have been sufficient. The public's disappointment with Sam Sheppard was that he dissipated his final years. If forces beyond his control prevented him from pursuing his beloved medicine, could he not have worked for prison reform or greater fair trial-free press equity?

Despite his ultimate acquittal, the 10-year legal odyssey of Sam Sheppard adds no luster to the judicial process. It emerges tarnished. Dickens's Mr. Bumble said, in *Oliver Twist*, back in 1838: "The law is a ass." Many reporters who covered the trials of men accused of the assassinations of President John F. Kennedy, Reverend Dr. Martin Luther King, Jr., and Senator Robert F. Kennedy concluded that "American justice works accidentally, if at all."

In the original 1954 Sheppard conviction Ohio officials may have been boobs at best, villains at worst. Yet the case of the deceased Sam Sheppard is now studied in law schools as having influenced the course of fair trial jurisprudence. In my college lectures in both law and journalism classes, students invariably have been fascinated—and challenged—by the complexity of the case. An individual can have all the earmarks of guilt but still be absolutely innocent.

Although some issues are still in dispute, important general guidelines have been established in the reporting of criminal trials. The epic Sheppard ruling by the United States Supreme Court has already profoundly influenced news reporting. The case of the front page personality in virtually every newspaper in America—and many overseas—still overclouds Ohio.

When Sheppard died, the *Cleveland Press*, which according to his attorney helped put him behind bars unjustly for 10 years, published a charitable editorial below its Scripps-Howard lighthouse symbol and slogan: *Give Light and the People Will Find Their Own Way*. The editorial was entitled "End of the Sheppard Story."

But is it really the end?

High school classmates still remember Sam as a handsome, athletic, fun-loving, promising youth who believed in motherhood, apple pie, and pledging allegiance to the flag. He became a successful doctor, married his childhood sweetheart, had a fine family, lived in a comfortable suburban home—until, like a Kafka victim, one night his life took a tragic turn.

The post-prison Sam Sheppard was an obsessed man whose mind always seemed somewhere else. Whenever I was alone with him, I invariably felt that by the way he periodically gritted his teeth, tightened his jaw, and seemed to ask pitifully: "Will my troubles never end?" It was almost like a child being accused of doing something that he did not understand. Recently I observed a shoplifter in a supermarket stealthily tucking a steak under his belt and buttoning his shabby coat. Desperately, he said to me, "Mister, gimme a break. I haven't had anything to eat in two days." His pleading tone and frightened eyes reminded me of Sam Sheppard in some ways. I said nothing and walked away.

I have another recollection of Sam Sheppard in the dead of winter, roaring around the Cleveland suburbs on his high-powered motorcycle with a broad grin on his still boyish face. He invited me to ride with him on the rear seat. Despite his perfect control, one ride was enough. Sam Sheppard enjoyed speed. Perhaps that was his way of securing emotional release. Likewise, in the dead of winter, coatless and hatless, he drove his convertible with the top down.

The car that I purchased from him I kept much longer than any sensible motorist should have. Subconsciously I must have sensed that I did not want to let go of Sam Sheppard until I had written this book, which I felt that I must do some day. In July, 1970, I drove the car to a Broadway dealer who advertised "Top prices for any make, any year car." After driving it around the block the wheeler-dealer said, "Why do you offer me a piece of junk like this? What did I ever do to you? I'd have to pay somebody to tow it away." I left in anger and turned the car over to a less contemptuous used car dealer, who assured me that he could sell it for at least $600. He was unable to do so for a year. I then had the car towed into two Lincoln service shops, but mechanics were still unable to locate the short circuit—just as no one could ever find the short circuit in Sam Sheppard's own life. A mechanic who had no idea of the car's checkered history bravely offered me 30 dollars for it. Since I was just finishing this book, I accepted the offer, probably because the word "30"—the traditional sign-off number used to denote the end of newspaper stories—somehow seemed symbolic to me.

If Sam Sheppard were living in our present world, would life seem any more demented to him than the world in which *he* lived? Today this murder case belongs to the law books, to history, and to the millions who will never forget Dr. Sam.

ACKNOWLEDGMENTS

I AM INDEBTED to many individuals for considerable professional and personal assistance from the germination to the completion of this book—a period of nine years.

Mr. Julian Bach, Jr., my literary agent, launched and shepherded me through it.

Mrs. Mary Fritchie and Mrs. Eleanor L. Kirkhus typed the messy manuscript.

Mr. Joseph Frank, my attorney, was a bulwark of warm and unfailing support.

Miss Susan Pollack and Miss Deborah Pollack, my daughters, and Mrs. Rose Frank made helpful editorial suggestions.

For earlier assistance I am grateful to Mr. Paul Holmes, especially for some illuminating letters and private discussions.

My thanks likewise to *Parade* editors, especially former managing editor Mr. Edwin Kiester, Jr., and photographer Mr. Ben Ross, the latter for unique photographs.

Mr. F. Lee Bailey, Dr. Stephen Sheppard, Dr. Richard Sheppard, and Mrs. Ariane Tebbenjohanns Sheppard, and above all, Dr. Sam himself contributed immeasurably, long before the book was even conceived.

Along the way many others helped, too, including Mrs.

Libby Jackson, the late Mr. Gene Lowall, Miss Susan Roberts, Dr. Richard S. Gubner, Mrs. Leon H. Guide, and Mrs. Queena P. Fineman.

Unique thanks are due to the late Mr. Abraham L. Chanin, the pioneer lecturer at the Museum of Modern Art who, even when fighting for his own life, urged me to write the Dr. Sheppard story—as a play. He was right: The story *does* belong on the stage—no movie nor television performance ever caught the real Sheppard drama. His gifted wife Margit Chanin, a leading private art dealer, helped at first by not listening and then by being compelled to listen too much.

If I have neglected to thank any others, here or elsewhere, for their help, I trust that they will understand and forgive my unintentional oversight.

Should errors have crept into this book, my excuse is that there are still some missing pieces of the Sheppard puzzle and that the author—like Dr. Sam—is a frail mortal.

Index

A CHILLING DETECTIVE STORY
OF MURDER AND MADNESS

AN EX-COP MUST FIND A CRAZED KILLER . . .
BEFORE THE COPS CATCH UP WITH HIM!

NATIONAL BOOK AWARD NOMINEE

THE DEATH OF THE DETECTIVE

MARK SMITH

This is a novel about murder, corruption, defilement and violence—every seamy reality you have ever read about in the daily papers . . .

The Detective is an ex-cop who left the force because he was too honest. Now, he must find an escaped mental patient with a terrible grudge who will kill anyone in his way. Here are two human beings, stalking each other in the American hell called Chicago, the city where people suffer and bleed; love and die. One is the pursuer, one the pursued; one the murderer, one the avenger; one the madman, one the detective.

"A COMPLETE SUCCESS . . . ABSOLUTELY WORTH READING . . ." *The New York Times Book Review*

AVON 26567 $1.95

Where better paperbacks are sold, or directly from the publisher. Include 25¢ per copy for mailing; allow three weeks for delivery. Avon Books, Mail Order Dept., 250 West 55th Street, New York, N.Y. 10019. DDet 12-75